D1714577

Deterrence
and the Crisis
in Moral Theory

San Francisco State University Series in Philosophy

Anatole Anton
General Editor

Vol. 8

PETER LANG
New York • Washington, D.C./Baltimore
Bern • Frankfurt am Main • Berlin • Vienna • Paris

Gabriel Palmer-Fernandez

Deterrence and the Crisis in Moral Theory

An Analysis of the Moral Literature on the Nuclear Arms Debate

PETER LANG
New York • Washington, D.C./Baltimore
Bern • Frankfurt am Main • Berlin • Vienna • Paris

Library of Congress Cataloging-in-Publication Data

Palmer-Fernandez, Gabriel.
Deterrence and the crisis in moral theory: an analysis of the moral literature on
the nuclear arms debate/ Gabriel Palmer-Fernandez.
p. cm. —(San Francisco State University series in philosophy; vol. 8)
Includes bibliographical references and index.
1. War—Moral and ethical aspects. 2. Just war doctrine. 3. Nuclear warfare—
Moral and ethical aspects. 4. Deterrence (Strategy). I. Title. II. Series.
B105.W3P37   172'.422—dc20   94-33707
ISBN 0-8204-2621-0
ISSN 1067-0017

Die Deutsche Bibliothek-CIP-Einheitsaufnahme

Palmer-Fernandez, Gabriel:
Deterrence and the crisis in moral theory: an analysis of the moral literature on
the nuclear arms debate/ Gabriel Palmer-Fernandez. –New York; Washington,
D.C./Baltimore; Bern; Frankfurt am Main; Berlin; Vienna; Paris: Lang.
(San Francisco State University series in philosophy; Vol. 8)
ISBN 0-8204-2621-0
NE: San Francisco State University: San Francisco State...

The paper in this book meets the guidelines for permanence and durability
of the Committee on Production Guidelines for Book Longevity
of the Council of Library Resources.

© 1996 Peter Lang Publishing, Inc., New York

Printed in the United States of America.

Then Calchas spoke again. "The wind," he said,
"Was sent by Artemis; and he revealed
Her remedy—a thought to crush like lead
The hearts of Atreus' sons, who wept, as weep they must,
And speechless ground their scepters in the dust."

The elder king then spoke: "What can I say?
Disaster follows if I disobey;
Surely yet worse disaster if I yield
And slaughter my own child, my home's delight,
In her young innocence, and stain my hand
With blasphemous unnatural cruelty,
Bathed in the blood I fathered! Either way,
Ruin! Disband the fleet, sail home, and earn
The deserter's badge—abandon my command,
Betray the alliance—now? The wind must turn,
There must be sacrifice, a maid must bleed—
Their chafing rage demands it—they are right!
May good prevail, and justify my deed!"

Then he put on
The harness of Necessity.

Aeschylus, Agamemnon, 199-218

To Ralph B. Potter
who taught me what ethics is all about

Contents

Deterrence and the Crisis in Moral Theory

Acknowledgments

Debts of gratitude are a pleasure to pay, and the following are among the most pleasurable of all. As a graduate student I benefited from the excellent teaching and good counsel of a number of individuals whose influence over the years has formed the foundation of my approach to the moral problem of war. I was first introduced to the study of morality and war in Fr. David Hollenbach's course "Christian Social Ethics" at Weston School of Theology in the Fall term of 1982. Later, a seminar taught by Professor Ralph Potter of Harvard University, though on an unrelated topic, convinced me to undertake further work on the problem of war. Potter's commitment to careful, disciplined, and detailed moral analysis has served as a model to which I have tried to conform. I was fortunate during my graduate studies to have Ralph Potter as advisor. Few others, I think, would have respected my need for independence of thought and satisfied my desire for frequent and informal conversations on this as well as on many other topics in ethical theory and everyday life. My debt to him is obvious from the dedication of this book. In the Spring term of 1987, I had the good fortune to serve as Fr. J. Bryan Hehir's teaching fellow on a course on the nuclear arms debate. His approach to the massive and complex body of literature on this subject has provided me with an insightful and reliable guide. Richard B. Miller's excellent book, *Interpretations of Conflict: Ethics, Pacifism, and the Just-War Tradition*, provided a model for writing about, as well as much needed motivation to return to, the moral problem of war.

I want to express my gratitude also to Kimberley Patton and John Lanci. They know the origins of this book and served as its first midwives. Professors Arthur Dyck and Stanley Hoffmann read an earlier draft of this study and pressed me to pursue further work on the morality of war. Sarah Verrill Lown endures my irascibility and near constant distraction from our common life occasioned by this as well as other projects. The brightness her loving-kindness brings to my gloomy character might be equalled only by our wonderful summer retreats in Turbat's Creek, Kennebunkport, Maine. My editor at Peter Lang, Dr. Heidi Burns, put her superb skills to work on this manuscript and made the tedious work of revision both pleasant and instructive. Professor Anatole Anton provided detailed and incisive comments without which greater weaknesses would have remained in this study. My colleagues in the Department of Philosophy & Religious Studies at Youngstown State University together create an excellent learning and work environment: Drs. Chris Bache, Cynthia Brincat, Brendan Minogue, John-Christian Smith, Linda "Tess" Tessier, Bruce N. Waller, and Victor Wan-Tatah. My department head, Dr. Thomas Shipka, hastened the completion of this work not only by granting me release time from teaching duties, but also through his good and infectious example of diligence. My research assistants, Toni Bisconti and Carrie Pitzulo, as well as Skip Slavic, assistant to the directors of the Ethics Center at Youngstown State University, where I serve as the associate director, gave much of their time and talent to this project. Finally, I am indebted to Youngstown State University for its financial support through a University Research Council Grant.

G.P.-F.
Youngstown, Ohio
September, 1995

The San Francisco State University Series In Philosophy

This series is designed to encourage philosophers to explore new directions in research, particularly directions that may lead to a re-integration of philosophy with the sciences, the arts and/or the humanities.

The series is guided by three premises:

1. The intellectual division of labor into distinct academic disciplines is a product of changing historical circumstances and conditions (including developments within the disciplines themselves).

2. The current intellectual division of labor has outlived its usefulness in many ways.

3. There is a pressing need to re-integrate the metaphysical and evaluative concerns of philosophy with current work in both the natural and social sciences and their associated technologies, the humanities and the arts.

Works in this series are intended to challenge social and philosophical preconceptions that block the re-integration of philosophy with other disciplines and at the same time to maintain unquestionably high standards of scholarship. The eighth volume in our series, *Deterrence and the Crisis in Moral Theory*, exemplifies our intentions. Despite the apparent end of the cold war, global militarization remains an on-going process with no end in sight. With the stakes in this process determined by the increasing prevalence and accessibility of thermonuclear weapons, the need for a critical guide to the moral issues raised by these political and technological developments turns out to be more urgent, more complex, and more profound, if Professor Palmer-Fernandez is right, than moral philosophers and theologians have heretofore imagined. Indeed, the very decision to bear the economic, social, and ecological costs of the production of nuclear weapons for the purpose of deterrence has profound moral dimensions. *Deterrence and the Crisis in Moral Theory* is a fascinating study of how questions of applied ethics which arise in the context of military policy force us to recognize the need for a deeper understanding of ethical theory itself. As well as pushing us to ask deep questions about fundamental assumptions of ordinary moral theory, Palmer-Fernandez argues that the ethical questions concerning nuclear war push us to accept the conclusion that only the concept of an ultimate moral dilemma, a concept which is out of place in existing ethical theories, whether they be deontological or consequentialist, can do justice to the military and technological realities of the present. Though he ultimately defends a consequentialist approach to the moral questions surrounding a policy of nuclear deterrence, Palmer-Fernandez also argues that, so to speak, these policies have an ineradicable "moral cost," that there is a tragic dimension to the decisions forced upon us by the nuclear age. In the course of his argument, Palmer-Fernandez is led to challenge a number of the assumptions of typical moral theories concerning, for example, the relation between intentions and action, and the nature of the conflict between an ethics of character and the moral claims of politics. The implications of his work are, then, that the division of labor which separates moralists and theologians from political scientists, military planners and diplomats must be questioned. Moreover, the ordinary idea of technological progress must be questioned not only because of the potentially tragic consequences that may result from such progress, but also because of the actually tragic dilemmas with which technological progress in the military sphere forces us to live on a daily basis.

Anatole Anton, *General Editor*
San Francisco State University
Department of Philosophy
1600 Holloway Avenue
San Francisco, CA 94132

Foreword

Richard B. Miller

This book is about the differences between private and political morality, and how those differences are intensified in debates about the ethics of nuclear deterrence. With admirable clarity and rigor, Gabriel Palmer-Fernandez argues that nuclear deterrence presents us with a crisis in moral reasoning, forcing us to choose between moral purity or political necessity. In either case the stakes are high, with each choice involving enormous trade-offs. Purity—refusing to threaten nuclear reprisal and risk nuclear devastation—may require nations to disarm, leaving them vulnerable to outside dangers and mendacious threats. Necessity—the need to maintain self-defensive measures—may involve a commitment to do wrong to prevent the (political) heavens from falling.

If we recognize the kinds of responsibilities that surround public roles, the author insists, it becomes clear that the kinds of expectations that surround the ideals of moral integrity in personal affairs are unhelpful in the arena of political morality. Thus, public policy ought to be freed somewhat from the deontological constraints that normally shape the morality of private life and personal conscience. This is especially true, Palmer-Fernandez argues, when it comes to the task of protecting a nation from outside aggression or intimidation. He thus maintains that the possession of and commitment to use nuclear weapons in order to prevent their use creates a set of issues that defy standard attempts to impose agent-centered expectations on public policy, opening the way for consequentialist considerations in the assessment of nuclear deterrence and political morality in general.

Over the past three decades the issues surrounding deterrence and political responsibility have engaged some of the best minds in theological ethics and, more recently, moral philosophy: John Courtney Murray, Paul Ramsey, Michael Walzer, the U. S. Catholic bishops, John Finnis, Joseph Boyle, Germain Grisez, Gregory Kavka, and David Gauthier. The reader will find incisive discussions and criticisms of their works here, along with an instructive account of the history of deterrent policy and the moral quandaries that informed shifts in defense strategy from the 1950s through the 1980s. Palmer-Fernandez carries out this analysis in a constructive fashion, building upon the lessons to be learned from his examination of academic discussions and policy debates. In addition to the issues that surround the differences between private and public morality, he calls our attention to three sets of questions that are woven together in the ethics of deterrence.

First is the question of the logical relation between actions and intentions. Do we derive the morality of intentions by first determining the morality of actions? Is what is wrong to do also wrong to intend? If we derive the morality of intentions by first determining the morality of actions, then public officials must conceive a set of morally acceptable actions to carry out in the event that deterrence fails. In this model, a justified deterrent presupposes a set of policy decisions informed by just-war criteria. Otherwise the preventive aims of deterrence are implicated in plans for an unacceptable course of action. If, on the other hand, we can assess intentions in light of their autonomous consequences, then another route suggests itself. On this second model, we ought to begin by determining whether the intention to protect a nation from intimidation or aggression is acceptable, and then reason derivatively about the morality of performing actions that fulfill that intention should requisite conditions arise. In either model, the conceptual point is plain: Given the fact that deterrence involves forming intentions *both* to prevent war *and* to act should deterrence fail, the proper method for assessing intention in relation to action is of no small importance when considering the morality of defense policy.

Second, what are the relevant similarities and differences between conventional and nuclear war? Ought we conceive of nuclear war, and the morality of nuclear war, according to the paradigm of conventional war and the just-war tradition? Or is nuclear war and its horrors so great as to defy any attempt to smooth over the differences between these kinds of wars? Those who conceive of nuclear war according to the paradigm of conventional war typically urge public policy makers to develop a nuclear war-fighting capability. Those who insist upon radical differences between the two types of war argue that nuclear war should never be fought and that attempts to conceive of such wars along conventional lines make them likelier (and the world more dangerous).

Debates about whether to increase or decrease the differences between conventional and nuclear wars are linked to a third set of questions: What are the differences between plans to fight a war and plans to deter war? Do plans that make fighting war more practicable weaken the preventive aims of deterrence? Lying behind these questions is the fact that deterring war involves preparation to fight a war, but with a paradoxical intention. Deterrence involves preparing to go to war in order to prevent war from being fought. Given this paradox, does it make sense to think of the ethics of deterrence according to the framework of the ethics of war? Or does the preventive aim of deterrence invite a different set of categories for moral analysis?

Palmer-Fernandez argues that recent discussions about the ethics of deterrence have involved some careless thinking about these various questions. He argues that we can salvage the institution of nuclear deterrence from incoherence if we are able to grant some consequentialist concessions to public policy and craft a theory of intention that draws from an understanding of the responsibilities that political leaders face in their roles as public officials.

Yet this book is about more than the vertiginous issues surrounding nuclear deterrence. Indeed, to read this work as a book about practical morality alone would be to read it superficially. Palmer-Fernandez is also arguing a theoretical point about the nature of moral dilemmas, the task of having to choose between two fundamentally incompatible yet compelling alternatives. As I have said, these two ways are marked by a concern for the purity of individual conscience and a concern for outcomes in the arena of public life. Palmer-Fernandez draws upon some broader features of our liberal culture to suggest that we ought not see this dilemma as fatal or paralyzing: We should acknowledge the merits of moral pluralism, the existence of rival moral theories in Western culture. One way to ease the anxieties that surround the dilemma posed by deterrence is to understand that, in general, conscience-based and consequences-based moralities each have distinct roles to play given the different exigencies that private individuals and public officers must confront.

Readers familiar with Reinhold Niebuhr's *Moral Man and Immoral Society* will recognize parallels with Palmer-Fernandez's line of thought. As the author makes clear, the tensions that surround nuclear deterrence are scarcely new. But the problems that surround nuclear war and deterrence raise questions that were unknown to Niebuhr in the 1930s, and invite careful inquiry along practical and theoretical lines. In the spirit of Niebuhr's realism, Palmer-Fernandez fashions a trenchant moral and political analysis, one that brings traditional Western thought and crisp analytical rigor to bear upon problems posed by modern life.

Indiana University
Bloomington, Indiana
October, 1995

1 Introduction

A satisfactory moral assessment of war addresses several distinct but interrelated topics. According to an ancient view, the subject matter of ethics is largely determined by the question of how people ought to live their lives. I am of the opinion that much of what ethics is about involves considerations of character as well as of a coherent plan of life. Better to cultivate in ourselves a gentle and pure disposition toward others, than not. For the Christian, this view takes the form of a deeper and more searching requirement that one's life shall detract nothing from the majesty of God and the well-being of our neighbor. At the same time, there are other, perhaps equally important, considerations that need to be taken into account. Even under normal political conditions, a contrary set of moral claims arises requiring "the cunning of the serpent" and a certain experience and wisdom in the management of power.

The moral assessment of war must also consider the plurality of our ordinary morality intuitions and their corresponding principles. Some of our intuitions are, I think, outcome-centered, giving great moral weight to the effects of our actions on those goods and values we seek to secure. These seem to have a singularly important place in public matters, especially defense policy, where there are very high stakes for a large population. But not all acts that are or might be recommended because of their consequences have an intuitive justification. There are contrary intuitions and principles that prohibit certain acts, regardless of what happens. These can be recognized by all but the morally obtuse. The complexity of and conflicts between these rival intuitions are reflected in my analysis and conclusions. The point I wish to make is simple and was long ago recorded by Heraclitus: life is more than diversity; it is a perpetual conflict between different claims which cannot be brought together in any neat and tidy way. Philosophers and theologians who say otherwise have simply overlooked, or for the sake of theoretical coherence ignored, this fact.

My interest in war is part of a broader attempt to understand the shape and limits of practical morality. Many recent discussions on the moral problem of war have centered on the philosophical bases of individual responsibility in war and the rules of war. In this study I devote considerable attention to the continuities and discontinuities between the ideals of character and the moral claims of the political community upon the national leadership. Discussion on the relation between character and politics usually center on a distinction between private and political, sometimes also referred to as public, morality. That distinction is important and carries with it wide-ranging implications. It is especially important in a pluralistic democracy where the diversity of ideas, both secular and religious, of the good life or the virtuous character conflict, or might conflict, with each other in a profound way.

1.1 AIMS OF THIS BOOK

I have two primary aims in this book. First, I wish to examine the judgments of just-war theorists on the morality of the use of nuclear weapons and the practice of nuclear deterrence, and to show how these judgments are linked by different mediating concepts and factual assumptions. I propose to analyze the dominant views on the subject of the morality of modern war, to compare them with each other, and to consider objections that have been or might be brought against them. My second aim, both more controversial and substantive, is to argue that nuclear weapons and war-fighting plans engender disturbing moral dilemmas. The moral judgments we bring to bear upon the use of these weapons and the practice of deterrence recommend incompatible courses of action and no fully rational and coherent way to choose between them is available. The incompatibility of recommended courses of action prompts us to question fundamental ways of thinking about morality and some of our ordinary morality intuitions about the relation of intentions and actions. While this is primarily a study in applied ethics, I am also interested in general moral theory, especially in the very important question of the possibility of a comprehensive and unified moral theory.

Until about 1950, a continuous and long-standing tradition existed that defined a *casus belli* and left little doubt concerning the moral justification for the recourse to force. This tradition was sanctioned by church and international law, and with the exception of various groups that dissent on grounds of conscience or religion, it was generally accepted. By providing rational restraints on the recourse to and use of force, the tradition of the just war furnishes a set of criteria for the counsel of individual conscience, the direction of public discussion, and the formation of government policy on the use of military force and the conduct of soldiers in war.

Since the advent of nuclear weapons, however, the just-war tradition has been challenged both from within and without as moralists reflect on the massive and indiscriminate power of modern means of warfare. During the last several decades innumerable books and articles have appeared which appraise the morality of nuclear weapons. Each seeks to persuade its reader to adopt a particular moral outlook and recommends to the public and government what ought to be done here and now about the new instruments of war. The result is widespread diversity and disagreement. Among just-war moralists there is no collective opinion on the values and goods worth defending by the threat or use of nuclear force (life, liberty, territorial integrity, political sovereignty), the ends to which nuclear arms policy ought to be directed (disarmament, be that bilateral or unilateral, arms control, the correction, balance or deterrence of an adversary's nuclear or conventional forces), or the justification of such policy (moral, political, or strategic). More generally, there is no agreement on the possibility of applying in a meaningful and coherent way the received moral tradition to a nuclear-armed world.

Discussion on the question "Can modern war be just?" is now in its fifth decade. It was first addressed, in the 1950s, by theologians and church councils, Catholic and Protestant alike. Most of them appealed to the language of the just-war tradition. This language of moral discourse is evident in the extensive and sometimes sophisticated Christian moral literature of the 1960s and '70s on the problem of nuclear war, and in the influential and widely discussed 1983 Pastoral Letter of the American Catholic bishops. During the Vietnam War, an increasing number of secular philosophers became interested in practical-moral rather than abstract-theoretical problems. The inadequacy of pure philosophy to address widespread dissatisfaction with U.S. policy in Southeast Asia led philosophers to rethink their discipline in a more socially responsible way. Their contribution to discussions on the problem of war is not only gladly received by the theologically trained, but also invaluable for the nuclear arms debate. Philosophers bring to bear upon the problem of modern war their sharp analytic tools, their fondness for hypothetical examples to test the limits of our customary ways of thought, and an unwavering commitment to reason rather than dogma as a source for moral guidance. Many of the authors I treat in this study belong to the former group, but I make frequent use of the excellent philosophical literature available on the problem of war.

There are four possible positions one might adopt on the morality of the use of nuclear weapons and the formation of deterrence intentions: (1) the use of nuclear weapons and the practice of deterrence are morally impermissible; (2) the use of certain nuclear weapons and the practice of deterrence are morally acceptable under specific limiting conditions; (3) the use of nuclear weapons is wrong, though deterrence for the aim of dissuading a similarly armed adversary is, under present conditions of world affairs, morally acceptable; and (4) the use of nuclear weapons is morally permissible, but not the practice of deterrence. As far as I know no one has held this last view, nor do I believe it can have any serious justification. Therefore it will not be discussed.

I refer to the views I examine in this study as the Disarmament Party (chapter 3), the War-Fighting Party (chapter 4), and the Deterrence-Only Party (chapter 5). The differences among these three views are the result either of certain moral principles or factual assumptions by which a particular party links judgments on the use of nuclear weapons and on deterrence intentions. For example, the disarmament party links these judgments by way of a prohibitive moral principle which draws a moral equivalence going from action to intentions. This principle says that it is immoral to intend what is immoral to do (the Wrongful Intentions Principle [WIP]). It also rests on the factual assumption that nuclear weapons are qualitatively different from conventional arms (Principle of Discontinuity [PD]). While the war-fighting party adopts the prohibitive WIP, and so endorses the moral equivalence of action and intentions, it does not assume that all nuclear weapons are qualitatively different from conventional ones. At most, it might claim that nuclear weapons are different only in degree. So it rejects PD. Absent this factual assumption, the war-fighting party allows within the parameters of WIP for the use of certain nuclear weapons and deterrence intentions. The deterrence-only party adopts the factual assumption that nuclear weapons are a class different from conventional ones, and in this way prohibits their use. But representatives of this party think that deterrence intentions are permissible because, under present conditions, not to form those intentions might allow for a moral evil much greater than whatever evil is produced in forming the requisite intention. They believe the urgency of present security needs overrides the prohibition on intending what is immoral to do. So they accept PD but retreat from WIP.

Substantive differences among these parties emerge from two other sources. First is a party's primary reliance on one or the other of two dominant styles of moral reasoning available in contemporary ethical theory: either an outcome-centered or agent-centered approach, more commonly referred to as consequentialism and deontology, respectively. Both of these styles of reasoning give incompatible content to the structure of morality. Roughly speaking, an outcome-centered moral theory is primarily concerned with the consequences of a given policy. It sometimes draws from social-scientific, especially economic, models of analysis—the theory of choice, for example—and attempts to predict and to assess the effects of a particular policy or course of action as it relates to certain predetermined values—e.g., self-interest, value preference, or human well-being. On this view, morality is dependent on the expected net utility or other morally relevant consequences produced by different policy alternatives. The agent-centered approach, on the other hand, views morality as an area of analysis distinctively autonomous of the social sciences. It is primarily concerned with giving an independent account of the rightness of acts and establishing clear principles that impose more or less universally binding constraints on action, regardless of consequences.

Both of these approaches to moral reasoning have an undeniable intuitive appeal, and the moral agent is oftentimes caught between equally compelling and incompatible ways of reasoning about morality: one clearly has to do with what *happens* to certain values or goods when we adopt a course of action as a policy position, and the other with the nature of what we *do* to others. The difference between these ways of reasoning illustrates the theoretical problem of relating the special obligations of those who are entrusted with the welfare of our public institutions and with guaranteeing a secure social environment, to ordinary constraints and prohibitions on action. It is an important question whether an agent-centered moral theory primarily concerned with the internal state of the agent (sentiments, intentions, character, and condition of the will) and the intrinsic nature of acts (What kind of act is it? It is a promise? Or is it a lie?) can successfully address the special moral features of public office.

The values that enter policy decisions is another source from which substantive differences arise between the various parties. Generally speaking, the two fundamental values that collide in the moral literature on nuclear arms policy are those of national self-defense, which give rise to specific role-duties incurred by the national leadership, and of human life, usually presented under a theory of rights, which yields constraints on what we can morally do to others—for example, that persons not be threatened or treated in harmful ways. Each of these values gives compelling support for adopting courses of action incompatible with each other, and a decision between them, though necessary, might seem necessarily arbitrary. This is so because to choose either value means to act against the rejected value, even though we have compelling moral reasons not to do so. If human beings were so created that a single value outweighs all other possible values, then one might envision a decision procedure able to resolve practical conflicts of this kind. I myself doubt that such a value exists. I also doubt that all values have a common source to which one can appeal to resolve practical conflicts. However, in chapters 2 and 4.2, I argue that an outcome-centered approach is able to guide us in policy decisions in ways impossible for an agent-centered approach. It is therefore, by my account, the preferred approach to policy evaluation.

1.2 THE POST-COLD WAR WORLD IS NOT POST-NUCLEAR

The debates about the morality of nuclear deterrence and war examined in this book were waged with great vigor and urgency in the decades preceding the fall of the former Soviet Union. Because this study examines the moral literature that emerged as a response to the strategic doctrines of the Cold War, the reader might opine that the relevance of this study is at best historical. I do think there is a historical value to this topic. But that value does not exhaust the relevance of the moral literature on nuclear arms policy nor the moral problems posed by these weapons of mass destruction.[1]

At present, the major military powers possess a combined total of well over fifty thousand nuclear weapons, testing and production of nuclear weapons and of fissionable materials are still pursued by the major powers, and more and more countries, especially in the Third World, wish to possess them. As former CIA Director James Woosley warned Congress, "more than twenty-five countries, many of them hostile to the United States and our allies, may have or may be developing nuclear, biological and chemical weapons—so called weapons of mass destruction—and the means to deliver them."[2] In the post-Cold War world the nuclear club has only increased its membership, and a nuclear-free world is at best a distant hope.

Thomas Reed, former secretary of the Air Force, in 1991 urged maintaining a "sizeable nuclear arsenal" targeting "every reasonable adversary" and cautioned that "more nuclear-weapons states are likely to emerge in the Third World. With such weapons they can seek to deter the United States and others from interfering with their regional aggressions." These nations, Reed argued, should not be "allowed to believe that they can embark on major aggression against the United States, its deployed forces, or its allies and friends while enjoying sanctuary from American weapons, including nuclear weapons."[3] Similarly, in his January 1994 report to the President and Congress, Les Aspin, Bill Clinton's first secretary of defense, said,

> The United States cannot rely solely on arms control to mitigate this threat [of nuclear war]. The old Cold War tools of deterrence can still help the United States respond to the threat that these nuclear weapons would pose in the hands of, for instance, a government in Russia that revived an adversarial relationship. This requires the United States to maintain a nuclear posture that clearly demonstrates that no nation would succeed in achieving its military or political objectives if it initiated a conflict with the United States and its allies.[4]

The post-Cold War world is decidedly not post-nuclear. Nuclear weapons poised for (either direct or indirect) indiscriminate attack against whole cities are still very much with us. I am inclined to think that these weapons will be with us until a more powerful generation of weapons is developed. The military and political use of those weapons will either be made to fit our nuclear modes of thought—deterrence, escalation control, survivability, and so forth—or will stimulate new strategic theories that, in turn, might or might not create distinctive moral concerns.

Either way, the theoretical problems forced upon us by efforts to think morally about nuclear weapons and the institution of deterrence are more than a historical curiosity. Those problems are still with us and are, moreover, of lasting significance because they raise important questions about some fundamental assumptions of traditional moral theory—e.g., regarding the relation between intentions and action, the incompatibility of ordinary morality intuitions and their corresponding principles, the conflict between an ethics of character and the moral claims of politics, the range of a coherent moral theory, among others.

1.3 CAN A MORALIST SPEAK ABOUT WAR?

As a moralist, I am engaged in the sustained analysis of a human experience that critical reflection cannot fully capture. In the heat of war, the soldier in the battlefield or the technician in a missile silo is not likely to engage in the kind of examination I, in the tranquility of my study, think is required for a proper understanding of war. There is no common ground, some will say, between the practice of war and a moralist's reflection. Moreover, as John Keegan says in the opening lines of his brilliant portrait of war, I have "not been in a battle; not near one, nor heard one from afar, nor seen the aftermath."[5] My closest acquaintance with war was the few shots I as a young boy heard off in the distance in the city of Havana shortly after the fall of the Batista regime. The soldier or statesman might well think this personal fact sufficient to disqualify me from serious writing on the subject of war. In this, perhaps more than in most other areas of life, it is experience that counts.

Paul Fussell has given these claims a forceful and poignant expression. In a defense of the nuclear bombings of Hiroshima and Nagasaki, Fussell argues that the experience of war provides an indispensable perspective on the subject, "an experience of having to come to grips, face to face, with an enemy who designs your death."[6] No matter how much one reads, reflects on, or speaks with those who have encountered an enemy "face to face," the unique insight into the reality of war that such an experience provides is simply unavailable to the uninitiated. "What is at stake," he says, "in an infantry assault is so entirely unthinkable to those without experience of one, even if they possess very wide-ranging imaginations and sympathies, that experience is crucial in this case." In battle we might find ourselves having "to compromise the pure clarity of [our] moral vision by the experience of weighing [our] own life against other people's."[7]

Yet the experience of war, while necessary for a full sympathetic appreciation of its reality, is not a sufficient condition for the task at hand. It may, in fact, bring us too close to the action. We should then lose sight of the whole reality of war by the particularities of experience. War consists not only of assaults, battles, and victory or defeat, but also of complex political conditions over time, as well as the rules and judgments that always accompany human activities. Although war does suspend some of the rules that guide human conduct, even when it is hell, it still remains a rule-governed activity. The fact that in war the ordinary rules of conduct and peaceful constraints of human groups are temporarily ruptured does not entail a condition without order. It entails only a departure from ordinary conduct.

The reality of war is not, nor can it be, exhausted by the activity of soldiers, statesmen, and strategists. War is a social practice defined by an environment of ideas that surround it, which, in turn, is influenced by social and cultural developments, and the opinions of humankind. As Michael Howard puts it:

> to abstract war from the environment in which it is fought and study its technique as one would those of a game is to ignore a dimension essential to the understanding, not simply of the wars themselves but of the societies which fought them.[8]

Some of the ideas that come to bear upon the reality of war and its waging are technological. These determine not only the instruments and capabilities—the hardware—of war, but also the conceptual orientation we bring to it.[9] Other ideas have to do with the theory of the state and the doctrine of national self-determination. There are some ideas that have to do with peace, and how best to achieve it. For example, at least since the time of Immanuel Kant, liberal political philosophers have held that liberal nations are less likely to go to war with each other than illiberal regimes. Liberal nations will gradually move from a state of wild, lawless freedom to a federation of free states that will maintain itself effortlessly and in perpetuity.[10] There is another set of ideas that, perhaps now more than ever, comes to bear upon the reality of war. These are moral or humanitarian ideas having to do with the character of persons and right restraint that define the limits of morally permissible action. These ideas form the special province of the moralist and are, therefore, my main concern.

There is a code of conduct supported by a moral argument that soldier and civilian, academic or not, can readily recognize. This code is often ignored or broken, in times of peace as well as during war. Whether it be a code of honor, of knightly chivalry, or a professional code does not matter much, because the fact is that it is always there. It forms part of the fabric of everyday life, and every soldier, general, and strategist appeals to it, sometimes unconsciously, when asked why a particular course of action was chosen over an alternative. Both in peace and in war human activity requires justification, and when things go wrong we look for reasons and for those who are or might be accountable. We will argue about these things. We will give praise and blame to those deserving of them. But the moralist does not have to teach the soldier what murder, cruelty, terror, and looting are, nor why they are wrong. He already knows.[11] And he knows also when he has been the perpetrator of a crime, even when the crime provides a military advantage.

There is, I believe, something right in the claim that direct experience offers a vantage point moral reflection is unable fully to capture. It is nonetheless a mistake to think that direct experience is decisive for understanding war's reality, and this in at least two ways. First, direct experience is not a necessary condition for competent moral judgment. Indeed, to require direct, personal experience of a particular kind of human activity for participation in moral discourse tends to undermine the objectivity of moral statements. That position would presumably regard first-person accounts as the only reliable source of moral knowledge. Second, even if we assume a gap to exist between the practice of war and a moralist's reflection upon it, few would consider this gap to be absolute.

To think otherwise makes war so autonomous from every other area of life that no decision-maker, save the military, could offer an intelligent opinion.

1.4 OUTLINE OF THE ANALYSIS

It is not the purpose of this study to assess the morality of past or hypothetical wars, nor to elaborate a set of prescriptions for the proper way to wage war. My purpose will be achieved if the following chapters provide a critical guide to the complex moral issues of modern war which compete for our attention.

This study may be read in at least two ways: as an introduction to the application of an ancient moral doctrine to the nuclear age, or as a history (albeit not a chronological account) of the modern understanding of the just war. Both can be approached from my three-fold typology found in chapters 3-5. In these chapters I treat some of the most prominent figures in the debate on the morality of nuclear arms policy from the 1950s to the 1980s—perhaps the most important public debate ever—and in two sections of this study, 3.1 and 4.1, make some connection between their analyses and the empirical facts of the nuclear debate. In addition, this study can be read as a contribution to the on-going, though now not especially heated, debate on the just-war perspective on the instruments and plans for major war. Finally, the more fundamental question about the relation of force and morality and the problems that this relation brings in the context of the nuclear age to ethical theory figure prominently in several sections: 2.1-2, 3.2, 4.2-3, 5.1.

Accordingly, this book offers a critical appraisal of the arguments for and against the use of nuclear weapons and the practice of deterrence. Chapter 2 examines a central problem in moral discourse about war. It attempts to articulate a discontinuity between our ideas about what kind of persons we ought to become and the claims that come to bear upon political office. The discontinuity between these dominates much of the analysis in this study.

Chapters 3 through 5 present the three parties in the debate and also advance an argument for a consequence based evaluation of political action. In chapter 3, I examine a non-consequentialist argument against the use of nuclear weapons and the practice of deterrence. My concern is to introduce and to assess the factual assumption that nuclear weapons are different in kind from conventional weapons and the claim that one may not intend what is immoral to do, PD and WIP, respectively. Chapter 4 presents an alternative non-consequentialist position on the nuclear arms debate, that of limited nuclear war and of counterforce deterrence. This position draws on the moral equivalence going from what is permissible in war to what may be sanctioned in deterrence intention. Having rejected this equivalence in chapter 3, I now advance a slightly different argument against it. My main point here is that the logic of this party requires that civilians be targeted as a means to the goal of a counterforce deterrence. That threat to civilian life is contrary to this party's endorsement of the absolute principle of discrimination. Chapter 5 has a double focus. It examines the attempt of the deterrence-only party to make deterrence compatible with the moral limits on the use of force, part of which is based on a rejection of WIP, and develops the discussion on moral dilemmas introduced in chapter 2.

The final chapter offers some concluding reflections on the effect of dilemmas on how we should think about moral problems, whether they concern individual action or social policies. If moral dilemmas of the kind described here are not real, then we can trust that with careful deliberation there will always be one right choice a person can take without the possibility of remorse or regret. If they are real, as I hold they are, then the residual requirement that is not acted on gives us good reason to imagine how we might feel after our choice is made. Thinking about morality in this way forces us to look at moral theory in a new way.

NOTES

1. The continued relevance of the moral problems posed by nuclear weapons is made clear in Carl Kaysen, Robert S. McNamara, and George W. Rathjens, "Nuclear Weapons After the Cold War," *Foreign Affairs* (Fall 1991), 108: "There are several reasons why it is desirable to reduce the number of nuclear weapons even further. Perhaps the most basic one is the fundamental immorality of relying on the threat of death and destruction to civilians and the urban fabric of civilization on the scale that even a few tens of modern nuclear weapons would produce. Such a strike would put at risk not only the citizens of the nuclear powers involved but millions of citizens of even distant nonbelligerent states affected by the fallout of radiation, as Chernobyl made clear. The world has lived with a similar immorality ever since Germany and then Britain and the United States relied on air attack of cities as a major instrument of war. But the basic point remains and at bottom reflects the deeper moral difficulty of relying on war as an instrument of state policy." It is important to note that these authors think there is "no need for most of the world's nuclear weapons" (109). They do not say there is no need for *any* of those weapons. Because they think these weapons are immoral yet see a need for some of them, Kaysen, McNamara and Rathjens counsel the continued reliance on an immoral practice.

2. James Woosley, Testimony before Senate Committee on Governmental Affairs, "Proliferation Threats of the 1990s," February 24, 1993, *Boston Globe*, June 12, 1994.

3. Quoted in Joseph Gerson, *With Hiroshima Eyes: Atomic War, Nuclear Extortion and Moral Imagination* (Philadelphia, PA: New Society Publishers, 1995), 174.

4. Les Aspin, *Annual Report to the President and the Congress* (Washington, DC: Department of Defense, 1994), 59.

5. John Keegan, *The Face of Battle* (New York: Penguin Books, 1978), 13.

6. Paul Fussell, "Hiroshima: A Soldier's View," *The New Republic* (August 22 & 29, 1981), 27.

7. Fussell, "Hiroshima," 27, 30.

8. Michael Howard, *War in European History* (Oxford: Oxford University Press, 1976), ix.

9. See, for example, Martin Van Creveld's excellent study, *Technology and War* (New York: The Free Press, 1989).

10. Joseph Schumpeter advanced a variant of this view when he argued that a capitalist democracy "steadily tells against the use of military force and for peaceful arrangements, even when the balance of pecuniary interests is clearly on the side of war." *Capitalism, Socialism, and Democracy* (New York: Harper Torchbooks, 1950), 128. More recently, Michael W. Doyle has suggested that Kant's theory of a pacific union of liberal states has been borne out by the events of the past two-hundred years. As more nations adopt liberal institutions, the closer we approximate a warless world. "Kant, Liberalism, and Foreign Affairs," *Philosophy and Public Affairs* 12 (Summer/Fall 1983), 203-235, 323-353.

11. I find the construction "he or she" and its variants cumbersome. So I use "she" in some and "he" in other places.

2 Dilemma in the Moral Logic of War

You may be quite sure, gentlemen, that if I had tried long ago to engage in politics, I should long ago have lost my life, without doing any good to you or to myself. The true champion of justice, if he intends to survive even for a short time, must necessarily confine himself to private life and leave politics alone.

Socrates, *Apology*, 31e.

Those then who think that the natures of the statesman, the royal ruler, the head of state and the master of a family are the same, are mistaken. [B]y examining the elements of which [the state] is composed we shall better discern in relation to these kinds of rulers what is the difference between them.

Aristotle, *Politics*, Bk.I

No highly developed sensibilities are required to give an account of what is morally wrong with the slaughters at Guernica and Shanghai, the air campaigns against Dresden, London, Tokyo, the nuclear bombings of Hiroshima and Nagasaki, or the massacre at My Lai. Civilians were directly and intentionally killed as a means to a military goal. And that, most commentators agree, is not war but murder. In some situations, however, our judgments might not be as firm because the principles which underlie them either remain obscure or justify action we know is, at the same time, in some real way morally wrong. Our intuitions rebel against the latter idea, partly because we should then have to admit a contradiction in our principles, but more importantly because we find ourselves to have run into some profound limitation on human action.

In this chapter I sketch the broad lines of a fundamental dilemma that arises in the moral evaluation of the practice of deterrence and of nuclear war, namely: the dilemma between the moral claims of politics and the moral standards appropriate to, and more commonly used to appraise, conduct in private life. Part of my argument in this study is designed to show that there is a profound conflict between the moral requirement on politics to protect the life of the community and the moral requirement on us all not to threaten the lives of those who have done no wrong. To do so,

I draw upon what I believe is a fairly strong and long-standing, even if not always explicit, consensus among writers on the morality of war that a division of sorts obtains between those principles by which we appraise the conduct of individuals in private acts and those relevant to acts of a political nature.[1] But first I must address the question whether genuine moral dilemmas are possible.

2.1 MORAL DILEMMAS

Moralists often overlook those situations wherein incompatible alternatives for action are each strongly prescribed by some moral requirement and no rationally satisfactory way to choose between them is available. Such a situation is one of a moral dilemma. A moral dilemma is a situation where a person has compelling moral reasons to adopt two or more incompatible courses of action and none is overridden in any significant way.

Philosophers and theologians admit that there are instances of apparent moral dilemmas, as when, for example, there is some subjective doubt about what is to be done in a given set of circumstances or a person succumbs to character weakness—intemperance, incontinence, and the like. But most philosophers and theologians refuse to admit that genuine moral dilemmas can ever occur. As Alasdair MacIntyre puts it, "there is an objective moral order, but our perceptions of it are such that we cannot bring rival moral truths into complete harmony with each other."[2] We often find ourselves torn between morally incompatible courses of action because, he says, we have inherited mere fragments or scraps of heterogeneous moral traditions which have been severed from the social context that gave them meaning and order.

One important purpose of a moral theory is to provide some decision procedure for choosing one over other possible courses of action in a situation of conflict. Such a procedure may be impossible because when moral requirements conflict, the agent cannot avoid the transgression of one of the conflicting moral requirements. If that is the case, then the purpose and, more importantly, the possibility of a coherent moral theory are radically challenged.

It is worth noting, even if only briefly, some typical claims made on behalf of this view. The *locus classicus* of the refusal to admit the possibility of moral dilemmas is Aristotle's doctrine of the unity of the virtues.[3] This doctrine implies that there can be no conflict among the virtues. St. Thomas Aquinas adopts a variant of this view in his discussion on law, and explicitly precludes the possibility of moral dilemmas. Since law is a dictate of right reason ordered to a single end, incompatible propositions are impossible. However, Aquinas does admit that conflicts of duties can arise.[4] He says that the principles of a moral system cannot all be obeyed in all situations, and if that is what the claim for the possibility of moral dilemmas means, then the claim is true. But he defuses the possible force of this claim by a distinction between two kinds of conflict of duties, or, as he called them, "perplexities." There is a perplexity *secundum quid* and a perplexity *simpliciter*; that is, a perplexity conditional upon some wrongdoing and one which is not. The latter is, for Aquinas, inconceivable, but he admits the possibility of the former.

Aquinas employs this distinction in his response to three perplexities given by St. Gregory. Two of them concern persons who have made injudicious vows and find themselves, because of their vows, having to do what they have a moral duty not to do. The third perplexity involves a priest who obtains the cure of souls through simony, and must either exercise this wrongful authority or wrongfully desert his flock. The former is contrary to the moral requirement not to exercise ecclesiastical authority wrongfully. Evil means may not be used even for a good end. Yet failure to cure the parishioners' soul is contrary to the moral requirement not to abandon one's flock particularly in time of need. A conflict of duties such as this one is possible and real, Aquinas maintains. Yet it is not a genuine dilemma; rather it is a perplexity that arises only on the condition of a prior wrongdoing.

Kant also refuses to admit the possibility of moral dilemmas. He says:

Now duty and obligation in general are concepts which express the objective practical necessity of certain actions, and as two opposite rules cannot be necessary at the same time, but if it is a duty to act according to one of them, it is then not only not a duty but inconsistent with duty to act according to the other; it follows that a conflict of duties and obligations is inconceivable.[5]

Kant's point is that when there is a duty (and hence a moral necessity) that a certain action be performed, then there cannot also be a duty (and hence a moral necessity) to perform an action incompatible with the first. He acknowledges that there are conflicting grounds of obligation which might enjoin one to perform incompatible actions. But when this is so, one of them is not a necessary or is a weaker ground of obligation and does not morally obligate one to act accordingly. So, there are no genuine moral dilemmas.

These claims, however, are insufficient to explain why a perplexity *secundum quid* is not a genuine moral dilemma or why a conflict of duty is inconceivable. If the requirement for a moral dilemma is that a person be faced with two incompatible courses of action and this conflict is present for St. Gregory's priest, regardless of his prior wrongdoing, then he faces a genuine moral dilemma. Even if we assume there was no wrongdoing on his part, a dilemma (or perplexity *simpliciter*) is still possible, even if it is not actual–for example, that the duty to cure this soul is incompatible with the requirement not to abandon one's flock because the priest has made an error in belief or calculation. Like other conflict situations, a perplexity *secundum quid* requires choice. In this instance, it is a choice between incompatible courses of action. The fact that there is some wrongdoing or error does not diminish or eliminate the dilemma. Agamemnon may have been in error when he thought the expedition to Troy would be frustrated if he did not offer his daughter Iphigenia as sacrifice. But that he believed this to be true was sufficient to put him in a situation in which either course of action he pursued would violate a moral requirement for which he had compelling moral reasons to adopt. Nor can we say that dilemmas arise only on account of some prior wrongdoing. Sartre's student, who must choose between abandoning his dependent mother or becoming a freedom fighter, was not at fault for his mother's condition nor the war with Germany. Yet he still has to choose between conflicting moral requirements.

What needs to be shown in order to refute the possibility of a moral dilemma is either that the definition—namely, that a moral dilemma is a situation where a person has equally compelling, non-overriding moral reasons to adopt two or more incompatible courses of action—is seriously flawed; or that our judgments about cases of perplexities *secundum quid* are in some significant respects different from our judgments on perplexities *simpliciter*; or yet, and less likely, that the world is such that morality can never require an agent to adopt incompatible courses of action.

I present evidence in this study that supports the claim that genuine moral dilemmas are not only possible, but actual. Our moral concerns with what *happens* as the result of our actions and with the nature of what we *do* to others pull us in quite opposite directions. Absent a resolving principle, no matter what we do the moral transgression of the rejected alternative is unavoidable. Neither agent-centered nor outcome-centered moralities can escape this feature of our moral experience. They cannot escape it partly because values often have different motivational sources—e.g., endorsing dishonorable tactics for the sake of some political objective or failing to secure that objective because of the dishonor it involves—that cannot be brought together by a single evaluative rule.[6]

There is another tradition in modern ethical thought that allows moral conflicts a more significant role, even if it also refuses to admit the possibility of genuine moral dilemmas. Typical of this view, is F. H. Bradley's essay "Duty for Duty's Sake." Bradley's account of moral conflict in this essay begins with an argument against the Kantian concept of "duty for duty's sake." Being a purely formal principle, this concept, Bradley argues, is without content and so cannot move from the universal level to particular duties. He then goes on to observe that the concept of "duty for duty's sake" is unable to account for the common occurrence of conflicting duties which only a "pedant, if not a fool"[7] would try to decide by applying the categorical imperative.

The core of Bradley's argument lies in his claim that there are different duties that often require conflicting courses of action. He acknowledges that there are some duties higher than others. For example, he says that there are "duties above truth-speaking and many offenses against morality which are worse," and cites the case of an imprisoned Italian who, lest he betray his comrades during torture, cuts his veins. "So to kill oneself in a manner which must be called suicide may not only be right but heroic," even if it is a breach of the categorical imperative.[8] But it is unclear from what Bradley says whether this act or any duty or overruling principle cancels the lower duties and so resolves the conflict, or the conflict remains in full force. If the latter, then Bradley allows the possibility for genuine moral dilemmas. However, I suspect that this is not so, since for Bradley the conflict of duties that arises at the moral level is transcended by religion, which I gather is able to offer a harmonious whole. Through faith and through faith alone can conflicts of duties be resolved. Yet this is a religious and not a moral argument. Capable of resolution, conflict of duties are never genuine moral dilemmas.

In recent years increasing attention has been given to the possibility of moral dilemmas. The stubborn claim that moral dilemmas are merely apparent, that there must be some overruling universal principle, value, or point of view that captures our deepest moral convictions and is able to solve cases in which a person morally ought to do one thing and morally ought to do another when both things cannot be done, has been seriously challenged. The field which has come to be called applied ethics has shown that compelling reasons can be given for incompatible courses of action on a wide variety of topics: euthanasia, paternalism, abortion, preferential treatment, capital punishment, among others.

In the current literature one argument we find for the possibility of moral dilemmas says that often in practical resolutions of conflicts there is a moral remainder (either regret, remorse, or guilt). This remainder, so the argument goes, suggests that even when we act on one of the conflicting moral requirements, the rejected alternative is not eliminated or overridden in any significant way. As Bernard Williams puts it, even if we think "we acted for the best," the phenomenon of regret shows that it is a mistake to think that "one ought must be totally rejected in the sense that one becomes convinced that it did not actually apply."[9] No matter what one does in dilemmatic cases, a moral transgression is unavoidable.

One clear illustration of a genuine moral dilemma is given by Jean-Paul Sartre and concerns a student of his who presented the following situation:

His father was quarrelling with his mother and was also inclined to be a collaborator; his elder brother had been killed in the

German offensive of 1940 and this young man, with a sentiment somewhat primitive but generous, burned to avenge him. His mother was living alone with him, deeply afflicted by the semi-treason of his father and by the death of her oldest son, and her one consolation was in this young man. But he, at this moment, had the choice between going to England to join the Free French forces or of staying near his mother and helping her to live. He fully realized that this woman lived only for him and that his disappearance—or perhaps his death—would plunge her into despair. He also realized that, concretely and in fact, every action he performed on his mother's behalf would be sure of effect in the sense of aiding her to live, whereas anything he did in order to go and fight would be an ambiguous action which might vanish like water into sand and serve no purpose. For instance, to set out for England he would have to wait indefinitely in a Spanish camp on the way through Spain; or, on arriving in England or in Algiers he might be put into an office to fill up forms. Consequently, he found himself confronted by two very different forms of action; the one concrete, immediate, but directed towards only one individual; the other action addressed to an end infinitely greater, a national collectivity, but for that reason ambiguous—and it might be frustrated on the way. At the same time, he was hesitating between two kinds of morality; on the one side, the morality of sympathy, of personal devotion and, on the other side a morality of wider scope but of more debatable validity. He had to choose between the two.[10]

Sartre's response to the young man is that "You are free, therefore choose—that is to say, invent. No general morality can show you what you ought to do; no signs are vouchsafed in this world."[11] But this response is far from clear. It confuses what one will do with what one ought to do. The student, as any other person in a similar situation, must choose. But that he must choose does not imply that he can invent morality. In the absence of some resolving principle to appeal to freedom raises more questions than are settled. How, for example, do we know what we *ought* to do when moral requirements conflict? In fact, doesn't this response return the young man to his original perplexity? He does not know which moral claim takes priority, how he ought to act. And no matter how he does act, his action involves him in the moral transgression of the rejected alternative.

This young man faces a conflict between the moral claims of family and nation. Looked at from the point of view of each claim, the young man is required to adopt incompatible courses of action: one to do all he can to free the French nation from a murderous force by joining the resistance, and the other to stay home and care for his afflicted mother. The one may involve him in violence of an extreme kind, in coercion, extortion, inspiring fear, and doing, as Sartre says in the play *Dirty Hands,* "whatever [the party] require[s] of me,"[12] while the other will nourish his affection and dedication to a loved one. He must decide between playing a dirty but necessary part for the vindication of justice, possibly thereby facing an untimely death and exposing his family to possible punishment by the occupying force, or staying home. Either course of action has compelling reasons on its behalf, none overrides the other, nor is there a principle by which he can choose which way to go in this dilemma.

Ultimately the dilemma this young man faces is one between different and incompatible sets of virtues. He is required to choose between the virtue of justice and that of friendship or loyalty to family, between a life as a member of a resistance movement serving an instrumental purpose for a political end, and a life of care, gentleness, and protection of loved ones from untoward fortune. Each of these sets of virtues is animated by different conceptions of the good, nourishes different kinds of relations, and brings about different ways of life. Is there some decision procedure by which we can advice this young man which way he morally ought to choose in this situation?

I have no ready-made answer, nor do I think there is a felicitous way out of the dilemma this young man faces. But there is, I think, an important point to be made regarding a dimension of the moral life that is lived through our social institutions. In the following section I concern myself with what seems to me a significant discontinuity between private and political morality, that is, between the principles and demands of personal action and the special moral status of action in a public role.

2.2 THE MORAL DIVISION OF LABOR

In the normal run of events the threat and use of force, the declaration and waging of war, do not arise in private life but in the execution of state policies. The recourse to force, either domestic or international, brings certain moral requirements for which private decisions cannot provide an adequate basis for justification.

The most striking feature of war is the destruction of human life and culture on the part of those who are entrusted with the care of the common good, but who nevertheless believe that the violence and death they bring about is somehow justified. War is a condition between belligerent states waged for the sake of a political objective by means which otherwise constitute riot, piracy, terror, butchery, random violence, and murder. War is never a private act for the sake of personal goals. If war ever is a private matter or a means to such goals, then it enjoys no justification. It should then be intrinsically and always evil. Some very powerful moral logic must be at work in the justification of war to turn what is evil and sinful into a morally obligatory act. Much of how the "moral logic of war"[13] works depends on a distinction between and the relative moral autonomy of two spheres, that of public and of private life, which yields what Thomas Nagel calls an "ethical division of labor."[14] It should be noted that while my concern here is with the judgments we make about war, the moral division of labor ranges extentionally over a class of acts much broader than those having to do with the declaration and waging of war. This division has typically and rightly been noted in discussions on political and professional ethics, for example, in medical, legislative, and legal ethics, and in the problem of dirty hands.

In a discussion on the distinctiveness of public office, Nagel says:

the constraints of public morality are not imposed as a whole in the same way on all public actions or on all public offices. Because public agency is itself complex and divided, there is a corresponding ethical division of labor, or ethical specialization. Different aspects of public morality are in the hands of different officials. This can create the illusion that public morality is less restrictive than it is, because the general conditions may be wrongly identified with the boundaries of a particular role. But in fact those boundaries usually presuppose a larger institutional structure without which they would be illegitimate.[15]

Conduct that appears wrong from the point of view of ordinary morality and is justified when performed by a public official is the central feature of the moral logic of war and depends on the notion of role. I shall argue that persons in public roles should be guided not by the whole of morality, but by that segment of morality which is primarily concerned with future consequences. But first, what is a role?

The notion of role was first developed by social scientists to evaluate patterns of expected behavior within social groups, institutions, and societies. These patterns exhibit a number of reasonably stable functions and relations with a predictable degree of empirical uniformity to certain rules or norms. There are, for example, the roles of teacher, lawyer, doctor, minister, soldier, and so on the occupant of which, according to the definition, is expected to act with almost singular regard to the rules and norms of the respective role. In his classic work, *The Study of Man*, Ralph Linton spoke of roles as "patterns for reciprocal behavior between individuals or groups of individuals" on whose presence "the functioning of societies depends."[16] More recently, Erving Goffman defined role as "consisting of the activity the incumbent would engage in were he to act solely in terms of the normative demands upon someone in his position."[17] And Dorothy Emmet defined a role as "a part someone plays in a pattern of social activities."[18]

As understood by these writers, the performance of roles is in some real way connected with how one ought and ought not to act in certain situations. Thus Linton writes that roles entail "a collection of rights and duties,"[19] and Goffman emphasizes the "normative demands" a role places upon its incumbent. The affinity between the social-scientific description of role and the realm of morality is made more explicit in Emmet's discussion. She writes, "as a directive for behavior in certain kinds of relationship, role is structured by rules; if not by explicit and sanctioned rules, at least by implicit understandings, and maxims, or rules of thumb, as to how such a person would behave in this kind of relationship."[20]

From the moral point of view, what is important about the idea of role is that it prescribes a form of conduct particular to one's function or office within an institutional setting that is distinguished from those rules of conduct that come to bear upon purely personal relations. The idea of role entails for morality a class of special considerations which are decisive for justifying, from the moral point of view, the forms of action appropriate to public office, within certain limiting constraints. Two of the elements which give rise to the special considerations of these roles or offices are these:

(a) A person in public office is responsible for some acts which no private citizen as such is ever justified in doing.

(b) Public functionaries are required to protect the aggregate interests and values of a very large population. They assume rights and obligations which ordinary citizens do not have.

Both (a) and (b) stress the point that there are different principles and distinctive values in public office from those we find in private life. This difference requires a procedure for justification which cannot depend on common intuitions of right and wrong nor on those categories usually associated with private action—such as friendship, personal interests, integrity—nor religious, ideological, or class beliefs as an adequate defense of policy choices. A justificatory procedure for public policy cannot be established by an appeal to standards, however widely held they may be, of personal conduct.

There are at least two reasons why what has justificatory force in private action has no such force in matters of public policy. First, there is an empirical condition that surrounds public office and the performance of public roles that is not included in the conditions of private action. Roles or offices are always part of a social institution. Assuming that the institution is morally justified, say, because of the good it seeks to bring about or because it is intrinsically just, then those roles required for the work of the institution are also morally justified. Call the form of moral justification that moves from institutions to roles and then to role-duties and their performance transitive. Second, given that the justification of a role is derived from that of its institution, the standards appropriate to determining the morality of a role is derived not from the standards of private action, but from the ends of the institution which particular roles and actions seek to secure.

Action performed under the auspices of a role brings with it the requirements of publicity in reasoning open to the scrutiny of the community that is beyond what we commonly and can reasonably expect in private action, and of neutrality in the normative grounds on which policy decisions ought to be judged. It was Kant who first emphasized the connection between morality and publicity, and presented the latter as a fundamental test of public morality. "All actions," he said, "that affect the rights of others are wrong if their maxim is not consistent with publicity."[21] Thus when public officials act under the requirement of publicity, they must justify their actions on publicly accessible grounds, and this not only to give an account for policy choices, but also as a rational defense on their behalf. Moreover, in a liberal state the justification of policy decisions must be neutral with regard to the variety of conceptions of the good life. The multiplicity of ways in which life can be fulfilled has in modern times pressed the state and its functionaries to recognize the real possibility of interminable disagreement among reasonable persons over the idea of the good life. Such disagreement has led to the liberal doctrine of neutrality as the normative grounds for governing the public relations between individuals and the state as a procedure of justification distinct from the ideals that govern the private relations between individuals and other institutions.

By contrast, justification of private action typically makes use of a style of reasoning that is primarily concerned with certain dispositions of character that are said to be virtuous and ennobling, such as temperance, integrity and love, or terms which point to their opposites. On this view morality is reflexive. It is fundamentally concerned with an imagined best way of life, together with a conception of the sort of person one ought to become, and the virtues and goods necessary for that life. This view suggests that when we deliberate on and choose a particular course of action we are, at the same time, deliberating on and choosing to become a certain kind of person. Our choices and actions are important not because they are instrumental for some sought-after result, but because they are in a real way constitutive of the sort of person we become. As John Finnis puts it, "Self-constitution is a foreseeable, intrinsic, and necessary effect of one's free choice."[22] Now, can those terms which have their natural place in private life apply meaningfully to our moral judgments on public policy? What seems to matter most in public policy is not so much the moral character of the agent and the reflexive effects of choices, but the consequences of alternative policies for the aggregate and sometimes disparate interests and values of a large population.

The difference I want to make here can be illustrated by a logical distinction between dispositions and occurrences drawn on the basis of the words we typically employ when we are talking about the properties we infer are present in a person because of what she does in a given situation and the effects of a course of action.[23] Examples of the first category are words that commonly point to character-traits: patient, diligent, trustworthy, faithful, conscientious. These terms may properly be referred to as disposition-words that are particular to our moral assessment of persons as persons. However, when we turn to action by a public functionary done on behalf of the state, a different family of evaluative terms arises. We want to know, for example, the effectiveness of a given policy in bringing about a desired end, be that end economic welfare, national security, rather than the dispositional state of a moral agent. Here the concern is not with the attributes of a person's character but with the qualities of a policy as it relates and embodies public ends to which the state is morally bound to secure.

Machiavelli captured perhaps better than anyone else the distinctive and relatively autonomous justification of political action when he said: "You must realize this: that a prince, and especially a new prince, cannot observe all those things which give men a reputation for virtue, because in order to maintain his state he is often forced to act in defiance of good faith, of charity, of kindness, of religion."[24] In 2.3, I suggest how this view goes too far in separating the public and private spheres. But Machiavelli's point is important. What is often unacceptable in light of the principles of private conduct ought to be separated from the evaluation of public action, and the morality of public office must be fundamentally concerned with outcomes. Not to hold consequences of policy decisive for the morality of public office would be a grave dereliction of the politician's responsibility for the overall well-being of the political community. Political morality permits and often requires that our judgments be more instrumental, more willing to allow ends to justify means than does private morality.

The distinction between a purely personal morality and that of an institutional role was made in no uncertain terms in Bradley's famous essay, "My Station and Its Duties." Bradley says: "my station and its duties teaches us to identify others and ourselves with the station we fill; to consider that as good; and by virtue of that to consider others and ourselves good too."[25] A simple morality of personal relations under the guidance of an ideal conception of character cannot take account of the different kinds of relations in which we stand to other people, nor the impersonal element that arises, today perhaps more than in Bradley's time, in highly routinized and differentiated social institutions. Accordingly, the role-agent cannot do the work of, nor is she responsible for, the whole of morality, but only for that segment of morality which falls within the moral claims of her role.

In a few sections of this study I try to show that policy decisions on the practice of nuclear deterrence are best arrived at on the basis of a consequentialist framework. Because consequentialism takes account of the special requirements of public office better than any available alternative and is able also to compare conflicting values, I reject in 3.2 the deontological or agent-centered argument against deterrence and suggest a consequentialist defense for this practice. But that consequentialism is better than any alternative theory does not entail that ordinary constraints are superseded and moral dilemmas thereby resolved. In the next section I try to support this point and in chapter 5, especially in 5.2, I look at the problems that arise for this style of moral reasoning when applied to nuclear deterrence.

2.3 THE RELATION OF ROLE TO ORDINARY MORALITY

In the foregoing section I described some ways in which the morality of private life and that of public roles are distinct. Not only do each of these seek different ends, but also the way that action is justified in one is inapplicable to the other. I briefly noted two logically distinct modes of justification, transitive and reflexive.³ In this section I explore the possibility of some constraints on the consequentialism I have defended.

When one says that there is something morally special about public roles, one must account for the way in which an individual's description of a given situation is altered by roles. I assume that most people want to improve their moral status, that part of what it means to be human is to seek the moral perfection that is attainable within the natural powers each of us possesses in varying degrees. Because our individual moral history is constituted by the choices we make, we should want to make good ones, those which dispose us towards our fellow human beings in certain morally praiseworthy ways. I further assume that praiseworthy dispositions are partly the result of the in-born faculties of thought and action. Proper exercise and right cultivation of these in-born faculties yield certain universal moral laws which form a harmonious system of moral claims.

While there is consensus among moralists schooled in the Aristotelian and Christian moral traditions to make the above statements fairly uncontroversial, my description of role morality introduces some ways of thought and action that though desirable in public officials are contrary to the convictions of ordinary morality. In this study I argue that political decisions, especially those decisions having to do with war, rent us apart between the ideals of character—having to do with honesty, conscientiousness, love for all humanity—and effectiveness in politics. If the argument is correct, then it seems morality is not a harmonious system of claims, but is rather divided in its purpose. Such division is, I think, more serious and troubling than that between agent-centered and outcome-centered styles of reasoning. It points to a moral pluralism which renders incompatible ways of life, such as those present in Sartre's example, equally worth choosing.

The distinction between the special moral obligations of a political role and ordinary morality has frequently been noted by liberal thinkers, even those with a strong vein of universalistic morality.[26] Kant, perhaps the most enthusiastic supporter of this kind of morality, was willing to concede that in a condition short of perpetual peace national leaders have in international relations the moral duty to act on behalf of the national interest.[27] Liberal indulgence towards what will work in a condition of suspicious and sovereign states allows on consequentialist grounds for conduct that would rightly be judged unprincipled in private life. States and their functionaries are, within liberal morality, licensed to set aside ordinary deontological constraints on action for the sake either of achieving good outcomes or avoiding bad ones. The dilemma this poses is a moral one. It is best interpreted as a practical problem confronting someone who wonders what ought to be done under a given set of circumstances, and at once acknowledges and feels the force of deontological constraints on what we can morally do to others as well as the impersonal demands of public office in the affairs of state. This dilemma is unavoidable in the exercise of political power, and shows up the different structures of morality animated by incompatible conceptions of the good. What is the relation of role to ordinary morality, that is to morality which is not contingent on one's role or function within an institutional framework, but concerns obligations that apply to persons as persons?

Both Bradley and Machiavelli draw a sharp line between role-related and ordinary morality. But Bradley, unlike Machiavelli, later tempers his view. In a remarkable criticism of his defense of role-morality, Bradley warns that "the community in which [one] is a member may be in a confused or rotten condition, so that in it right and might do not always go together. And the very best community can only insure that correspondence in the gross; it cannot do so in every single detail."[28] There are good reasons for caution in a theory of role morality. Strict adherence to it might tend towards a conservative, sometimes totalitarian, conception of social roles, favoring existing social institutions even when these might have weak or no moral justification. Historical examples of what Hannah Arendt describes as the "banality of evil" are sufficient to persuade any morally decent person of this possible and very awful defect in an unconstrained theory of role morality. Other less dramatic but nonetheless disturbing examples of the level of suffering ordinary individuals will inflict upon others have been documented in social psychological experiments on obedience to authority.

It would be a mistake, however, to deny the merits of role morality on these accounts. When properly exercised, a role is a useful device for the distribution of social responsibility within an institutional framework and for ensuring provisions of a theory of justice, such as making fair awards and giving equal respect to all relevant parties. A fully developed theory of role morality can also incorporate elements of a theory of just appropriation by which the products of labor are fairly distributed within a given population. In addition to these merits, the justification I have given of role-duties and their performance precludes the possibility of Eichmann-like evil insofar as the ends institutions pursue must be morally good. But in those cases when a role-duty requires action that is morally unacceptable, the role-agent is always, in a democratic system at least, free to resign. The role-agent can thereby use a role as a vehicle for expressing a commitment to a certain way of life.

To get a better handle on the issue at stake here, let me recast the problem. If decisions on policy—for example, whether or not to go to war, given the ends that might be at stake in a particular conflict—are made entirely on the moral claims of a public role, then policy has, strictly speaking, a consequence-based evaluation. The question of what is morally acceptable in policy, and the relation of means to ends are thereby settled on a comparative evaluation of outcomes. This is contrary to ordinary, more deontological, morality intuitions concerned with the inherent moral qualities of an act. Moreover, if policy decisions are made entirely on the basis of role requirements, then the justification of public policy seems merely conventional and restrictions on what we can morally do to others are to be determined by the gains or losses under alternative policies, that is, on total outcome. In a choice, say, between torturing someone and thereby extracting some very important information and the loss of a necessary military victory, the former seems the preferred alternative. This is, of course, unacceptable on deontological grounds. But there is no reason to think that this or any other similar course of action is on a consequence-based system necessarily the preferred act.

Few of us are totally immune to deontological constraints on what we can morally do to others, even when engaged in violence of an extreme kind. For example, in Camus' play, *The Just Assassins*, we have record of an event in late Tsarist Russia in which a revolutionary group decided to assassinate an official of the state, the Grand Duke Sergei. On the assigned day, the young man chosen for the mission held a concealed bomb and approached the Duke's carriage. But when he came close to the carriage he noticed the Duke held two small children on his lap, and decided to abort the mission. Camus has one of the comrades say, "even in destruction there is a right way and a wrong way—there are limits."[29] The problem is how to relate the limits or constraints on action to a consequence-based evaluation of a political role.

What is morally instructive about Camus' example is that even when the presumption against violence is temporarily suspended the moral distinction between killing and murder, between what we can justifiably do to another under a given set of circumstances and what is prohibited no matter the consequences, is not canceled. If this is true, then an important theoretical point is illustrated, namely: that constraints on action have a certain priority over utility, even when the disutility of aborting a crucial mission is large. I don't think I can account for the force nor the generation of deontological constraints. Nor do I think it is necessary to show this. It is sufficient for my purposes to know that certain rules of conduct are somehow always there, and that the forms of relations that govern one's conduct apply also in the most ruthless kind of human activity. That some code of conduct, no matter how minimal, is present for those who find compelling reasons to suspend ordinary presumptions against what we can morally do to others is enough to suggest that however restricted our choices may be there is a set of considerations that always comes to bear on our choices and absolutely prohibits certain kinds of action.

A second point is illustrated by Camus' example. At least some of the moral requirements that come to bear on political action overlap with the moral requirements of personal morality. Whether the former is derived from the latter or both sets of requirements are derived from a common source is a question that, I think, cannot be settled with our existing knowledge about morality. But that public or political and personal morality overlap in some significant sense does not entail that they share the same structure. A public functionary is still required to do things which, from the viewpoint of personal morality, are impermissible. There is, as Nagel says, either "the addition or the removal of restrictions in public morality [that] can therefore explain the discontinuity" between them.[30] A significant element of public morality is derived from the moral claims of politics upon the office-holder. These claims not only yield a structure of morality formally different from personal morality, but are also sufficient to produce genuine dilemmas. Under certain conditions the special character of a public role can give compelling support for a course of action that would not be allowable for persons as persons to undertake.

NOTES

1. Consider the following statements. In his *Summa Theologiae*, II-II, Q. 40, art. 1, St. Thomas Aquinas says that "it is not the business of a private individual to declare war. Moreover it is not the business of a private individual to summon together the people, which has to be done in wartime. And as the care of the commonweal is committed to those who are in authority, it is their business to watch over the commonweal of the city. And just as it is lawful for them to have recourse to the sword in defending that commonweal against internal disturbances, so too is it their business to have recourse to the sword of war." And in II-II, Q. 64, art. 3, he says that it is not permissible for a private person to kill a criminal. This "right belongs only to the one who has care of the whole community. The care of the public good has been entrusted to rulers who have public authority and so only they, and not private persons, may kill criminals." See also Augustine's dialogue with Evodius in Bk. I of his *De Liberio Arbitrio*. Elizabeth Anscombe expresses the same view when she says in Walter Stein, ed., *Nuclear Weapons: A Catholic Response* (New York: Sheed and Ward, 1961), 49: "The right to attack with a view to killing is something that belongs only to rulers and those whom they command to do it. [I]t does belong to rulers precisely because of that threat of violent coercion exercised by those in authority which is essential to the existence of human societies."

2. Alasdair McIntyre, *After Virtue* (Notre Dame, IN: University of Notre Dame Press, 1981), 134.

3. Aristotle, *Nicomachean Ethics*, Bk. VI.13.

4. St. Thomas Aquinas, *Summa Theologiae*, I-II, 19, art. 6, ad. 3; II-II, 62, 2; III, 64, art. 6, ad 3; *de Veritate*, 17, art. 4, ad 8.

5. Immanuel Kant, "Introduction to the Metaphysics of Morals," in T. K. Abbott, *Kant's Theory of Ethics*, 5th ed., (London: Longmans, Green, and Co., 1898), 280.

6. This is Thomas Nagle's point in "Fragmentation of Value," in *Mortal Questions* (Cambridge: Cambridge University Press, 1979).

7. F. H. Bradley, "Duty for Duty's Sake," in *Ethical Studies* (Indianapolis, Indiana: Bobbs-Merrill, 1951), 95.

8. Bradley, "Duty's Sake," 96.

9. Bernard Williams, "Ethical Consistency," in *Problems of the Self: Philosophical Papers 1956-1972* (Cambridge: Cambridge University Press, 1973), 184.

10. Jean-Paul Sartre, "Existentialism is a Humanism," trans. P. Mairet, in *Existentialism from Dostoyevsky to Sartre*, ed. W. Kaufmann (New York: Meridian, 1957), 295-96.

11. Sartre, "Existentialism," 297-98.

12. Jean-Paul Sartre, *Dirty Hands*, trans. Lionel Abel, in *No Exit and Three Other Plays* (New York: Vintage Books, 1949), 136.

13. The expression is Ralph Potter's in his "The Moral Logic of War," *McCormick Quarterly* 23 (1970), 203-33.

14. Thomas Nagel, "Ruthlessness in Public Life," in *Mortal Questions*, 85.

15. Nagel, "Ruthlessness," 85.

16. Ralph Linton, *The Study of Man* (New York: Appleton-Century, 1936), 113.

17. Erving Goffman, "Role Distance," in *Encounters: Two Studies in the Sociology of Interaction* (Indianapolis, Indiana: Bobbs-Merill, 1961), 85.

18. Dorothy Emmet, *Function, Purpose, and Power: Some Concepts in the Study of Individuals and Societies* (London: Macmillan, 1958), 26.

19. Linton, *Study of Man*, 113.

20. Dorothy Emmet, *Rules, Roles, and Relations* (Boston: Beacon Press, 1975), 158.

21. Immanuel Kant, *Perpetual Peace and Other Essays*, trans. Ted Humphrey (Indianapolis, Indiana: Hackett Publishing Co., 1983), 135.

22. John Finnis, *Fundamentals of Ethics* (Oxford: Clarendon Press, 1983), 141.

23. The distinction between disposition-words and occurrence-words is taken from Bernard Mayo, *Ethics and the Moral Life* (London: Macmillan & Co. Ltd., 1958) 135ff. However, my use of these terms is slightly different from his.

24. Niccolo Machiavelli, *The Prince*, trans. George Bull, (New York: Penguin, 1961), 101. Giovanni Botero expressed the same view when he said, "it should be taken for certain that in the decisions made by princes, interest will always override every other argument; and therefore he who treats with princes should put no trust in friendship, kinship, treaty nor any other tie which has no basis in interest." *The Reason of State*, trans. P. J. and D. P. Waley, (London: 1965), 41. Cited in Quentin Skinner, *The Foundations of Modern Political Thought* (Cambridge: Cambridge University Press, 1978), vol. 1, 249.

25. Bradley, "My Station and Its Duties," *Ethical Studies*, 117.

26. Catholic natural law moralists also uphold the distinction. John Courtney Murray, for example, says: "Society and the state are understood [in the ethic of natural law] to be natural institutions with their relatively autonomous ends or purposes, which are predesigned in broad outline in the social and political nature of man. These purposes are public, not private. The obligatory public purposes of society and the state impose on these institutions a special set of obligations which, again by nature, are not coextensive with the wider and higher range of obligations that rest upon the human person." *We Hold These Truths* (New York: Sheed and Ward, 1960), 286.

27. Immanuel Kant, *Perpetual Peace*, see the Preliminary Articles, especially 2, 3, and 4.

28. Bradley, "My Station," 138.

29. Albert Camus, *The Just Assassins*, in *Caligula and Three Other Plays*, trans. Stuart Gilbert, (New York: Knopf, 1958), 258.

30. Nagel, "Ruthlessness," 79.

3 The Disarmament Party

> If anyone were to declare that modern war is necessarily total, and necessarily involves direct attack on the life of innocent civilians, and, therefore, that obliteration bombing is justified, my reply would be: So much the worse for modern war. If it necessarily includes such means, it is necessarily immoral itself.
>
> John C. Ford, "The Morality of Obliteration Bombing."

Within the range of views available in the moral debate on nuclear arms policy, one group of just-war moralists declares that modern war is immoral. This is so, they claim, because modern weapons violate the principle of non-combatant immunity (also referred to as the principle of discrimination). If to kill non-combatants is wrong, and modern war inevitably involves such killing, then war is morally wrong. Moreover, since one can never intend what is immoral to do, the threat to retaliate with nuclear weapons, upon which rests the doctrine of deterrence, is itself immoral. It follows that the only morally acceptable position is that of immediate and unilateral disarmament.

In this chapter I examine some of the central features of the nuclear pacifism of the disarmament party. The pacifism of this party is different from absolute pacifism in that the latter rests on the view that it is always immoral for a person to use force against any other, regardless of conditions or consequences. More radically, this view maintains that it is immoral for the state to use force against another state, whether for the defense of self or others. Absolute pacifism is both a principled and abstract moral position. Nuclear pacifism, on the other hand, is contingent upon certain empirical conditions having to do almost entirely with the technology and strategy of modern war. On this view, state recourse to force might be justified if there is a just cause and the means it employs are also just. But this view holds also that modern weapons and war-fighting plans are intrinsically unjust, and so no war that employs those weapons can ever be just. Thus nuclear pacifism rests not upon a principled moral position—i.e., it is always immoral to use force—but on an interpretation of our present technological and military capabilities.

The initial force of nuclear pacifism lies in its emphasis on individual conscience and the requirements of good moral character. It then draws from these the moral principles for state action. I argue, however, that some features of this position are highly unsatisfactory. In 3.1 I argue that the empirical assumption that nuclear weapons are a class apart from conventional, nonnuclear weapons leads the disarmament party into a paradox which it is unable to resolve. I suggest that absent a moral theory independent of conventional modes of thought, the morality of nuclear weapons and war must be examined within familiar moral territory even if doing so might tend to justify the selective use of highly discriminating nonconventional weapons. Then in 3.2 I look at an agent-centered or deontological argument against the possession of a nuclear arsenal for the purpose of deterring a similarly armed adversary. In my examination of the idea of a "common morality" and of the Wrongful Intentions Principle, I show that neither precludes a moral pluralism in which outcome-centered or consequentialist considerations, among others, can be brought to bear upon the moral appraisal of nuclear deterrence. This has both theoretical and practical results. In the final sections, 3.3 and 3.4, I look at questions of a different kind. While my main concern in this book is with the possession and use of nuclear weapons, I want briefly to consider the morality of producing these weapons and whether preparing to fight a nuclear war is contrary to the humanitarian principles of international law. The arguments advanced in these sections reinforce the nuclear disarmers' pacifism.

3.1 THE PRINCIPLE OF DISCONTINUITY AND ITS PARADOX

On 12 January 1954, Secretary of State John Foster Dulles delivered a speech at the Council of Foreign Relations in New York that outlined the Eisenhower administration's nuclear deterrence strategy. Titled "The Evolution of Foreign Policy," this speech, which came to be known as the "massive-retaliation speech," called for a complete change in attitude toward defense in the nuclear age. In a passage that would frequently be quoted, Dulles maintained that "the way to deter aggression is for the free community to be willing and able to respond vigorously at places and with means of its own choosing." That meant reinforcing existing defenses with "the further deterrent of massive retaliatory power," the power of a strategic nuclear arsenal.[1] Eisenhower himself had made it very clear that he did not intend to limit the use of nuclear weapons to strategic warfare. "The United States," he said, "cannot afford to preclude itself from using nuclear weapons even in a local situation, if such use will best advance U.S. security interests."[2] "Where [nuclear weapons] are used on strictly military targets and for strictly military purposes, I see no reason why they shouldn't be used just exactly as you would use a bullet or anything else."[3]

To support the policy of massive retaliation, the Eisenhower administration embarked on a program which aimed to give the nation's armed forces what it referred to as the "New Look." It called for deep cuts in conventional forces and a massive buildup in nuclear weapons and long-range bombers able to strike targets deep in enemy territory. As a result, between 1953 and 1957 Army personnel was reduced from 1.4 million to an even million, and Navy personnel from 765,000 to 650,000. The Air Force, on the other hand, expanded from 913,000 to 975,000 men and women, and from 110 to 137 wings. In addition, the administration sought the development of intercontinental and intermediate-range ballistic missiles, particularly of the Atlas, America's first ICBM, and the Thor. By the end of the 1950s, the U.S. had developed a solid-fueled ICBM, the Minuteman, and a submarine-launched ballistic missile, the Polaris, later much favored by the Kennedy administration.

Also during the 1950s and early 1960s, discussion on nuclear strategy became the concern of an audience much wider than the narrow circle of military and political elite. The emerging public debate of that time expressed in no uncertain terms the mounting anger, frustration, and great anxiety that security and defense in the nuclear age depended on what the British historian E. P. Thompson later called the "logic of exterminism."[4] It is no surprise that popular movements calling for unilateral nuclear disarmament appeared first in England and the European Continent. The painful experience of two world wars and the still fresh memory of the effects of obliteration bombing are sufficient testimony to the misery and destruction brought by modern instruments of war. Opposition to the deployment and use of nuclear weapons came from trade unions, churches and other religious groups, and professional societies alike.

This was the beginning of the great public debate, fought with increasing fervor over the next several decades, among citizens and intellectuals, in Europe and the United States. The opposition of popular movements to nuclear weapons and the call for immediate disarmament were expressed with equal conviction and considerable rigor of analysis by professional moralists. The single most influential scholarly work first to advance this position is that edited by Walter Stein under the title *Nuclear Weapons and Christian Conscience*,[5] with contributions by noted moral theologians and philosophers such as Elizabeth Anscombe, Peter Geach, R. A. Markus, and others addressing some of the most significant moral dimensions of the nuclear debate. The main argument of this volume is later also advanced by Anthony Kenny in *The Logic of Deterrence* and then by John Finnis, Joseph Boyle, and Germain Grisez in their *Nuclear Deterrence, Morality, and Realism*. Focusing on some of the general features of nuclear pacifism as a distinct just-war position in the nuclear debate, I will not examine the minor differences among these nuclear pacifists. Rather, I will direct my analysis at the core of their argument. It is important to begin by noting two things.

First, Stein's volume addresses itself primarily to Catholics, making use of Papal and episcopal statements that are binding for their co-religionists. The authors of this work are aware that the common conscience of the West, and especially the principles of international law and the rules of war, are schooled by the Christian faith. This is true also of Kenny and of Finnis and his collaborators. Kenny's work is less self-consciously addressed to a Catholic or religious audience. However, he acknowledges the contributions of the Christian tradition to the theoretical framework within which he considers the rights and wrongs of nuclear force. Finnis's volume is dependent upon what its authors refer to as "the tradition of common morality," "the Jewish and Christian morality which, though often violated, provided standards of moral assessment formative of our civilization and still accepted by many."[6] Although it may be said that the arguments in these volumes have a special relevance for Catholics, they are no less relevant to individuals of humane sentiments everywhere. Kenny and Finnis, Boyle, and Grisez agree with Stein when he says that "one does not need to be a Christian—nor indeed any theist at all—to recognize in these [nuclear] threats a deracination from humanity, and from the humanity within ourselves."[7]

Second, the pacifism advocated by this group is not of the traditional, absolute kind that judges all uses of violence as morally evil. Stein emphasizes that the authors of his volume do not claim that "war can never, in principle, be justified," or that "there are powerful motives in justice."[8] They do not deny the moral legitimacy of the profession of arms. Other things being equal, the authors agree that the use of force for national self-defense might not only be justified, but perhaps obligatory. "We deny," Stein says, "the pacifist position, and maintain that states have the right, and the duty, to protect their communities against an unjust attack."[9] Kenny also rejects absolute pacifism, calling it a "moral error." He claims that absolute pacifism might prevent a government from fulfilling its duty to protect the rights and liberties of its subjects and could lead individuals to neglect their "allotted task in a just war."[10] It is possible, he says, "to have a right to go to war, and to wage war morally, provided that certain conditions are fulfilled."[11] Similarly, Finnis and his collaborators say that "our moral theory by no means entails pacifism."[12] They argue that it is always wrong to choose to kill a human being. But some forms of killing, they say, are not always wrong. The right to life of innocent persons "ought to be defended, even by deadly force." This idea extends to the protection of a just social order that, when unjustly challenged, can make the use of force morally justifiable within certain strict limits.[13]

However, these authors are unanimous in their agreement that the use of nuclear force is profoundly immoral. Technological advances in the instruments of war and nuclear war-fighting plans draw a sharp line between conventional and nuclear war. The latter, based on a program of "massive nuclear bombardment," would bring about the "virtual annihilation" of the human race. Could it really be supposed, Stein asks, that such a war "might be justified?"[14] The central submission of the disarmament party is, in the words of the Stein volume, that "the concept of nuclear war has obliterated the concept of military defense."[15] Thus, the conclusion is drawn that "there is no *moral* alternative to an unconditional renunciation of the deterrent."[16] This is so, Stein maintains, because "whatever the aim (i.e., victory for a just cause), the immediate aim would include a deliberate destruction of non-combatants—would include a commitment to *mass-murder*."[17] Along similar lines, Kenny argues that the use of nuclear weapons would involve the "deliberate killing of the innocent, and therefore be murder by the traditional rules of the just war."[18] And according to Finnis, Boyle and Grisez the norm excluding the killing of civilians is a bedrock prohibition of the common morality of our civilization.

I noted in chapter 1 that the moral assessment of nuclear weapons involves two distinct and independent judgments. One has to do with the morality of the *use* of nuclear weapons; the other involves a judgment on the *possession* of these weapons. Much of what I have to say in this study concerns the various ways in which just-war moralists bring these two judgments together by way of certain moral principles and factual assumptions. The disarmament party's condemnation of the use of nuclear weapons rests primarily on an application of the traditional just-war principle of non-combatant immunity coupled with an interpretation of the empirical, i.e., military and strategic, facts that underlie nuclear war-fighting plans. Stein, Kenny, and Finnis agree that any first or retaliatory use of strategic nuclear weapons cannot be regarded as a legitimate act of war because it would involve the indiscriminate killing of millions of non-combatants. Much like the effects of obliteration bombing in WW II, even if the distinction between combatants and non-combatants is recognized, it is almost certain that any strategic nuclear attack against built-up areas will result in large-scale killing of civilians.

For example, with the increase in explosive power and the radiation effects of nuclear weapons, a single one-megaton groundburst bomb exploded over a major metropolitan area will bring about nearly a quarter of a million deaths, most if not all of whom will be civilians. No matter what use is made of strategic weapons, their limitless capacity for destruction coupled with a doctrine of massive retaliation in which *cities themselves* are targeted makes them woefully murderous. To use these weapons deliberately against civilians or to allow non-combatant deaths as a side-effect to a targeting policy said to aim only at military or other legitimate targets is, according to these authors, inconsistent with morality and must be condemned by all who profess to respect the traditional rules for the conduct of war. This judgment is common to most representatives of the just-war tradition, whether they are pacifist or not.

Existing nuclear arsenals, however, include also tactical, battlefield nuclear weapons designed for use against enemy frontline troops and support forces the effects of which can be highly discriminating and in a real sense similar to the effects of nonnuclear weapons. Thomas Schelling has observed that with the development "of small-size, small-yield nuclear weapons suitable for local use by ground troops with modest equipment the technical characteristics of nuclear weapons have ceased to provide much basis, if any, for treating nuclear weapons as peculiarly different from other weapons in the conduct of limited war."[19]   An attack on a military installation in an uninhabited area using battlefield nuclear weapons—say, a neutron bomb having a maximum yield below 500 rads or an M110 shell with a yield of one kiloton and a range of 13 miles—surely will not produce the collateral damage to civilian populations of strategic weapons. Can these low-yield and highly accurate nuclear weapons truly be compatible with the principle of discrimination?   Are they capable of hitting a specified military target with little if any blast and radiation effect to the surrounding civilian population and natural environment? If the effects of these small-yield weapons are comparable to those of conventional weapons, can the moral condemnation of strategic weapons apply to battlefield, frontline nuclear weapons?

Debates about tactical nuclear arms policy bring into consideration several factors which call for a judgment more complex than that required for the moral assessment of the use of strategic nuclear weapons. Some defense analysts have argued that limited war-fighting and war-winning strategies represent a moral improvement over countercity nuclear warfare.[20] We should expect that if a case can be made for the use of tactical weapons, then it might seem to follow that the nuclear pacifist is justified only in a condemnation much narrower in scope than the full nuclear arsenal. If, on the other hand, the use of small weapons is prohibited, we shall have to know in what respects low-yield, tactical nuclear weapons used, say, between ships at sea or armies in isolated terrains are of the same kind as ICBMs. For the disarmer's condemnation of all nuclear weapons to be valid, it requires a factual assumption very different from the claim that the use of nuclear weapons is morally impermissible because they are instruments of mass and indiscriminate destruction. Do the facts about strategic weapons set apart morally all nuclear weapons regardless of their explosive power? In other words, are all nuclear weapons of one and the same kind?

Stein, Kenny, and Finnis are aware that this question can pose a serious challenge to the position they advocate. If the claims of the disarmament party are premised on the factual assumption that nuclear weapons are indiscriminate and we can isolate a class of weapons that does not fail the discrimination test, then nuclear pacifists will have to show how the variety of ways in which different nuclear weapons can be used is not morally relevant. These authors think that while the above distinction has some empirical basis, whatever difference there may be between battlefield and strategic nuclear weapons is not sufficient to justify a moral distinction between nuclear weapons that *cannot* from those that *can* morally be used. They are willing to entertain the hypothetical case of the "fleet at sea." But for them, the grave evils that would follow from crossing the nuclear threshold by the use of any nuclear weapon are sufficient to proscribe their use.

Nuclear disarmers assume that there is no morally relevant difference between *any* (tactical) and *all* (strategic) nuclear weapons. Were such a difference to be accepted, then the conclusion that the use of nuclear weapons is morally prohibited would not necessarily follow. If there is a class of nuclear weapons the effects of which are no different from the effects of weapons used in nonnuclear wars, and such wars can be just according to traditional concepts, then the restricted use of low-yield nuclear weapons would have to be similarly judged. After all, a torpedo armed with a small nuclear warhead of .01 kiloton has no greater explosive power than a single A-6 Intruder attack plane conventionally armed. And if the latter is morally acceptable according to traditional criteria, so too must be the former. Some use of nuclear weapons should then be morally tolerable.

This conclusion is not reached by these authors because they assume that nuclear weapons are radically discontinuous from conventional, nonnuclear weapons. We can take advantage of this assumption to introduce a point that is of considerable use in reflecting on the nature of nuclear weapons and war. The assumption that nuclear weapons are *qualitatively* different from nonnuclear weapons is so prevalent that it may be regarded as fundamental to the moral debate on nuclear arms policy. I state it as follows:

> The Principle of Discontinuity: Nuclear weapons are qualitatively different from their nonnuclear counterparts. They are *sui generis* in the sense that any use of them renders inapplicable the traditional notions of politically-instrumental war, military victory, and moral limitations on the use of force, e.g., civilian immunity.[21]

According to this principle, the advent of nuclear weapons challenges our convictions about military reality and the morality of war. This is so because the singular nature of these weapons is radically incompatible with the received tradition. Military ideas and axioms, received moral and juridical concepts, all fail to accommodate the existing reality. Any attempt to apply prenuclear modes of thought to nuclear weapons only tends to obscure the latter's unique and singular nature. In the past, nations went to war to preserve or promote a certain way of life. War was conceived of as a legitimate instrument of national policy and justified in terms of achieving specific policy goals. But the massive and indiscriminate power of destruction unleashed by nuclear weapons could never successfully attain any of those goals. Their use in war would defeat any rational purpose.

Now what is the moral significance of the Principle of Discontinuity (PD)? What follows morally once PD has been accepted? Many who condemn the use of nuclear weapons on the grounds that *any* use of either tactical or strategic weapons is radically discontinuous with traditional forms of warfare, however correct they might be in this empirical claim, either ignore or are unaware of a paradox engendered by PD that profoundly weakens their position, a paradox for which, I will argue, other than abandoning PD, there is no satisfactory solution. And to do so would amount to an abandonment of the factual basis of the disarmament party.

The usual way of thinking about the basic discontinuity between nuclear weapons and traditional conceptions of war is to claim that the inherent indiscriminateness of the former cannot be accommodated to the latter's requirement that weapons be capable of discriminate use. Anthony Kenny, for example, says that "what is *special* about nuclear weapons is that they are uniquely well adapted for the obliteration of populations."[22] This judgment is echoed in Stein when he says that, unlike conventional war, the use of the nuclear arsenal would mean "total war."[23] Similar statements have also been made by members of the political and strategic communities. Bernard Brodie, for example, was among the first to draw our attention to the unique nature of nuclear weapons when he said, early in the nuclear age, that the power and destruction of the new weapons made them essentially unusable for war. "Thus far the chief purpose of our military establishment has been to win wars. From now on its chief purpose must be to avert them. It can have almost no other useful purpose."[24] Brodie's worry was that those responsible for military policy had not come to the recognition that in the nuclear age the nature of war has radically changed. Along similar lines, Hans Morgenthau stated, in 1977, that "one of the characteristics of the nature of nuclear weapons [is] that their destructiveness is so enormous that it has simply destroyed, disintegrated like an atomic bomb, the very conceptions [of war] from the beginning of history to the beginning of the nuclear age."[25] And Leon Sigal writing in *Foreign Affairs*, said: "the sheer destructiveness of nuclear war has invalidated any distinction between winning and losing. Thus, it has rendered meaningless the very idea of military strategy as the efficient deployment of force to achieve a State's objective."[26]

The immediate conclusion typically drawn from PD by nuclear disarmers is that since the break between nuclear weapons and the morality of war cannot be mended, the use of these weapons is morally impossible. This gives rise to a curious paradox. On the one hand, the empirical claim that nuclear weapons are *sui generis* and so cannot be contained within familiar terms renders meaningless the traditional limitations of war, both moral and political. The moral function of sanctioning and restraining military activity is now lost in light of the new instruments of war. On the other hand, the moral condemnation of nuclear weapons and war rests upon prenuclear categories of thought which on the basis of PD are claimed to be inapplicable to the nuclear age. It seems to me that a convincing and coherent condemnation of nuclear weapons must somehow be linked to what we already know about the morality of war. For example, a reasonable division between morally permissible and impermissible targets of attack is essential to the justice of a war. But if that division is said to be inapplicable or meaningless to the new technology of war, then the basis for the moral assessment of war has been radically removed. Yet if it were possible, or at least defensible, to apply traditional moral categories to nuclear weapons, then it would not be a simple matter to condemn them *all* nor to uphold their alleged uniqueness. In the first case, we are deprived of our moral bearings. In the second, we shall have to compare (at least some) nuclear weapons in terms favorable with those of prenuclear war.

The problem is not so much the empirical claim that nuclear weapons are in a very real sense a class apart from conventional instruments of war. The evidence might well confirm this claim. The real problem is one of principle: it is incoherent to adopt PD and then to condemn nuclear weapons on conventional moral grounds. Not only is this the wrong way to get an argument against the use of nuclear weapons, but it is also to create a hopeless situation in our theoretical understanding of war in which we are unable to render a sound moral appraisal of the new instruments of war. If I am correct that adoption of PD is incompatible with the traditional concepts for understanding the morality of war, is a conceptually integrated assessment of war possible?

I think it is. One could develop a moral basis for the assessment of nuclear war independent of conventional categories. This would allow for PD and for a principled condemnation of nuclear weapons that is not drawn from prenuclear forms of thought. But whether it is or is not possible, let alone convincing, to develop an independent basis for the moral assessment of nuclear weapons is a question no one to my knowledge has satisfactorily answered. Perhaps some time in the future an "adjusted" moral theory will be developed which can be compatible with PD. But as things stand now such a theory is not forthcoming. It seems to me, then, that absent a moral theory compatible with the factual claim of PD, the moral argument against the use of nuclear weapons needs some other basis.

A second and, I think, more promising procedure is to show how the moral problems posed by the use of nuclear weapons are unlike the normal range of permissible conduct in war. This would be accomplished by determining what is *morally* peculiar about the use of these weapons without necessarily making any *empirical* claims about them of the sort captured by PD. What happens to the combatant/non-combatant distinction as we progress along a continuum ranging from wars that manage to preserve this distinction reasonably well to wars which tend to bring harm to entire populations and those whose victims may also include future generations? Call the first kind *conventional*, the second *total*, and the last *absolute* war. Here the difference among these three kinds of war is drawn on the scope of intended or potential victims rather than on the technology of war. So construed, wars are potentially just or unjust as a result of what they do to present or future populations and not on the basis of a controversial factual claim about the inherent qualities of a weapon.

To admit this way of distinguishing different kinds of war has important moral consequences. Well before the introduction of nuclear weapons, the principles of the just war force us to consider the defensibility of war as it approximates different levels of violence. Traditional limitations on the conduct of war prohibit the deliberate killing of non-combatants regardless of the scope or yield of particular weapons—whether it be an arrow, a bullet, or a bomb. On this view, conventional wars are permissible so long as destruction is limited to legitimate targets and the risks of moving to higher levels of violence are relatively low. That conventional wars do not entail total war might be due either to the absence of technology necessary for total destruction of an enemy population or, present such technology, to the restraint practiced by the belligerent powers to limit the kinds of weapons employed. In total war, however, the combatant/non-combatant distinction is seriously jeopardized regardless of the sort of weapons used. The practice of mass-bombing during WW II and other cases of recent nonnuclear conflicts—Vietnam, Beirut, Afghanistan, and Iraq—tend towards the erosion of the distinction conventional war preserves. Such erosion of the conventional distinction is often also characteristic of ideological, revolutionary, and guerrilla war where the fighting is taken to an entire people or segment of a civilian population in which no distinction between combatant and non-combatant is made. To the extent that total war fails to discriminate between legitimate and illegitimate targets, it cannot be just according to the principle of non-combatancy.

This line of reasoning may be extended to absolute war where violence is brought not only to an enemy population, as in total war, but also to large populations not involved in hostilities—e.g., neutral nations—and to future generations of any population, enemy or not. To bring about destruction of an absolute kind, the weapons employed need not necessarily be nuclear. Chemical, biological, and other present or future weapons may be capable of the kind of destruction defined above. Wars in which destruction is absolute become the focus of an entirely different kind of reflection. This shift of focus occurs because such wars are contrary in a very profound way to the interests of the human race. They threaten not only the survival of a particular people, as do total wars, but also of the totality of human life.

The distinction I have drawn here places the question of the defensibility of war on two different bases. Conventional and total wars draw upon traditional moral concepts of the justification and limitation of force. Both may be said, provisionally, to be moral or immoral according to widely held principles. But as we move from total to absolute war, it becomes more and more difficult to defend the recourse to force. The violence and destruction of absolute war place larger segments of total populations at increasing levels of risk. This increased danger makes the justification of force very difficult or impossible to reconcile with any moral or prudential interests. The moral principles of the just-war tradition allow us to conceive of situations in which, given certain limitations, some interests or values may be overridden in order to satisfy other ones having wider and more fundamental importance. Fundamental interests of aggregate bodies must first be secured so that the interests of particular persons may be pursued in a relatively tranquil and secure environment. For example, protecting national liberty so that individual life-projects may be brought to completion.

Absolute war, however, exceeds any purposes that may be linked to the prudential or moral interests of human beings. It is thus immoral because of its failure to distinguish between legitimate and illegitimate targets of attack, and irrational by risking a level of violence that would destroy the natural and social conditions requisite for the pursuit of goods or values widely cherished by rational individuals. For a credible moral defense of the use of any nuclear weapon, it must be shown that its use can be confined to the limits of conventional war, and escape the risk of total or absolute destruction. While I think it possible on the basis of the scheme I have outlined here to give a justification for the use of highly discriminating nuclear weapons in selective targeting policies, the risks of escalating from justified to unjustified violence—i.e, from conventional to absolute destruction—tend to divorce nuclear force and other forms of *indiscriminate* warfare from the pursuit of any rational goal.

I have argued that the nuclear disarmer's condemnation of the use of any type of nuclear weapon rests on a factual claim that, even if correct, leads to a logical contradiction. To escape the contradiction we must either develop a basis of appraisal independent of traditional moral categories, while accepting PD, or reject the factual claim about the uniqueness of nuclear weapons and assess nuclear weapons on familiar moral territory. Since no independent moral theory is available, we are, it seems to me, left with the latter alternative, even if this choice leaves open the possibility for some, however very weak, justification for the use of limited nuclear force. In 5.3 I argue against this possibility but for different reasons.

3.2 DETERRENCE, COMMON MORALITY, AND THE WRONGFUL INTENTIONS PRINCIPLE (WIP)

The old idea of war as an arbitrament of arms by which nations adjudicate conflicts insoluble by non-violent means has, in the nuclear age, given way to a contest of wills by which the great powers forestall the always-present possibility of recourse to nuclear force. Once described by John Foster Dulles as "one of the great advances of our time," the strategy of nuclear deterrence by threatening an unacceptable level of damage to a potential adversary is said to provide an alternative to nuclear war. Robert Tucker has observed that a policy of deterrence insures that "peace-loving nations may realize the purposes otherwise frequently realized only through a defensive war without ever having to engage in such a war."[27] If the use of large-scale, indiscriminate nuclear weapons is both immoral and irrational, how are we to think about the conditional intention to use them? In other words, what is the moral status of nuclear deterrence?

In this section, I examine the most crucial argument made in *Nuclear Deterrence, Morality, and Realism*. Finnis, Boyle, and Grisez claim that what they call the "tradition of common morality" is the theoretical framework in which nuclear deterrence should be assessed. Such assessment, they say, will inevitably conclude that nuclear deterrence is morally prohibited and should therefore be abandoned immediately. My argument is that the substance of what these authors call common morality is not what they say it is. Moreover, even if they were correct about the substance of common morality, WIP, which they claim is a central part of this tradition and applicable with equal force to private and public morality, does not lead to a conclusive condemnation of the possession of a nuclear arsenal for the sake of deterring a similarly armed adversary. Crucial to my argument is the claim that neither common morality nor WIP necessarily precludes a moral pluralism that regards consequentialist considerations, among others, as relevant to the moral assessment of the policy of nuclear deterrence. I begin with the authors' critique of consequentialism.

Part Four of *Nuclear Deterrence, Morality and Realism* is devoted to a defense of common morality and its norm prohibiting the intentional killing of civilians. Having already argued that morality is fundamentally concerned with intentions and choices,[28] the authors now go on to do two things. One is to reject consequentialism. The other is to argue that there is a diversity of basic forms of human good that are incommensurable with each other. Therefore, any attempt to employ a decision-rule in order to choose between different goods or to maximize one over another of these goods will not work. This last point is important and powerful, and the authors use it as the basis of their attack on consequentialism.[29]

The rejection of consequentialism consists of three parts. First is an examination of the prodeterrence views of Michael Walzer and Gregory Kavka, and the antideterrence views of Robert Goodin, Douglas Lackey, and Jefferson McMahan.[30] For Finnis, Boyle, and Grisez, the fact that consequentialism among these writers leads to opposing conclusions illustrates the main problem with the consequentialist approach. Second, even if consequentialist reasoning could arrive at a morally correct conclusion, the argument will be unsound because the essential problem with consequentialism lies in its comparative evaluation of goods of different kinds. The authors think this makes consequentialism *senseless*. Finally, the authors argue that consequentialism is *incoherent* because it requires that two incompatible conditions be simultaneously met.

Finnis, Boyle, and Grisez claim that comparative evaluation of different policies in the nuclear debate is impossible because the negative outcomes of unilateral disarmament (which they say could lead to the enslavement of the West) and nuclear deterrence (which is likely to make nuclear war and hence devastation more probable) cannot be compared in consequentialist terms and because the probabilities of these outcomes cannot be determined. If one tries to compare the outcome of foreign domination, should deterrence be abandoned, with the prospects of nuclear devastation, should deterrence be maintained and fail, each seems, the authors say, "the more repugnant while one is focusing upon it."[31] But what if it were possible to assign to each alternative policy a value? Would this offer a way to determine which is the lesser evil and thereby give some rational basis for an intelligent choice between them? And what if the probabilities of the occurrence of these evils, namely, foreign domination and nuclear devastation, could be predicted? Is a procedure that can determine the relative values of outcomes and their probabilities plausible?

Jefferson McMahan suggests that we can judge the values of outcomes under the policies of deterrence and disarmament. He argues that devastation is a worse outcome than domination for most people in the U.S. and elsewhere in the world, as well as for future generations. Abandoning the deterrent would not "increase the probability of Soviet domination by *significantly more* than it would decrease the probability of nuclear war."[32] Since nuclear devastation is a worse outcome than foreign domination and abandoning the deterrent has a lower probability of leading to nuclear war than maintaining nuclear deterrence without having a significantly higher probability of foreign domination, it follows that unilateral disarmament, coupled with a strong nonnuclear defense, is the superior alternative and therefore ought to be adopted as a matter of policy.

Finnis, Boyle, and Grisez, however, think that McMahan's approach fails because he has not provided the factual premises necessary for the judgment that foreign domination is "less bad" than nuclear devastation, nor for establishing the probabilities of these outcomes. Indeed, they claim that the argument McMahan thinks the most plausible, namely, that abandoning the deterrent would not significantly increase the likelihood of foreign domination, is found implausible by "virtually every Western military and political leader, the vast majority of their people, and almost all consequentialists."[33] More strongly, the authors think that any weighing of outcomes necessarily fails because it rests largely on the claim that goods are interchangeable. But "the values of life, liberty, fairness, and so on, are diverse. How many people's lives are equivalent to the liberty of how many—whether the same or other—persons? No one can say."[34] On this view, the range of rational application of a comparative method is very restricted. Goods could be measured if and only if either human beings have some well-defined, dominant end in life for the sake of which all other goods and activities are chosen, or the different goods human beings pursue have some common denominator on the basis of which a comparison could be made. Absent either of these, the effort to measure and trade-off goods is, as Finnis says, "senseless in the sense that it is senseless to try to sum up the quantity of the size of this page, the quantity of the weight of this book, and the quantity of the number six," where we are comparing incommensurable kinds of quantity: namely, volume, weight, and cardinal numbers.[35]

What is wrong with this argument?[36] The diversity of goods and their incommensurability need not necessarily prevent us from making rational choices when basic goods and values conflict in concrete cases. Assume a situation in which the only alternatives available are life or liberty.[37] Even if these are diverse and incommensurable goods, it is possible that reasonable and morally decent individuals will differ in the importance they attach to them such that when these goods come in conflict one of them will appear preferable to the other. A person might think life is more desirable than liberty. At least while having life, this individual might think, one is still able to pursue other goods and life-projects that make life meaningful: tradition, community, family, friendship, worship, knowledge, and play. Such an individual will indeed agree that the goods of life and liberty are incommensurable, and so they cannot be brought under a decision rule. But it is possible, she will say, to choose between them without having to reduce one to the other. For example, in any conflict between two goods or values, say, life and liberty, a given course of action might yield a greater amount of gain in the former than loss in the latter, while choosing otherwise might yield unacceptable loss in both. So domination and loss of political liberty might be preferable to annihilation. Those under totalitarian rule may well be aware that the opportunities available to them are narrow and their liberties restricted. But that surely is no reason to choose death. After all, restricted liberties under totalitarian rule might not be a permanent state of affairs, while death is. It is therefore reasonable to think that life under foreign domination if not fully liveable, is at least tolerable, just as do those who presently live under totalitarian regimes. Moreover, if we assume that we have an important moral obligation to preserve the integrity of our natural environment and to ensure the existence of future generations, we shall be further persuaded to choose life over liberty. Failure to choose the former, and assuming that nuclear war would be absolute war in the sense defined in 3.1, would lead to the extinction of the human race.

But the point Finnis, Boyle, and Grisez want to make with the incommensurability claim is that there are no rational standards by which we can determine in situations of conflict which good or value is to be favored over others. This seems to leave us in a condition of despair. Consider Grisez's own example of parents who on the evening before Thanksgiving deliberate whether to spend the next morning in a leisurely family breakfast or to join a special Thanksgiving liturgy at church.[38] The choice is between the basic goods or values of leisure and religion. Let us say that the parents are inclined to the breakfast, which will presumably honor the good of leisure. But they find themselves also inclined to go to church, a choice which will honor the good of religion as well as instruct the children in the way of their faith. Let us further say that the father, who is a golf enthusiast, is equally inclined to play some golf the following morning, and this choice honors the goods of play and of community with his fellow golfers. Faced with such a situation, Grisez refuses to recognize that there is any procedure by which we can determine which good shall take priority over the others in particular cases. For him, no rational choice can be made. So, absent any rational procedure or standard, one must presumably choose arbitrarily.

This is what I mean by a condition of despair. Assuming their incommensurability, conflicts of goods or values cannot ever be fully rationally resolved. Values have no common denominator nor is there an independent value one could appeal to in order rationally to choose. Yet a choice between the conflicting values must be made, even if the choice is to retreat into quietism. How, then, is one to choose? In situations of value-conflicts any choice will yield a loss in the rejected good or value. Finnis, Boyle, and Grisez agree that if life is set against liberty (or equality against friendship, or any other combination of basic goods) and no comparison between them can be made, then there is really nothing rational that can be said. I think this overstates the problem, and the situation is not as hopeless at it seems upon first inspection. While I do not think there is a felicitous way out of this problem, the following can be suggested as a more or less rationally satisfactory approach.

What Finnis, Boyle, and Grisez understand by the incommensurability of goods is that there is no standard we can use to adjudicate the conflict of goods *antecedent* to choice.[39] This is true. But we can imagine the loss and regret an agent would (or might) experience *subsequent* to choice and use that as an indicator for which side of a conflict is to be favored. On Grisez's example of parents deliberating on Thanksgiving eve how to spend the following morning, all of the possible alternatives have strong reasons on their behalf. But what is lost in any one of them is greater or less than what is lost on the others. If we assume that these parents are conscientious individuals who are committed to the well-being of their children, and they believe the religious education of their children is more important than the father's satisfaction of the value of play, then the choice to go golfing will drop out of consideration. Otherwise what they are committed to will not be preserved and its loss to the family will be greater than the loss in leisure to the father. The commitment to the children's religious education sets a (subjective) preference scale such that when the good of religion comes in conflict with some other good a comparison between them is possible. To choose leisure or play would be a much greater loss in terms of this family's preferences than to choose religion.

We can achieve some refinement in reference to loss if we distinguish between *recoverable* and *irrecoverable* loss. An agent will resolve a conflict between two incommensurable goods, A and B, by affirming one over the other. Whichever way the agent chooses, some loss is registered. This is a result of the incommensurability of goods. But not all losses are equal. There are at least three kinds of losses that can readily be identified: (i) some may lead to a long-term increase in the rejected good; (ii) some may be recuperated; and (iii) others are permanent. Both (i) and (ii) are recoverable, while (iii) being a permanent loss is not. A typical argument for (i) says that some nonmaximizing choices may be utility-maximizing such that to affirm A over B may also lead to a long-term and relative overall increase in the latter, whereas to resolve the conflict by choosing B will register only a loss in A without any significant gain in B.[40] Thus proposals that resolve conflicts by choosing the alternative that will increase both goods, although in different ways, have at least one sound reason on their behalf over choosing a course of action that increases marginally only one of the goods in conflict. (ii) is a variation of (i). It requires only that the loss be regained either by reversing one's initial choice—e.g, that as the father is teeing off he changes his mind, returns home, and drives with the family to church—or through some compensatory act. In both cases the point seems to have some force because the loss registered in the rejected alternative is in some real way recoverable.

(iii), however, is unique. The choice cannot be reversed nor the loss compensated. In a value-conflict where the rejected alternative suffers irrecoverable loss a rational agent will choose a course of action which forestalls such consequence. Let us say that on Grisez's example choosing the good of play or leisure over the good of religion will lead to a permanent loss of the latter. Or, more to the point: assume that in a conflict between the goods of life and liberty choosing the latter alternative will lead to an irrecoverable loss of the former. Even if a comparative evaluation of loss neither makes these goods commensurable nor appeals to some alleged common currency or independent value, it is not necessary to conclude that any choice between them must be arbitrary. So we avoid the despairing condition. That under certain choices the loss of a basic value will be irrecoverable is sufficient reason to reject its alternative.

There are other reasons why a rational agent would choose as I have described. For example, since personal preference scales and commitments change over time it would be irrational to preclude permanently the possibility of realizing a basic good or value one might in the future favor over others. I think these remarks are sufficient to suggest that even if the incommensurability claim is true (which I think it is) and we cannot reduce one good to another, nor measure, count, and weigh them, a comparative evaluation is not senseless in the way Finnis says it is nor must we resign ourselves to making arbitrary choices. As Isaiah Berlin so aptly put it, we are not barred from seeking "to adjust the unadjustable."[41]

The preceding remarks have focused on one-person value-conflicts. The following questions now emerge: What counts as a good public justification for choosing one good over another? If we admit the same plurality and incommensurability of goods in public as we do in private life, are state functionaries accountable for policy decisions in a way analogous to decision in personal life? In both public and private life there is a felt need to resolve conflict. At least this much is common to all value conflict. But in modern, liberal societies what justifies choices in private and interpersonal conflicts are insufficient grounds for choices having to do with public life. Given that the demands of social order require that a rational, publicly accessible answer be given for particular policy choices, some basic distinction between private and public justificatory procedures needs to be made. In 2.2 I argued that such a distinction might turn on the impersonal nature and other special features of public office. Personal preferences or convictions will then not fully provide the required bases for public choice. We must achieve some other, more impartial procedure that nonetheless corresponds in some real way to the force of personal conviction and is thereby able to relate public choices to ordinary morality intuitions. That procedure is one that will regard as relevant and important in the moral evaluation of policy choices not only, as Thomas Nagel says, what one *does*, but also what *happens*. If some comparison of outcomes is possible without reducing one good or value to another, and accountability in public life will take consequences of actions as morally important, then the argument for the senselessness of consequentialism loses much of its force.

I turn now to the third attack on consequentialism. Finnis, Boyle, and Grisez think consequentialism is incoherent because it cannot account for the possibility of making a morally wrong choice (which is different from an immoral or a mistaken choice, where the former involves a certain moral evil and the latter involves some nonmoral error—e.g., intentional unfairness versus error in calculation, respectively). For convenience, I will call this argument the IC (incoherence of consequentialism).[42] Finnis states IC as follows:

[O]n the proportionalist explanation of "right" and "wrong," wrong choice would be not merely wrong but unintelligible and, as a *choice*, impossible. One can choose only what appears to one to be good; but if, as proportionalists claim, (i) "wrong" entails "yielding (or promising) less good," and (ii) there are choices which can be identified as yielding or promising less good than some alternative choice(s), then it becomes inconceivable that a *morally* wrong (as distinct from a merely mistaken) choice could ever be made. How could anyone *choose* an act which he can see yields less good than some alternative open to him?[43]

Grisez's formulation of IC is:

What is perceived as definitely less good or more bad simply cannot be chosen, because one can only choose what appeals to intelligent interest, and that which is seen as being definitely less good or more bad than something else has no appeal. [N]othing is chosen except insofar as it seems good. Alternatives under consideration which one sees to promise less, simply drop out of consideration. What reason could there be to choose the less good or the more bad? None.[44]

And in *Nuclear Deterrence, Morality, and Realism,* IC is stated as:

The choice of some possibility can be morally significant and required only when an alternative possibility can remain appealing. Now, an alternative to the required possibility can remain appealing only by promising something not available in the required possibility. For nothing can be chosen except in so far as it is judged good. But if one alternative is seen to promise unqualifiedly greater good, or unqualifiedly lesser evil, the other alternative(s), promising only unqualifiedly less good or unqualifiedly lesser evil, lack any appeal and cannot be chosen.[45]

According to IC, consequentialism defines a wrong choice as one that involves "less good" than some alternative. The problem with this, say the proponents of IC, is that a morally significant choice is one in which, considered in themselves, the goods or values in conflict are all *equally worth choosing.* But if one can see that a certain course of action promises less good than its alternative, one could not choose it. Hence consequentialism cannot make sense of nor account for the possibility of making morally wrong choices.

I will comment on the phrase "morally significant choice" and why consequentialism as a theory of moral judgment fails to provide the conditions for such a choice. According to Finnis, Boyle, and Grisez a morally significant choice is one that has all the necessary but not sufficient reasons required for choosing any of the available alternatives. Now since consequentialism compares these alternatives and finds one of them as offering the most good, and this has all the required kinds of reasons in its favor, no choice between it and the other possibilities is possible. But, these authors say, this assumes that two incompatible conditions can be simultaneously met. First, if consequentialism is a theory of moral judgment, it must account for the possibility of a morally wrong choice. Second, consequentialism requires that the alternative which offers the most good be known. What is incompatible in these conditions is that if the second is satisfied and it is known that one of the available alternatives is better or more desirable or offers the best proportion of good over bad, then the first condition cannot be met since a morally wrong choice requires that the goods in conflict be equally worth choosing. But if all of the reasons favor one alternative, then there cannot be a morally wrong choice. Consequentialism, therefore, is incoherent.

Let me illustrate the point with a simple example these authors provide.[46] Assume a young couple is shopping for a house and is concerned with its price, size, and proximity to a school. There will be many houses that will satisfy one or another of these concerns, but no house that satisfies them all. If this couple adopts a consequentialist approach to decision-making, then no house is unqualifiedly better than any other. But if they find a house that satisfies all the above concerns, then they "simply *cannot* choose another house unless [they] become interested in some additional factor" about houses.[47] The reason why this couple cannot choose to buy a house that is less attractive, i.e., "less good," in the relevant sense is because, having found one that satisfies all concerns, i.e., is unqualifiedly good, no other house will be appealing. Losing their appeal, none of the other houses can be chosen, and so a morally wrong choice is impossible.

Further assume that this young couple also has a strong disposition towards altruism. They believe that buying a house that is cheaper than that which satisfies all the required conditions will permit them to give the difference in price to their favorite charity, say, an international children's fund. As consequentialists, they now face the choice between using that difference to buy the preferred house or to give it to charity. Choosing to buy the preferred house will bring about the best consequences in terms of house-hunting, while giving the money to charity will have the best consequences from the point of view of altruism. Comparing these two outcomes, the couple recognizes that giving the money to charity will yield the most good. Hence it is to be favored. Nevertheless the couple decides to buy the preferred house and to suppress their disposition to altruism. Can consequentialism account for this choice?

Proponents of IC would respond as follows. Consequentialism requires the choice which will result in the best state of affairs, and that undoubtedly is the choice to buy a less attractive house and to give the remainder to charity. Since the couple knows which choice will yield the most good, not to choose accordingly is to make an unintelligible choice. But this reasoning is unsound. To buy the house that will satisfy all the relevant concerns or to give to charity is a choice between two equally appealing goods or values that emerge from different points of view. When viewed from the perspective of house-hunting, buying the preferred house has all the necessary reasons on its behalf and is the superior choice, while viewing house-hunting from the perspective of charity the purchase of a less expensive house is equally attractive and is the preferred choice. So this couple faces a conflict between two courses of action each of which is equally worth choosing from the point of view of different values. Now, consequentialism does not require this couple when considering which house to buy to choose from the perspective of altruism. It requires only that they choose that which will bring about the best state of affairs from a given perspective, not from every possible perspective. It may be that this couple thinks their decision on house-hunting ought to take account of the value of altruism. If consequentialism requires that all choices take into account this and every possible value or point of view rather than what is relevant for a particular choice, then this couple's choice is indeed unintelligible and consequentialism cannot account for the possibility of a morally wrong choice. But consequentialism does not require that every choice be made from an omniscient point of view. Even if this point of view were possible, it would not be necessary. What is required is that the couple choose the alternative with the most good. However, what is the "most good" is determined from the perspective of different values.

My point is that consequentialists only need to argue that whatever choice one makes brings about a better state of affairs than if one chooses otherwise. This mode of reasoning allows for a plurality of points of view and values some (or all) of which may disagree on which choice will bring about the most good. Considered in themselves, buying the preferred house and giving to charity are both equally worth choosing, and so the condition for a morally significant choice is met. Proponents of IC assume that consequentialism allows only for a single point of view or value when considering the alternatives present in a situation. Were this assumption true, there would be only a single course of action having any appeal. But this assumption is false. Consequentialism allows for conflicting points of view each of which favors one over the other alternatives present in a situation. This means that not to choose as is required from the particular point of view of a given is to make a morally wrong choice. Consequentialism does lead to opposing conclusions, and this may indeed make it inconsistent, controversial, or mistaken. Consequentialism may even be in a real sense incoherent. But it is not incoherent on the basis of IC.

My argument so far has been that if consequentialism is to be rejected, it cannot be for the reasons these authors give. Finnis, Boyle, and Grisez have failed to show that consequentialism is either senseless or incoherent. Hence there is no reason to accept their claim that nuclear arms policy cannot be morally assessed in consequentialist terms. Nonetheless, disarmers have recourse to another, and wider, principle to support their condemnation of the possession of nuclear arms: WIP.[48] Stein puts it as follows: "It is a general moral principle that if an action is morally wrong, it is wrong to intend to do it, even if one never gets the chance to carry out one's intention. If an action is wrong no matter what the circumstances, it is wrong to intend to do it in any, no matter how carefully limited and specified, circumstances."[49] Kenny also assumes this principle when he asks whether it is a defensible ethical position "to threaten what it would not be legitimate to do."[50]   But among this group of just-war nuclear pacifists, it has been Finnis, Boyle, and Grisez who have made the most use of WIP. These authors say: "[A]ccording to common morality, intentions formed in the heart can be seriously wrong even if they are never carried out. Thus the principle: *one may not intend what one may not do.* [T]his principle has its truth for reasons that hold even when the intent in question is not wrong, and indeed even when the resolve, willingness, or will to might not be called an intention in ordinary language."[51]

In what manner WIP is a central feature of common morality these authors do not say. But I do think WIP is generally true and captures certain strong moral intuitions about the relation of actions and intentions. However, I will argue that these authors' use of it is incorrect and that its application to nuclear arms policy is defective. It is an interesting question whether this is true only of nuclear deterrence intentions or, more generally, of the role of intentions in public policy. I begin with the following question: Why should one think that the possession of a nuclear arsenal for the sake of deterring a similarly armed adversary is morally wicked?

One important answer to this question is that there is a necessary conceptual link between actions and intentions such that if an action is said to be morally wrong so too is the intention to engage in such an action wrong. We can say, generally, that if X is wrong the intention Y to do X is wrong also. That is: if I intend to do some action X, if and when the occasion for X arises, and X is wrong, then the intention Y to do X is wrong. Accordingly, if the use of large-scale nuclear weapons is wrong, then the intention to retaliate if attacked is morally proscribed. In other words, one may never intend what is immoral to do, that is, if X then Y. It is the relation of implication that forces the conceptual link between actions and intentions.[52] Hence the validity of WIP.[53]

But is WIP appropriate to the assessment of nuclear deterrence? Finnis, Boyle, and Grisez argue that the intention behind nuclear deterrence threats is to massacre millions of civilians in a massive retaliatory strike. Since there is a strong moral prohibition on killing civilians, except as a side-effect and proportionate to legitimate military operations, and the policy of deterrence intends indiscriminate and disproportionate killing, it is a murderous policy and has to be abandoned immediately. This is a strong moral argument and it articulates the intuitive basis of WIP. However, I am going to challenge the relation of implication in this principle. I will argue that *intending* to do X, i.e., Y, is itself an action and hence subject to a moral appraisal independent of X. My argument depends on the claim that the premise on intentions in WIP can be given various equally plausible interpretations.

A defender of WIP will claim that the prohibition on the use of nuclear weapons is absolute. No matter what the circumstances are nor what consequences will follow, the use of these weapons has no moral justification. Consequentialists can agree with this prohibition but for different reasons—e.g., that there are no situations in which the use of nuclear weapons can be justified in consequentialist terms. But for the non-consequentialist the question arises whether the absolute prohibition on using these weapons extends to an absolute prohibition on intending to use them as a matter of policy. Suppose we think it does and say that it is absolutely prohibited to intend what is absolutely immoral to do. In that case, WIP yields the desired conclusion. But is the moral equivalence of action and intention methodologically correct and is it sufficient for a conclusive condemnation of nuclear deterrence?

I think not. There is no reason why the absolute prohibition on an act necessarily extends to its antecedent intention. Consider the following. An act can be wrong in one of two ways. Suppose that some action A violates a non-consequentialist principle P, and that such violation is sufficient for A being morally impermissible. For the non-consequentialist, this violation of P is sufficient for not doing nor intending to do A. Let us refer to this as an absolute condemnation of A. Contrast that with the understanding that when an action B violates a non-consequentialist principle P′ some morally relevant facts of a non-absolutist kind could count for the moral permissibility of B. For example, in a situation of choice a person might find that every alternative open violates some moral principle. If we agree that some violations are worse than others—e.g., that killing is worse than lying—it would be terribly mistaken to say that one morally cannot lie regardless of consequences. That is, in a situation of choice where all the available alternatives violate some moral principle, it is better to choose the alternative with the "least bad" consequences. In such a situation the violation of the least pressing moral principle is *prima facie* wrong but permissible, when all morally relevant facts are considered. An action then can be either absolutely or *prima facie* wrong.

Finnis, Boyle, and Grisez recognize the fact that one may be persuaded and justified in choosing the lesser of two evils. Following Cicero, they say that "any moral adviser may have to advise *against the worse* of the possible sins which someone is going to commit."[54] In this they seem to acknowledge that the moral permissibility of an act cannot be determined in isolation from the evil effects that would follow from any of the other possible courses of action present in a situation of choice. In other words, acting without regard to the effects of rejected options could bring about a greater evil than acting otherwise. Thus an action may violate a moral principle and be *prima facie* wrong. But when that action is evaluated in relation to the available options, each of which would bring about worse violations of more pressing moral principles, it is the right and morally advisable thing to do, *all things considered*.

If we accept that an action can be wrong in one of two ways, one of which gives us an absolute condemnation, and the other an acknowledgment that, though an action violates a moral principle, it may nonetheless be the morally maximal (perhaps obligatory) thing to do, then the conclusion Finnis, Boyle, and Grisez want to draw from WIP is not required. There may be good reasons in favor of forming an intention to do what is morally prohibited, when absent this intention conditions will result in a great evil. In this case, the intention might be wrong, given the moral equivalence of actions and intention, but it would be so only *prima facie*. So an action can be wrong absolutely, such as using weapons of mass and indiscriminate killing, but it does not follow that the intention to use these weapons for the purpose of deterring a similarly armed adversary is wrong also, *all things considered*. That is, the moral equivalence of actions and intention is not as strong as it appears at first sight because intentions involve an entirely different set of questions and considerations that are uniquely relevant to their justification. Let me illustrate with an example.

Assume two countries, A and B, both of which are threatened by a hostile nuclear adversary. Assume also that if these countries deploy a nuclear deterrent, the probability that either will be attacked is fairly small, and that absent a deterrent the probability of attack is significantly increased. Both countries decide to pursue a policy of deterrence and develop nuclear arsenals sufficient to deter the hostile nuclear power. But there are some significant differences between them.

Country A is persuaded of the moral equivalence of actions and intention—that it is wrong to intend what is wrong to do—and so the leaders of this country decide to adopt the following deterrence policy. First, no decision is to be made about what will happen in the event of a nuclear attack. And second, they develop a type of deterrence that seeks to deter the adversary from a nuclear attack only on one's territory by the deployment of large-scale, countervalue weapons. Under this deterrence policy, the conditional intention to use nuclear weapons has not been formed and its capabilities preclude the possibility of a disarming first strike. Nonetheless, the leaders of this country are aware that given the pressures which might arise under attack, the mere possession of a nuclear arsenal introduces a risk that, in spite of their beliefs about the equivalence of actions and intention, the weapons might be put to actual use. Moreover, given the features of its arsenal, this country is capable only of a countervalue retaliatory strike that will undoubtedly kill millions of civilians. The leaders of country B, however, develop a type of deterrence that extends to nonnuclear allies and consists of a flexible nuclear capability. They also form the conditional intention to use their weapons, and announce that they will do so if attacked. Which of these deterrence policies is the more promising means of avoiding nuclear war?

The deterrence of country B is obviously the superior one. Consider the following. Suppose that while the leaders of country A have tried to conceal the fact that they have not formed the conditional intention to retaliate, the hostile nuclear adversary learns of this. As a result, country A's deterrence is not credible and its adversary will not be deterred from nuclear or any other type of aggression. Because its adversary is not deterred, country A is more likely to be attacked than B and hence to be in a position to have to use its countervalue weapons. On the other hand, country B, having formed and announced the conditional intention, and developed the capability to respond to a wide variety of situations, remains safe from attack.

Now WIP, as formulated by Finnis, Boyle, and Grisez, does not condemn country A's deterrence. Absent the conditional intention to retaliate, no wrong has been committed. But country A is more likely to have to use its nuclear weapons than B. Yet if A forms the required intention, the probability of using these weapons would be significantly reduced. That is, present the conditional intention the possibility of using these weapons deliberately is increased, insofar as the means and resolve to use them are present, but the probability of use is decreased, since the adversary is not likely to attack, and if it does attack B has available a number of response options short of countervalue warfare. On the other hand, absent the intention the possibility of use is decreased while the probability of using nuclear weapons is increased. Given these conditions, would it be morally wrong for country A to form the required intention?

The fact that an action can be wrong in one of two ways is obscured by WIP. This principle assumes that what is true of an action is true also of the antecedent intention. But intentions and actions do not represent equal wrongs. Unlike other conditional intentions, nuclear ones carry with them the conviction that the probability for those conditions arising which would lead to the use of nuclear weapons is significantly reduced present the required intention and increased with its absence. Since the purpose of forming the conditional intention is to reduce the likelihood of having deliberately to use nuclear weapons, one is not required to assess the morality of deterrence on the (im)morality of use. What is important about this point is that the bridge drawn intuitively between actions and intention does not necessarily hold in the case of nuclear deterrence. It does not hold because the reason for forming a conditional intention to use nuclear weapons is the prevention of consequences that would constitute a greater evil than forming the intention. If this reasoning is correct, then conditional intentions can be morally appraised independent of the intended act. Deterrence intentions might be wrong, to the extent that if carried out they would bring about a grave moral evil. However, when intentions have important autonomous consequences, they are at most wrong only *prima facie*.[55] All things considered, nuclear deterrence intentions are a morally preferable means for avoiding the use of nuclear weapons than a deterrence without the conditional intention.

In conclusion, the moral appraisal of nuclear deterrence cannot avoid consequentialist considerations, even when one adopts a moral theory or principle that wants to exclude them. Somewhere along the line consequences have to be brought in, either directly or indirectly. The arguments I have given are, I think, sufficient to show that a rational choice is possible between goods or courses of action which, in themselves, are equally worth choosing and that consequentialism has something significant to offer the moral appraisal of deterrence policies. According to my account, there is no compelling reason to think that a deontological moral theory is superior to a consequentialist one, or to accept the claim that nuclear arms policy cannot or should not be assessed in consequentialist terms. The examples in 3.2 suggest that our intuitions about the moral equivalence of actions and intention are, at least in the context of nuclear deterrence, misleading, and that intentions should be assessed independently of their corresponding action, at least when they have important consequences.

3.3 THE MORALITY OF PRODUCING NUCLEAR WEAPONS

For the most part, philosophers and theologians have centered their moral assessment of nuclear arms policy on whether nuclear weapons diminish the chance of attack, either conventional or otherwise, and increase the chance of victory in the event of war. Most of my discussion in this book attends to those matters by focusing on the morality of the possession and use of nuclear weapons. My presentation would be incomplete, however, if I did not consider the morality of producing nuclear weapons, either for deterrence or use.

There are obvious economic questions involved in the production of nuclear weapons—the effects, for example, of weapons production on scientific innovation, international trade, inflation, unemployment, and so forth. Yet the economic effects of weapons policy is a rather complicated and as yet unsettled area of inquiry. But the fundamental moral question a nation must address is whether or not to produce nuclear weapons. What might a nation, say, the United States, gain or loose by producing nuclear weapons? What decision should it take in a choice between production and non-production of nuclear weapons?

Our response should not be borne out of fear. That surely seems to have been case in the 1940s when the United States initially sought the development and production of nuclear weapons, lest Hitler develop them first. But since the stillborn post-WW II plan to internationalize nuclear weapons, the idea of a United States, or a modern military power, without nuclear weapons is utopic. Nonetheless, the morality of producing nuclear weapons is a question worth considering.

There are at least two lines of reasoning one might take to the question at hand. The first is retrospective. It derives the morality of producing nuclear weapons from the morality of possessing them for the purpose of deterring a similarly armed adversary. In the forgoing section I argued that a nation possessing a nuclear deterrent diminishes the risk of suffering a nuclear attack, and thereby reduces the probability of using these weapons. If the possession of a nuclear deterrent serves this very important purpose, then surely it follows that the production of nuclear weapons is justified. The simple truth is this: we cannot *have* deterrence without *producing* an adequate nuclear arsenal.

A version of the retrospective approach is the argument from national self-defense, which can take different forms—e.g., defense of the political community, duty to preserve territorial integrity and political sovereignty, national self-determination, among others. The argument from national self-defense says that states have the duty to protect themselves and their vital interests from unjust aggression. States have this duty, so the argument goes, just because they are instrumental in protecting the right to life of their members and the political community they have built. Many of the authors treated in this study accept this argument or one of its variants. Because states have the duty to protect themselves from unjust aggression, they must develop those (morally legitimate) means necessary for national defense. For this view, the morality of producing nuclear weapons turns largely on the duty of states to protect themselves from unjust aggression.

One popular opinion about what comes from producing nuclear weapons is that by having them no war between the major powers occurred during the Cold War.[56] A stronger version of this opinion might say that the United States decisively deterred the former Soviet Union from nuclear aggression, and also emerged victorious from the most expensive and tumultuous period of the century. Soviet communism came to an end and democratic capitalism was endorsed by former Soviet states. "There have been 37 years of peace in Europe," Caspar Weinberger said in a lecture to the Massachusetts Medical Society in May 1982.

Despite the threat of the Soviet army, despite the threat of the Soviet's nuclear weapons, Western Europe has prospered. Its political freedoms have flourished, and its social institutions have grown stronger. Indeed, there has not been an equal period of uninterrupted peace on the European continent since the Roman Empire fell. At the risk of stating the obvious, the United States and the rest of the world have also avoided the scourge of nuclear fire. Deterrence thus is and remains our best hope of keeping peace.[57]

There are doubtful assumptions in the above opinion. For example, there is no evidence that the peace in Europe was the result of deterrence. It is a common and simple fallacy to mistake what is not the cause (i.e., deterrence) of a given effect (i.e., the peace in Europe) for the real cause. Europe has enjoyed other long (and some longer) periods of peace without nuclear deterrence. So, we are justified in believing that peace is possible without nuclear weapons and that there may be many other reasons why nuclear war did not break out.[58] Put another way, we cannot know the truth of deterrence—whether it deters war, nuclear or otherwise, keeps peace, and so forth. The concurrence of the nuclear threat and the peace in Europe does not prove that deterrence has worked.[59]

Suppose, for the sake of argument, that producing nuclear weapons and thereby having them available for deterrence has been to the great benefit of the United States. The proposition would be true only if we take the Cold War as the relevant time-frame. But if we extend the time-frame beyond the period of the Cold War, would the United States still gain from producing these weapons? Should we take that fifty year time-frame as indicative of how we might decide on the choice between production and non-production?

The second line of reasoning is prospective. It looks forward in time to what might be gained or lost by producing nuclear weapons. Having reached an estimate on what might (or will) eventually come from producing these weapons, it determines whether one ought to have them.

Obviously, if the relevant time-frame is the Cold War, then the alleged benefits are far greater than any loss incurred by production.

Now, suppose that by producing nuclear weapons we create the probability of using them in a major war. Suppose further than in each given year there is a small probability of such a war, and that the probability grows over time. It is a fact that over the past fifty years nuclear weapons have been used twice. So, let us say that the probability is one in every twenty-five years. If we now speculate about the use of nuclear weapons in the 21st century, we should have four such instances. Add the assumption that probability grows over time, say, .5 every fifty years, we get a total of five such instances in the next century.

According to this view, it is a statistical certainty that over time nuclear weapons will increasingly be used in major wars. Perhaps they will not be used again until the year 2049. But the certainty of their use only increases (however gradually) with time. This may well be what Jonathan Schell had in mind when he said that "unless we rid ourselves of our nuclear arsenals a holocaust not only *might* occur but *will* occur—if not today, then tomorrow; if not this year, then the next."[60]

The determination that nuclear weapons will be used in the future is a far more complicated matter, however. There are other matters that have the direct and terribly awful effect of increasing those probabilities. While I assumed only the intentional use of nuclear weapons, there are also unintentional uses—e.g., an unauthorized launch that elicits retaliation, a launch based on misinformation, or a launch by mechanical malfunction. To be sure, we have no past record of unintentional uses of nuclear weapons, but one can only assume that an unintentional use will occur in the future.[61] There are additional risks that should be considered in estimating the probabilities of a future use of nuclear weapons—e.g., nuclear blackmail or terrorism, proliferation of nuclear weapons, among others.[62] Furthermore, since even a medium size nuclear war (intentionally or unintentionally initiated) could, according to present estimates, produce devastating ecological, cultural, and human effects, we cannot exclude the possibility that once produced nuclear weapons will lead to very bad outcomes. The truth here is that we *ought not to produce* nuclear weapons. Because we ought not to produce these weapons, then morally *we cannot have them nor use them*. We are all thereby better off.

The above discussion is far from conclusive. But there are several points I wish to register. First, a balanced treatment of nuclear arms policy considers the morality of deterrence and use, as well as the morality of producing weapons of mass destruction that will certainly be used in the future. Second, because we have good reason to think deterrence was not the cause of peace and that a nuclear war will bring a devastating human and ecological loss, we would be better off never to have produced nuclear weapons. Third, because it is not proven that nuclear weapons deter, then the immense cost of producing them is unjustified. Fourth, the above argument reinforces the nuclear disarmers' pacifism. It rejects the possession and use of nuclear weapons. But the rejection is more radical. Nuclear weapons should never have been produced because of the future loss we will certainly incur as the result of having them.

Even if we have to live with nuclear weapons, as many authorities claim,[63] the world will be better off without them,[64] and so we should never have produced them. This view may be conjectural. But it is not more so than the fiction advertised by Weinberger and many others that says deterrence "works. It has worked in the face of major international tensions involving the great powers, and it has worked in the face of war itself."[65]

3.4 IS THE PREPARATION TO FIGHT A NUCLEAR WAR ILLEGAL?

If the argument of 3.3 is correct, then the preparation to fight a nuclear war is immoral. Because the world is better off if we do not produce nuclear weapons and nuclear weapons have no discernible military or political value, then we should not prepare to fight a war with nuclear weapons. The preparation for such a war is already tainted with the immorality of producing nuclear weapons. In this section I briefly consider the question whether the preparation to fight a nuclear war is illegal. To address this question I remark first on the use and then on the possession of nuclear weapons. The account I give on the legality of use and possession yields a negative verdict on the question at hand.

(i) using nuclear weapons is against international law. The most important declaration on the legal status of using nuclear weapons is United

Nations General Assembly Resolution 1653 (XVI). It declares that "any state using nuclear weapons and thermo-nuclear weapons is to be considered as violating the Charter of the United Nations, as acting contrary to the laws of humanity, and as committing a crime against mankind and civilization."[66] Resolution 2936 goes further by establishing a "permanent prohibition" on the use of nuclear weapons.[67] Although these and other General Assembly resolutions do not have the force of law, they do express the international consensus that the use of nuclear weapons is contrary to the humanitarian ideas that are fundamental to international law.

Despite General Assembly resolutions on the use of nuclear weapons, the legal challenges of using nuclear weapons have never really been fully addressed. There are treatises that prohibit nuclear weapons in Antarctica, Latin America, outer space, on the sea beyond national boundaries, and the Partial Test Ban Treaty outlawing the testing of nuclear weapons in outer space, under water, and within the earth's atmosphere. But there are no provisions in international law that explicitly forbid the development, manufacture, stockpiling, deployment, or use of nuclear weapons. If there is anything striking about the status of using nuclear weapons in international law, it is the silence on this matter of the legal community.[68] In the absence of any explicit prohibition, it appears that the use of nuclear weapons is permitted. As Field Manual 27-10 of the U.S. Army puts it: "The use of explosive atomic weapons, whether by air, sea, or land forces, cannot as such be regarded as violative of international law in the absence of any customary rule of international law or international convention restricting their employment."[69]

That opinion, however, is premature. The legality of using a weapon with such destructive potential cannot be left simply to the absence of any standard that explicitly forbids it. That silence may well be due not to the implied opinion that it is permissible to use nuclear weapons. Rather, the silence may be due either to partisan views in the nuclear debate or to the belief that during the Cold War nuclear weapons served the important purpose of deterring Soviet aggression. The legal community may well have been motivated by the fear of Soviet aggression to subordinate the use of nuclear weapons to considerations of national security and military necessity.[70]

It is important to note also that the lack of an explicit prohibition in international law on nuclear weapons does not mean that they are not illegal. The International Military Tribunal at Nuremberg made it clear that "[t]he law of war is to be found not only in treatises, but in the customs and practices of states which gradually obtained universal recognition, and from the general principles of justice applied by jurists and practiced by military courts."[71] One principle of the law of war that has obtained universal recognition is a provision attached in 1977 to Article 51 of the Fourth Geneva Convention of 1949. That provision states:

The civilian population as such, as well as individual civilians, shall not be the object of attack. Acts or threats of violence the primary purpose of which is to spread terror among the civilian population are prohibited. Indiscriminate attacks are prohibited. Indiscriminate attacks are: (a) those which are not directed at a specific military objective; (b) those which employ a method or means of combat which cannot be directed at a specific military objective; or (c) those which employ means or methods of combat the effects of which cannot be limited as required by this Protocol: and consequently, in each such case, are of a nature to strike military objectives and civilians or civilian objects without discrimination. Among others, the following type of attack [is] to be considered as indiscriminate: an attack which may be expected to cause incidental loss of civilian life, injury to civilians, damage to civilian objects, or a combination thereof, which would be excessive in relation to the concrete and direct military advantage anticipated.[72]

Had this provision of Article 51 been in place during WW II, the mass-bombing of London, Hamburg, Dresden, and Tokyo, as well as the atomic bombing of Hiroshima and Nagasaki would have been illegal, so too with any use of nuclear weapons that attacks civilians directly or "may be expected to cause incidental loss of civilian life." While this provision says nothing about nuclear weapons, it prohibits indiscriminate attacks—i.e., those attacks that cannot distinguish between military and civilian objects. But since such weapons cannot by their nature make the required distinction and will cause immense "incidental loss of civilian life," nuclear weapons are indirectly prohibited by the provision's restriction on indiscriminate attacks.

A second line of legal thinking leads to the same conclusion. Suppose that nuclear weapons can be targeted in accordance with the restrictions of Article 51. Must we therefore assume that nuclear weapons are legal means of waging war? The assumption that nuclear weapons may be used discriminately, however, does not make them licit. Weapons that aggravate suffering have long been forbidden by the world community. The Declaration of St. Petersburg, for example, forbids the use of "any projectile of a weight below 400 grams which is either explosive or charged with fulminating or inflammable substance."[73] It also forbids as against the laws of humanity the use of weapons that cause unnecessary and excessive suffering:

> Considering that the progress of civilization should have the effect of alleviating as much as possible the calamities of war; That the only legitimate object which States endeavor to accomplish during war is to weaken the military forces of the enemy; That this object would be exceeded by the employment of arms which uselessly aggravate the sufferings of disabled men, or render their death inevitable; That the employment of such arms would therefore be considered contrary to the laws of humanity.[74]

The principles of this Declaration were later incorporated in Article 22 of the Regulations annexed to the Fourth Hague Convention of 1907, where the right of belligerents to adopt means of waging war is not an unlimited right, rather it is a right restricted by the laws of humanity that seek to reduce the "calamities of war." Even if nuclear weapons may be used discriminately, the experience of Hiroshima and Nagasaki make it clear that nuclear weapons used in populated areas bring indiscriminate destruction from blast, fire, and radiation effects. Additionally, the prohibition on weapons that cause unnecessary and excessive suffering is also the basis for the prohibition against the use of poison and poisoned weapons in Article 23 of the Regulations annexed to the Hague Convention. Similarly, the Hague Declaration Respecting Asphyxiating

Gases of 1899 and the Geneva Gas Protocol of 1925 prohibit the use of any poisonous substance. The latter declares:

> Whereas the use in war of asphyxiating, poisonous or other gases, and of *all analogous liquids, materials or devices*, has been justly condemned by the general opinion of the civilized world; and To the end that this prohibition shall be universally accepted as part of International Law, binding alike the conscience and practice of nations; the High Contracting Parties agree to be bound as between themselves according to the terms of this declaration.[75]

Any nuclear explosion releases various poisonous substances, some of which endure for very long periods of time, including uranium which is highly toxic. As Schwarzenberger puts it: "[I]f the use of a poison on an arrow made it a poisoned weapon, the use of uranium in a nuclear weapon would appear to render the latter poisoned in the same sense."[76] Hence, because the use of nuclear weapons will bring immense loss of civilian life, either directly or indirectly, and are analogous to poisonous weapons by the radioactive fallout, the legal prohibition on weapons that aggravate suffering or on the use of "all [materials] analogous [to] poisonous gases" renders the use of nuclear weapons illegal.

(ii) the possession of nuclear weapons is against international law. If the use of any nuclear weapons is judged to be contrary to the humanitarian principles embodied in international law, then the possession of these weapons seems equally contrary to those principles and should therefore be judged illegal. In his remarks on this problem, Douglas Lackey has correctly observed that "[v]ery little evidence exists that the possession of nuclear weapons by nation states is illegal. Certainly there is no general custom that nations refrain from the development of nuclear weapons."[77] Nonetheless, it does appear that the prohibition on using nuclear weapons carries over to their possession. A number of relevant international documents seem to prohibit nuclear weapons short of actual use—e.g., the 1959 Antarctic Treaty, the 1963 Partial Test Ban Treaty, and the 1967 Treaty of Tlatelolco. Article 36 of the 1977 Geneva Protocol I Additional to the 1949 Geneva Conventions says: "In the study, development, acquisitions or adoption of a new weapon, means or method of warfare, a High Contracting Party is under an obligation to determine whether if employment would, in some or all circumstances, be prohibited by this Protocol or any other rule of international law applicable to the High Contracting Party."[78] If the use of nuclear weapons is contrary to the humanitarian principles of international law, then the "study, development, acquisitions or adoption" of those weapons appear to violate those principles. Whatever license a nation has on basis of its sovereignty to develop and stockpile effective measures to dissuade a potential adversary from aggression is restricted by the above treaties and by core humanitarian principles of international law.

A more compelling point can be made regarding the illegality of possessing nuclear weapons. In April 1972, The United States and the former Soviet Union signed an agreement to destroy all their arsenals of toxic and bacteriological weapons. That agreement accepted the declaration of the Geneva Gas Protocol of 1925 prohibiting "poisonous and other gases, and of all analogous liquids, materials and devices." Because nuclear weapons are analogous to "poisonous gases," a consistent position demands that weapons, including nuclear weapons, that are toxic should not be possessed.

(iii) the preparation to fight a nuclear war is illegal. I take it as an obvious matter of logical consistency that when a weapon cannot be used or possessed because it violates core humanitarian principles of international law, the preparation to fight a war with those weapons is similarly violative of those principles. If the use and possession of nuclear weapons are illegal, then one cannot prepare to fight with those weapons. The point of the humanitarian principles of international law is to exert a civilizing influence on war by protecting civilian populations, reducing the calamities of war, prohibiting the employment of weapons that aggravate suffering, and restricting the development and stockpiling of weapons to those that can be used. It seems then reasonable to infer that the research, development, procurement, stockpiling of nuclear weapons, as well as the preparation to use these weapons in war, may be regarded as in violation of humanitarian principles. Those who say otherwise carry the burden of proof.

NOTES

1. John Foster Dulles, "The Evolution of Foreign Policy," *The Department of State Bulletin*, 30 (Jan. 25, 1954), 107-110.

2. Quoted in John Lewis Gaddis, *Strategies of Containment: A Critical Appraisal of Postwar American National Security Policy* (Oxford: Oxford University Press, 1982), 190.

3. Quoted in Lawrence Freedman, *The Evolution Nuclear Strategy* (New York: St. Martin's Press, 1983), 78.

4. E. P. Thompson, "The Logic of Exterminism," *New Left Review*, May 21, 1980.

5. Also published simultaneously in the U.S. under the title *Nuclear Weapons: A Catholic Response* (New York: Sheed and Ward, 1961). It is noteworthy that in discussions on nuclear weapons and war in the U.S. at this time, no pacifism comparable to that expressed in this volume appeared. In the two symposia by American Catholics during the same time as Stein's, no sustained presentation of nuclear pacifism can be found. Those volumes are, *Morality and Modern Warfare: The State of the Question*, ed. William J. Nagle (Baltimore: Helicon Press, 1960) and *Christian Ethics and Nuclear Warfare*, eds. Ulrich S. Allers and William V. O'Brien (Washington, DC: Institute of World Polity, Georgetown University, 1961). The exceptions are John C. Ford's and Gordon Zahn's contributions to the Nagle volume. Contributions by American philosophers would not appear for nearly twenty years.

6. John Finnis, Joseph Boyle, Germain Grisez, *Nuclear Deterrence, Morality, and Realism* (Oxford: Oxford University Press, 1987), 66.

7. Stein, *Nuclear Weapons*, 31.

8. Stein, *Nuclear Weapons*, 35.

9. Stein, *Nuclear Weapons*, 125. It should be noted that Stein is at times tempted to a pacifism much broader than a nuclear one, but still premised on the same factual assumptions as the latter. He says that "military security is now altogether unthinkable—the alternative of non-violent resistance acquires an unprecedented practical attraction. What we used to dismiss as the panacea of political enthusiasts, now imposes itself as a strategy for the tough-minded. At least it can no longer be precluded from serious thought." Stein, *Nuclear Weapons*, 22.

10. Anthony Kenny, *The Logic of Deterrence* (Chicago: University of Chicago Press, 1985), 6.

11. Kenny, *Logic of Deterrence*, 8.

12. Kenny, *Logic of Deterrence*, 315.

13. Finnis, Boyle, Grisez, *Nuclear Deterrence*, 310, 87.

14. Finnis, Boyle, Grisez, *Nuclear Deterrence*, 125.

15. Stein, *Nuclear Weapons*, 20.

16. Stein, *Nuclear Weapons*, 23.

17. Stein, *Nuclear Weapons*, 29.

18. Kenny, *Logic of Deterrence*, 22.

19. Thomas Schelling, *The Strategy of Conflict*, 2nd ed., (Cambridge: Harvard University Press, 1980), 257. Schelling, however, argues that even though the basis for a physical distinction between nuclear and other weapons might be weak, it is still possible to make such distinction in a way relevant to the process of limiting war. See pp. 257-266.

20. See, for example, Colin Gray and Keith Payne, "Victory is Possible," *Foreign Policy* (Summer 1980), 14-27.

21. The idea motivating this principle has been expressed in differing ways by various authors. Among the first to observe the uniqueness of nuclear weapons was Bernard Brodie who, shortly after the explosion of the first atomic bomb over Hiroshima, said: "Everything that I have written is obsolete." Quoted in Fred Kaplan, *The Wizards of Armageddon* (New York: Simon & Schuster, 1983), 10. See the excellent discussion on this point by Kaplan in chapters 1 and 2 of his book. Robert McNamara concurs with Brodie when he says, in that oft-quoted statement of his, that "nuclear weapons serve no military purpose whatsoever. They are totally useless—except only to deter one's opponent from using them," in McNamara, "The Military Role of Nuclear Weapons: Perceptions and Misperceptions," *Foreign Affairs* 62 (Fall 1983), 79. Others express the same opinion about the uniqueness of nuclear weapons. Michael Walzer says: "The real ambiguity of nuclear deterrence lies in the fact that no one, including ourselves, can be sure that we will carry out the threats that we make. But at the same time, the reason for our hesitancy and self-doubt is the monstrous immorality that our policy contemplates, an immorality we can never hope to square with our understanding of justice in war. Nuclear weapons explode the theory of the just war. They are the first of mankind's innovations that are simply not encompassable with the familiar moral world." *Just and Unjust Wars* (New York: Basic Books, 1977), 282. Joseph Nye in his *Nuclear Ethics* (New York: The Free Press, 1986) says: "There is no precedent for the challenge that nuclear weapons present to our physical and moral lives." "One can construct and aim a nuclear weapon that is so small and accurate that it will do about the same damage as conventional iron bombs full of high explosives. But even those miniature nuclear weapons must never be treated as normal usable weapons, because politically and technically they are too closely related to their big brothers of mass destruction," ix, 105. Thomas Schelling says: "Even those who consider a nuclear fireball as moral as napalm for burning a man to death must recognize as a political fact a worldwide revulsion against nuclear weapons." "[T]he distinction is not physical but psychic, perceptual, legalistic, or symbolic." "What makes atomic weapons different is a powerful tradition that they *are* different." "The first conclusion to be drawn from this argument is that there is a distinction between nuclear and nonnuclear weapons, a distinction relevant to the process of limiting war." *The Strategy of Conflict*, 259, 260, 263. In *Living with Nuclear Weapons* (New York: Bantam Books, 1983), the Harvard Nuclear Study Group says: What is new about nuclear strategy is that "[f]irst, with modern means of delivery, nuclear weapons make defense in the traditional sense of physically shielding oneself from attack

extremely difficult, if not impossible." "So far, at least, there is no defense against their power." "Second, nuclear weapons have greatly accelerated the historical trend toward making civilian populations the targets, intentional or not, in war." "Nuclear weapons, for the first time in history, offer the possibility of destroying a country before one has defeated or destroyed its armed forces," 30-31. The American Catholic bishops in their pastoral letter say: "We live today in the midst of a cosmic drama; we possess a power which should never be used. This fact dramatizes the precariousness of our position political, morally, spiritually." *The Challenge of Peace: God's Promise and Our Response* (Washington, DC: United States Catholic Conference, 1983), par. 124. At least one distinguished scholar of international law has argued for the qualitative difference between conventional and nuclear weapons. See Ian Brownlie, *International Law and the Use of Force by States* (New York: Oxford University Press, 1963).

22. Kenny, *Logic of Deterrence*, 14, emphasis mine.

23. Stein, *Nuclear Weapons*, 23.

24. Bernard Brodie, *The Absolute Weapon* (New York: Hartcourt, Brace & Co., 1946), 76.

25. Hans Morgenthau, "The Fallacy of Thinking Conventionally About Nuclear Weapons," in David Carlton and Carlo Schaerf, eds., *Arms Control and Technological Innovation* (London: Croom Helm, 1977), 57.

26. Leon Sigal, *Foreign Affairs*, 1979.

27. Robert W. Tucker, *The Just War: A Study in Contemporary American Doctrine* (Baltimore: The Johns Hopkins University Press, 1960), 67.

28. Finnis, Boyle, Grisez, *Nuclear Deterrence*, 133-146.

29. For their attack on consequentialism, also see Germain Grisez, "Against Consequentialism," *American Journal of Jurisprudence* 23 (1978), 21-72 and *Christian Moral Principles* (Chicago: Franciscan Herald Press, 1983); John Finnis, *Natural Law and Natural Rights* (Oxford: Clarendon Press, 1980) and *Fundamentals of Ethics* (Oxford: Clarendon Press, 1983); Joseph Boyle, Germain Grisez, and Olaf Tollefsen, *Free Choice: A Self-Referential Argument* (Notre Dame, IN: University of Notre Dame Press, 1976). In my discussion I will follow Finnis, Boyle, and Grisez and not make a distinction between consequentialism, utilitarianism, and proportionalism. For these authors, this is merely a terminological matter and makes no difference to their rejection of these moral theories.

30. See Michael Walzer, *Just and Unjust Wars*; Gregory Kavka, *Moral Paradoxes of Nuclear Deterrence* (Cambridge: Cambridge University Press, 1987); Robert Goodin, "Nuclear Disarmament as a Moral Certainty," *Ethics* 95 (1985), 641-58; Douglas P. Lackey, *Moral Principles and Nuclear Weapons* (Totowa, NJ: Rowman and Allanheld, 1984); Jefferson McMahan, "Nuclear Deterrence and Future Generations," in *Nuclear Weapons and the Future of Humanity*, eds., Avner Cohen and Steven Lee (Totowa, NJ: Rowman and Allanheld, 1986).

31. Finnis, Boyle, Grisez, *Nuclear Deterrence*, 240.

32. McMahan, "Nuclear Deterrence," 328.

33. Finnis, Boyle, Grisez, *Nuclear Deterrence*, 247. I do not think that these authors are correct in their arguments against McMahan, since for me, as I believe is also the case with many people, nuclear devastation is obviously a worse disaster than foreign domination. On this McMahan says: "Since any two-sided nuclear war would be unlikely to remain limited, nuclear war would probably result in the deaths of most people in the U.S. and in allied countries. If most people would find life under Soviet domination worth living, then it follows that, for most of those who would be killed in a nuclear war, nuclear war would be worse than Soviet domination." McMahan, "Nuclear Deterrence," 322.

34. Finnis, Boyle, Grisez, *Nuclear Deterrence*, 240.

35. Finnis, *Fundamentals of Ethics*, 87. See also, *Natural Law and Natural Rights*, 113.

36. The following discussion builds on some points developed by Bernard Williams in "Conflict of Values" and "Moral Luck" in *Moral Luck* (Cambridge: Cambridge University Press, 1981).

37. I mention life and liberty only because they are the most relevant to discussion on disarmament and deterrence. These remarks, however, have a much broader range—e.g., conflicts between equality and liberty or friendship and justice.

38. Grisez, *Christian Moral Principles*, 156.

39. See Grisez, *Christian Moral Principles*, 156 and "Against Consequentialism," 45.

40. See, for example, David Gauthier, "Reason and Maximization," *Canadian Journal of Philosophy* 4 (1975), 427-30.

41. Isaiah Berlin, *Four Essays on Liberty* (Oxford: Oxford University Press, 1986), lv.

42. The following pages develop some points made by Robert McKim and Peter Simpson, "On the Alleged Incoherence of Consequentialism," *New Scholasticism*, 62 (1988), 49-52.

43. Finnis, *Fundamentals of Ethics*, 89.

44. *Christian Moral Principles*, 150, 153. See also "Against Consequentialism," 43-44:"[G]iven the commensurability required by the consequentialist's theory, no one *can* deliberately adopt any proposal other than that which the consequentialist says one should adopt—the proposal, namely, which promises the greater good. But this means that no one can do moral evil. A theory of moral judgment must leave open the possibility that someone deliberately makes a morally wrong choice."

45. Finnis, Boyle, Grisez, *Nuclear Deterrence*, 254.

46. Finnis, Boyle, Grisez, *Nuclear Deterrence*, 258.

47. Finnis, Boyle, Grisez, *Nuclear Deterrence*, 258.

48. In 5.2 I sketch an argument that questions the application of WIP to nuclear deterrent intentions. For now I want to show only that this principle can be given various interpretations and is therefore inconclusive for determining the moral status of nuclear deterrence.

49. Stein, *Nuclear Weapons*, 71. See also p. 92. The term "wrongful intentions principle," however, must be credited to Gregory Kavka, "Some Paradoxes of Deterrence," in *Moral Paradoxes*. For my discussion of Kavka's views, see 5.2 below.

50. Kenny, *Logic of Deterrence*, 47. See also "Counterforce and Countervalue," in *The Ivory Tower: Essays in Philosophy and Public Policy* (Oxford: Basil Blackwell, 1985): "On reflection, it is obvious that if the use of large-scale nuclear weapons is immoral then their possession as a deterrent must be so also. We must give up our nuclear deterrent not because by doing so we shall achieve some desirable aim, but because to retain it is wicked," 73, 74.

51. Finnis, Boyle, Grisez, *Nuclear Deterrence*, 79-80.

52. For a proof of WIP, see John W. Lango, "The Wrongful Intentions Principle," *The Monist*, 70, no. 3 (July 1987), 316-329.

53. "It is difficult to deny," says Kenny, "the moral principle that if it is wrong to do X, it is wrong to intend X." *The Logic of Deterrence*, 47. And Gregory Kavka says, this principle "seems so obvious that, although philosophers never call it into question, they rarely bother to assert it or to argue for it." *Moral Paradoxes*, 19.

54. Finnis, Boyle, Grisez, *Nuclear Deterrence*, 358. See also *Fundamentals of Ethics*, 88. For Cicero, see his *de Officiis* III, 28.

55. For a similar conclusion, see Robert McKim, "An Examination of a Moral Argument Against Nuclear Deterrence," *Journal of Religious Ethics* 13 (Fall 1985), 279-97.

56. Richard B. Miller has aptly called this view the "success thesis." See his *Interpretations of Conflict: Ethics, Pacifism, and the Just-War Tradition* (Chicago: University of Chicago Press, 1991), 169-73.

57. Caspar Weinberger, "Shattuck Lecture: Remarks by the Secretary of Defense to the Massachusetts Medical Society," *New England Journal of Medicine* (May 1982), vol. 307, no. 12, 767.

58. For a discussion on factors other than nuclear ones contributing to the absence of war, see McGeorge Bundy, "Existential Deterrence and Its Consequences," in *The Security Gamble: Deterrence Dilemmas in the Nuclear Age*, ed., Douglas MacLean (Totowa, NJ: Rowman & Allanheld, 1984).

59. It is also false that nuclear deterrence has worked against nonnuclear nations. For example, in the 1950s the United States' near monopoly of nuclear weapons did not deter North Korea from invading South Korea. In 1973 Egypt and Syrian were not deterred from attacking Israel, despite its nuclear capability. Similarly, Argentina was not deterred from invading the Malvinas nor, more recently, Saddam Hussein from invading Kuwait—although he probably knew that the United States and some European nations would see his actions as a threat to their

vital national interests—or firing Scud missiles at Israel.

60. Jonathan Schell, *Fate of the Earth* (New York: Avon Books, 1982), 183-84.

61. False alarms are almost commonplace. In the early years of the Cold War nuclear alerts were triggered by radar beams bouncing off flocks of geese, off clouds, or the moon. More advanced radar systems now produce computer mistakes. While no nuclear attack has ever been launched by mistake, that one such attack occur sometime in the future is an increasing statistical possibility.

62. At least 25 instances of nuclear threats occurred between 1946 and 1993. See, for example, Richard K. Betts, *Nuclear Blackmail and Nuclear Balance* (Washington, DC: The Brookings Institution, 1987); Barry M. Blechman and Stephen S. Kaplan, *Force Without War: U.S. Armed Forces as Political Instruments* (Washington, DC: The Brookings Institution, 1978); Michio Kaku and Daniel Axelrod, *To Win a Nuclear War: The Pentagon's Secret War Plans* (Boston: South End Press, 1987); Joseph Gerson, *With Hiroshima Eyes* (Philadelphia, PA: New Society Publishers, 1995). As more nations produce nuclear weapons, the greater the frequency of nuclear threats.

63. See, for example, the Harvard Nuclear Study Group, *Living with Nuclear Weapons*.

64. A variant of this view might argue that a nuclear weapons-free world is a preferable future over a world much the same as today's. See, for example, Michael MccGwire, "Is There a Future for Nuclear Weapons?" *International Affairs*, vol. 70, no. 2 (April 1994), 211-28.

65. Caspar Weinberger, "A Rational Approach to Nuclear Disarmament," in *The Ethics of Nuclear War and Deterrence*, ed., James P. Sterba (Belmont, CA: Wadsworth, 1985).

66. G.A. Res. 1653, 15 U.N. GAOR Supp. (No. 17), note 90, U.N. Doc. A/5100 (1961). The resolution also cautioned the following. "The use of nuclear and thermo-nuclear weapons would exceed even the scope of war and cause indiscriminate suffering and destruction to mankind and civilization and, as such, is contrary to the rules of international law and the laws of humanity; The use of nuclear weapons and thermo-nuclear weapons is a war directed not against an enemy or enemies alone, but also against mankind in general, since the peoples of the world not involved in such a war will be subjected to all the evils generated by the use of such weapons; Any State using nuclear and thermo-nuclear weapons is to be considered as violating the Charter of the United Nations, as acting contrary to the laws of humanity and as committing a crime against mankind and civilization."

67. *Declaration on the Non-use of Force in International Relations and Permanent Prohibition of the Use of Nuclear Weapons*, United Nations G.A. Res. 2936, 27 U.N. GAOR, Supp. (No. 30) 5, U.N. Doc. A/8730 (1072), par. 1.

68. On the silence of the legal community on nuclear weapons, see Richard Falk, Lee Meyrowitz, Jack Sanderson, "Nuclear Weapons and International Law," World Order Studies Program, Occasional Paper No. 10, Center of International Studies, Princeton University.

69. United States Department of the Army, Field Manual 27-10, *The Law of Land Warfare* (Washington, DC: U.S. Government Printing Office, 1956), par. 35.

70. See, for example, Josef Kunz, "The Chaotic Status of the Laws of War and the Urgent Necessity for Their Revision," *American Journal of International Law* 37 (1951).

71. International Military Tribunal, *Trial of the Major War Criminals Before the International Military Tribunal* (Nuremberg, Germany, 1948), vol. 22, 464.

72. Protocol Additional to the Geneva Convention of 12 August 1949 and Relating to the Protection of Victims of International Armed Conflicts. Protocol I, Part IV, Chapter II, Article 51, in *International Conventions on Protection of Humanity and Environment*, eds. Gunter Hoog and Angela Steinmetz, (New York: Walter de Gruyter, 1993), 289.

73. *Declaration Renouncing the Use in Time of War of Explosive Projectiles Under 400 Grammes Weight*, 11 December 1868, 297.

74. *Declaration*, 298.

75. Protocol for the Prohibition of the Use in War of Asphyxiating, Poisonous or Other Gases, and of Bacteriological Methods of Warfare, in Hoog and Steinmetz, *International Conventions*, 117 emphasis mine.

76. G. Schwarzenberger, *The Legality of Nuclear Weapons* (London: Stevens, 1958), 27.

77. Lackey, *Moral Principles*, 210.

78. Protocol Additional to the Geneva Convention of 12 August 1949 Relating to the Protection of Victims of International Armed Conflicts, in Hoog and Steinmetz, *International Conventions*, 284.

4 The War-Fighting Party

Mr. Dicks: You haven't taken away any weapons aimed at the urban industrial base of the Soviet Union, have you, but you have added weapons to the military targets? Is that a fair way of putting it?
General Burke: Yes[1]

It is idle to talk about our strategies being counter-force strategies, as distinct from counter-economy or counter-population strategies, unless planners were actually to take deliberate restrictive measures to refrain from injuring cities.

Bernard Brodie, *Strategy in the Missile Age*.

Nuclear deterrence is like traditional deterrence in that the conditional intention to wage war is a means by which one nation can dissuade another from doing what the former does not want the latter to do. But nuclear deterrence is unlike traditional deterrence at least in one significant respect. Deterrence of nuclear war is a permanent condition and nuclear weapons, unlike conventional weapons, are very difficult, some say impossible, to fit into a rational conception of use. The Eisenhower-Dulles policy of massive retaliation was one attempt to develop a doctrine of use. Critics argued that this policy called for the immediate launch of the entire U.S. nuclear arsenal as a response to any level of enemy aggression. The single target list is said to have included cities in the former Soviet Union, China, and satellite states, and to have made no distinction between military, industrial, and civilian targets. As Daniel Ellsberg noted, "If the SIOP [Single Integrated Operational Plan] were activated, we would have hit every city in the Soviet Union and China in addition to all military targets."[2] Expected fatalities of a massive nuclear retaliatory strike were estimated between 360 and 425 million people.[3]

In chapter 3, I argued that a policy of deterrence has some good moral reasons on its behalf. At least a deterrent that relies upon the conditional intention to use nuclear weapons is a morally preferable means for avoiding nuclear war than one without such intention. I also argued that the intuitive basis of the prohibitive WIP is methodologically deficient when applied to the practice of nuclear deterrence. To support this argument I assumed a difference in the kinds of reasons that justify action in private and public life. Justifying reasons in public life must take into consideration factors that may not necessarily be present in private life. The value of liberty and the importance of national self-defense justify policies (i.e., intentions) that are, or might be, morally unacceptable for persons as persons to perform.

In this chapter I examine the attempt of a group of just-war thinkers to make deterrence and the use of limited nuclear weapons compatible with the ethical norms that traditionally have been employed to appraise the morality of military force. Part of the theoretical appeal of the war-fighting party is that it recognizes the special duties of public functionaries and the corresponding moral division of labor that arises from the purposes public institutions are morally bound to fulfill.

Nonetheless, I argue in this chapter that the attempt to develop a morally acceptable doctrine of the possession and use of nuclear weapons fails because it is unable to reconcile the intention and use even of limited nuclear force with respect for the moral principle of discrimination. 4.1 reviews some of the major features of the strategic debate from the mid-1950s' doctrine of massive retaliation and the 1960s' assured destruction, to the 1970s' reliance upon a strategy of flexible response. The principal moral problem with massive retaliation is that it is a response disproportionate to any injury the United States or its allies might suffer prior to the activation of the policy. The case is somewhat different with assured destruction. This policy depends upon the use of cities as direct targets of attack and civilian populations as hostages. It thus violates the widely accepted principle of discrimination. A policy of flexible response seems to bring some moral improvement over massive retaliation and assured destruction insofar as it offers a variety of nuclear responses short of countercivilian war. But it destabilizes deterrence by increasing the probability of a disarming first strike and introduces an unacceptable risk of unlimited nuclear war through the escalation of responses. In 4.2, I sketch the views of John Courtney Murray and especially of Paul Ramsey. More than any other contemporary American moralist, Paul Ramsey is responsible for the retrieval of the just-war tradition and the attempt to render it relevant to the conditions of a nuclear-armed world. My aim in this section is first expositional and then argumentative. Near the end of

4.2 I begin what I think is a strong argument against Ramsey's views, and then complete the argument in 4.3.

I want to emphasize two points at the outset. First, the structure of the strategic and moral arguments for deterrence and limited use advanced by the authors I consider in this chapter are in a very real sense parallel to each other.[4] Strategically and morally, the important questions are these: What is the relation of nuclear weapons to politically instrumental force? And must deterrence necessarily depend on the conditional intention to use nuclear weapons against civilians? Both questions were addressed during the 1950s and 1960s in the context of a critique of the doctrine of massive retaliation and an exploration, albeit for different reasons, by strategists and moralists for ways to limit nuclear war. Also the strategic and moral paradox of the war-fighting party is essentially the same. The attempt to think through ways by which nuclear weapons may be used, the more thinkable and hence the more likely (and perhaps the more attractive) some forms of nuclear war begin to appear. Second, the fundamental difference between the views advocated by the writers considered in this chapter and those of the disarmament and the deterrence-only parties is a function of different factual assumptions about nuclear weapons and their reliance on both deontological and consequentialist styles of moral reasoning. An important consequence of these assumptions is that they introduce a level of complexity into policy recommendations that makes the adjudication of disputes highly improbable, in spite of the fact that representatives of these parties are working within the same political-moral tradition.[5] The relation of factual assumptions and reliance on different styles of moral reasoning must be made explicit if one wishes to understand the diversity and disagreement in the moral literature on nuclear arms policy.

4.1 THE SEARCH FOR OPTIONS

One of the first official actions of the Kennedy administration was to reject the Eisenhower-Dulles policy of massive retaliation, which it chose to interpret as an inflexible doctrine,[6] and to develop a variety of options tailored to probable military challenges from which the President could choose in a time of crisis. The desire for a nuclear policy other than massive retaliation makes good strategic as well as moral sense. If massive retaliation is the only existing doctrine of use and a belligerent nuclear power has a secure second-strike capability, then in a situation of armed hostilities neither nation could afford to unleash its weapons. To do so would be equivalent to national suicide. Additionally, a strategy of deterrence based on massive retaliation to small-scale, local aggression lacks credibility and may only deter the deterrer from the use of nuclear force. Finally, to obliterate population centers is evil. Options to the irrationality, incredibility, and immorality of this doctrine were, therefore, sought in the first decade of the nuclear age.

Exploration of flexible nuclear response and advocacy of a "no-cities" strategy, often accredited to Kennedy and his Secretary of Defense, Robert S. McNamara, were already under way by the early 1950s.[7] When Eisenhower took office in 1953, the United States had developed as a result of projects initiated under the Truman administration a range of nuclear capabilities from thermonuclear weapons to small-size tactical weapons for battlefield use. Although each of these types of weapons had its critics, their combined use could be presented as a comprehensive doctrine in which strategic weapons served the purpose of deterring nuclear aggression and tactical ones compensated for the West's shortage of conventional forces. Further steps in the direction of selective responses to enemy aggression were also taken in the early years of the Eisenhower administration.

For example, the October 1953 National Security Council Paper NSC-162/2 made a distinction between nuclear forces for strategic and tactical purposes. It did contain and emphasize the language of massive retaliation, but it also recognized that "as general war becomes more devastating for both sides the threat to resort to it becomes less available as a sanction against local aggression."[8] Further, on 20 November 1958, Eisenhower requested the Net Evaluation Sub Committee of the National Security Council to examine the possibility of different targeting strategies. Its task was to determine "the relative merits, from the point of view of effective deterrence, of alternative retaliatory efforts directed towards: (1) primarily a military target system, or (2) an optimum mix of a combined military-industrial target system."[9] David Alan Rosenberg noted that this study, entitled NESC 2009, took into account the requirements of counterforce and how this capability would relate to targeting lists.[10]

Along lines similar to NSC 162/2 and NESC 2009, just three months after the "massive-retaliation speech," John Foster Dulles acknowledged that massively retaliating with nuclear weapons "is not the kind of power which could most usefully be evoked under all circumstances."[11] In the January speech to the Council of Foreign Relations in New York (see 3.1), Dulles had blurred the distinction between area-bombing and alternative targeting strategies that were possible with improved munitions and delivery systems. But in his April article for *Foreign Affairs* he developed his thinking more in accordance with the requirements of NSC 162/2. Dulles indicated in a clear way that the central problem in the nuclear age is to deter attack, and this, he noted, "requires that a potential aggressor be left in no doubt that he would be certain to suffer damage outweighing any possible gains from aggression."[12] If the aim of deterrence is to introduce into the adversary's calculation adverse consequences that outweigh whatever gain may be won by aggression, then deterrence must rest upon the capacity for responses proportionate to different levels of armed hostility. As Dulles put it:

To deter aggression it is important to have the flexibility and the facilities which make various responses available. [The] free world must have the means for responding effectively on a selective basis when it chooses. It must not put itself in the position where the only response open to it is general war.[13]

At the time of Dulles's speech, civilian as well as some military strategists had already been working on the concept of limited nuclear war involving the controlled and flexible use of nuclear weapons and city-sparing targeting strategies. By the mid- to late 1950s, the names of Bernard Brodie, William Kaufmann, Henry Kissinger, Robert Osgood, Paul Nitze, Thomas Schelling in the United States, Basil H. Lidell Hart and Sir Anthony Buzzard in England, and in France Raymond Aron, among others, became synonymous with a new philosophy the basic proposition of which is that in an era when more than one power has the capacity for massive retaliation, the means of deterrence must "be proportionate to the objectives at stake";[14] and those objectives, given the destructiveness of modern weapons, must be of a limited scope. This philosophy drew upon the Clausewitzian principle that force must be subordinated to national policy and must therefore be restrained and controlled in order to serve specific political objectives by using means that are proportionate to the political stakes involved. As Kissinger noted, a "limited war is fought for specific political objectives which tend to establish a relationship between the force employed and the goal to be attained."[15] It is a war that seeks to exert a desired influence upon an enemy's will, not to conquer and to crush it.[16]

The most powerful critique against the doctrine of massive retaliation and the line of argument that would have the greatest influence upon the policy of flexible nuclear response was articulated by William Kaufmann in his essay, "The Requirements of Deterrence." This essay first appeared as Memorandum No. 7 of the Center of International Studies at Princeton University some ten months after Dulles's speech and was later expanded and incorporated into Kaufmann's *Military Policy and National Security*. Kaufmann's basic concern in this essay is to understand how one might deter an enemy who has a retaliatory nuclear capability. In the early 1950s Kaufmann had begun thinking about this problem, first at Yale's Institute of International Studies, then at the RAND Corporation in Santa Monica, and later at Princeton. Dulles's "massive retaliation speech" in 1954 gave him the perfect opportunity to express and clarify his ideas on deterrence.

According to Kaufmann, the essential feature of deterrence is that it be credible. To be so a deterrence posture must anticipate the widest range of action available to an opponent and provide quick and efficient responses to possible hostile action. It should try "to fit the punishment to the crime," to forestall, and if that fails to defeat, enemy aggression at whatever level it occurs, "but is not provocative enough to make him turn to contingencies of the last resort."[17]

Kaufmann's solution to the credibility problem was to develop "precise, discriminating, and discreet methods of destruction" able to compete with an enemy on his own terms.[18] Those methods include (i) the availability of large-scale conventional forces ready to move into battle with speed and strength, (ii) a counterforce capability able to confine the scope and method of nuclear war to a level less destructive than general war and more compatible with limited war objectives, while (iii) preserving a large invulnerable reserve force of nuclear weapons which could be used both as a bargaining lever and a constraint against escalation. The result of Kaufmann's work was the formulation of a doctrine known either as "counterforce" or "no-cities" or "war-fighting."

So before the Kennedy administration took office, the ideas about nuclear strategy by which it distinguished itself from previous administrations had already gone through significant conceptual development and later by way of individuals such as Paul Nitze, Alain Enthoven, and others, influenced Robert McNamara. Kaufmann's thinking on limited war contained the major elements of what later became known as the McNamara doctrine: limited war requires a large conventional force; weapons that "permit of discriminating and precise employment" in accordance with limited political objectives; a policy that sends "messages to the other belligerent to accept limitations of geography, weapons, and possibly time"; and a role for nuclear force "as a counter in the bargaining process."[19]

On 10 February 1961, less than three weeks into his tenure as Secretary of Defense, McNamara heard Kaufmann's counterforce briefing to the effect that massive retaliation is strategically unsound and immoral. The idea of targeting only military installations at first and withholding a large nuclear reserve force as a deterrent against general war made a strong impression on McNamara. Several days later, Alain Enthoven, Charlie Hitch, and Marvin Stern presented a paper to McNamara emphasizing a nuclear strategy that aimed at enemy military targets, avoided cities, and protected a reserve force. By the end of the month, McNamara had approved a nuclear war plan of counterforce/no-cities called the "General War Offensive Package."

McNamara first announced the new doctrine on 5 May 1962, at a secret session of NATO. The language he employed closely followed the ideas of his advisor and speech writer, William Kaufmann, and the philosophy that had been taking shape at RAND since the early 1950s. McNamara described the counterforce/no-cities doctrine as follows:

The United States has come to the conclusion that to the extent feasible, basic military strategy in general nuclear war should be approached in much the same way that more conventional military operations have been regarded in the past. That is to say, our principal military objectives, in the event of nuclear war should be the destruction of the enemy's military forces while attempting to preserve the fabric as well as the integrity of allied society. Specifically, our studies indicate that a strategy which targets nuclear forces only against cities or a mixture of civil and military targets has serious limitations for the purpose of deterrence and for the conduct of general nuclear war.[20]

In fact, on 16 June 1962, in his commencement address at the University of Michigan at Ann Arbor, McNamara reiterated that the

principal military objectives, in the event of a nuclear war stemming from a major attack on the Alliance, should be the destruction of the enemy's military forces, not of his civilian population. We are giving a possible opponent the strongest imaginable incentive to refrain from striking our own cities.[21]

Reaction to the new doctrine was largely negative, both at home and abroad. The French and other allies were reportedly incredulous, and NATO was less than enthusiastic about it. The new doctrine gave little value to the small independent nuclear arsenals Britain and France were building,[22] and was seen as a departure from the strategic policies of the past upon which the Europeans depended for their security. One of the goals McNamara had sought in his speech was to discourage the European allies from developing an independent nuclear deterrent, especially of the kind the French were building. McNamara thought that an independent deterrence might make the coordination of nuclear retaliation to enemy attack on Europe extremely difficult and also increase the risks of accidental war. But the French reaction indicated that they had all intentions to proceed with their own deterrence. As Raymond Aron noted, "Europeans discovered that their security was no longer based on automatic American nuclear response to any Soviet violation."[23]

McNamara's speech was also attacked on strategic grounds. Aiming American nuclear weapons at enemy military targets could give the strong impression that the United States was preparing for a first and disarming strike. This caused considerable worry in the former Soviet Union for at least two reasons. First, the Kennedy administration was rather ambiguous on whether or not the U.S. ruled out a nuclear first strike; second, at the time the strategic force of the former Soviet Union was markedly inferior to that of the United States. It was, moreover, conceivable that at a moment of international crisis the Soviet Union would unleash its weapons in an attempt to knock-out the U.S. counterforce arsenal and thereby lead the latter to retaliate massively. In short, critics argued that nothing could be more destabilizing for deterrence than targeting enemy military forces. By making nuclear war more thinkable, the probability of occurrence was significantly increased.

But advocates of the counterforce/no-cities doctrine claimed that the strategy expounded by McNamara had been misunderstood. What the Secretary spelled out in his speech was in accordance with operational policy as described in the 1961 revision of the SIOP, which already contained flexible and graduated options in the use of nuclear forces. Some of its major features included the separation of the former Soviet Union from China and satellite countries; targeting Soviet strategic forces rather than its cities; a reserve force for intrawar deterrence; protection of command-control facilities to allow for controlled response; and, at least in the initial stages of a nuclear war, the sparing of Soviet command and control systems.[24] McNamara's supporters also argued that by not giving targeting priority to cities, the new doctrine enhanced the credibility of deterrence and, if war should break out, considerably limited damage to the belligerents. William Kaufmann summed up McNamara's rationale for the new doctrine by stating that "it would be foolish automatically to destroy cities at the outset of the war when they could always be taken under attack by reserve forces at some later stage."[25]

Regardless of the alleged merits of the counterforce/no-cities doctrine, its success was short-lived. By the fall of 1962, McNamara began to favor an entirely different strategic posture. There were several reasons for this. The sort of counterforce use of nuclear weapons McNamara envisioned made sense only in the most improbable circumstances. McNamara acknowledged that a nuclear attack by the former Soviet Union would directly involve the bombing of U.S. cities. At the time of his speech, the former Soviet Union had no capability for mounting a counterforce attack. Even if they possessed this capability, Western, especially conservative, understanding of Soviet approach to deterrence gave little hope for the exercise of mutual restraints. Moreover, within his own Defense Department, intraservice battles over military programs and defense money, especially the Air Force's exploitation of the no-cities doctrine for the procurement of programs McNamara thought were unnecessary, further led McNamara to withdraw from his Ann Arbor position. In subsequent years, his statements clearly indicated a retreat from the counterforce/no-cities posture in favor of a stable deterrent based on mutual assured destruction.

By the end of his tenure McNamara had come about-face, advocating the very ideas which, upon coming into office, he had criticized and dismissing the no-cities doctrine as having only a very limited role to play. He found himself unable to resolve the central paradox in nuclear strategy between fighting and deterring a nuclear war. The dangerous implications of a counterforce policy eventually transformed his thinking from fighting and controlling a nuclear war to deterrence-only. The foremost lesson he drew from his experience is, as McNamara put it, that "nuclear weapons serve no military purpose whatsoever. They are totally useless—except only to deter one's opponent from using them."[26]

A great irony in the evolution of nuclear strategic thought is that some of McNamara's critics came eventually to accept the strategic posture they had once so strongly opposed. By 1967, NATO adopted a strategy of flexible response for much the same reasons McNamara gave in 1962. It included the possible first use of nuclear weapons and the attempt to limit and control the escalation subsequent to the initiation of use. The consensus which had been reached in the 1950s with the doctrine of massive retaliation, undermined in the early McNamara years, and then reaffirmed with the doctrine of assured destruction, was once again challenged in the late 1960s and early 1970s. The writings of individuals such as Albert Wohlstetter, Donald Brennan, Colin Gray, Fred Ikle, Paul Nitze, among others, signaled the return to counterforce, but with some differences.

First, the new wave of counterforce theorists charged that the doctrine of assured destruction relied entirely on the threat coupled with the technological capability to kill civilians. This brought widespread dissatisfaction with the moral basis of the received doctrine. Wohlstetter expressed the moral unease felt by many in the defense community when he concluded a series of articles for *Foreign Policy* by questioning the morality of measuring the "adequacy of our weapons in terms of the numbers of civilians they can kill" and charging that existing policy had made "murder respectable."[27] The same moral abhorrence with the civilian-killing features of assured destruction was also voiced by many in the Nixon and Ford administrations. Of course, McNamara and others in the Kennedy administration had similar moral problems with assured destruction, but they seemed to have reconciled themselves with the moral cost of deterrence by the alleged stability provided by the mutual threat to kill noncombatants.

However, the modifications in doctrine motivated by the moral dissatisfaction with assured destruction re-introduced a significant strategic paradox. As critics of flexible response had stated in the early 1960s, and as they once again were happy to point out, by trying to think through ways in which nuclear weapons can be made to fit acceptable doctrines of use, say, by aiming at military targets rather than civilian populations, nuclear war was being made more thinkable and so more likely. A counterforce doctrine was, some said, morally dangerous not only because it sanctioned with moral authority the limited use of nuclear weapons, but also because it destabilized deterrence and increased the likelihood of preemptive war.[28]

The other difference distinguishing the return to counterforce in the early 1970s were concerns about the assumed rationality of an adversary who would recognize the risks of any attempt to knock-out U.S. nuclear forces in a massive first strike and the possibility of deterrence failing. The new counterforce theorists responded to these concerns by stressing the need for plans and capabilities anticipating these and other contingencies and providing the President with selective responses to a wide spectrum of situations. As Richard Nixon asked in his 1970 annual report on foreign policy:

Should a President, in the event of a nuclear attack, be left with the single option of ordering the mass destruction of enemy civilians, in the face of the certainty that it would be followed by the mass slaughter of Americans? Should the concept of assured destruction be narrowly defined and should it be the only measure of our ability to deter the variety of threats we may face?[29]

The sharpest critique of the doctrine of assured destruction came from Fred Ikle in an article for *Foreign Affairs*. Like many of McNamara's advisers, Ikle was a RAND veteran. There, in the mid- to late 1950s, phrases such as "counterforce," "limited nuclear options," "nuclear war-fighting" had been coined. Now, as Director of the U.S. Arms Control and Disarmament Agency in the Nixon administration, Ikle brought them back into currency and rejected what he called the "dogmas" of assured destruction. He argued that the received doctrine of deterrence falsely and dangerously assumed the rationality of all leaders of nuclear-armed nations. It neglected the problem of leaders who are "willing to see their nation destroyed in pursuit of causes which only they and their henchmen espouse," as well as the persistent danger of a "fatal accident or unauthorized act." Ikle also attacked the policy of deterrence for its immorality. "The jargon of American strategic analysis," he said, "works like a narcotic."

> It dulls our sense of moral outrage about the tragic confrontation of nuclear arsenals, primed and constantly perfected to unleash widespread genocide. It fosters the current smug complacency regarding the soundness and stability of mutual deterrence. It blinds us to the fact that our method for preventing nuclear war rests on a form of warfare universally condemned since the Dark Ages—the mass killing of hostages.[30]

Ikle's suggestion was to replace the obsolete and immoral strategy of assured destruction with new technologies that permit the "assured destruction [of] military, industrial and transportation assets—the sinews and muscles of the regime initiating war."[31]

By the time James Schlesinger became Nixon's Secretary of Defense in July 1973, the shift towards options in accordance with limited-war principles and the development of requisite military capabilities were already well under way. This thinking was quite congenial to him. Schlesinger had spent much of the 1960s at RAND, and brought back to the

Pentagon with him those who one observer described as "the cohort of RAND alumni."[32] While at RAND, Schlesinger had argued for a "more rational posture than city-busting to create every incentive for the enemy to refrain from striking at one's own cities."[33] On January 1974 at a meeting of the Overseas Writers Association, Schlesinger announced what he referred to as a "new nuclear strategy" representing "probably the greatest change in U.S. nuclear missile strategy in a decade."[34]

The new strategy was meant to enhance the credibility of deterrence by satisfying four basic requirements. One requirement was a survivable nuclear force able to retaliate massively against the economic base of the enemy. This, of course, was not new. Holding civilian populations hostage for intrawar deterrence and bargaining had by now become conventional wisdom. But the other three requirements were somewhat novel. First was an "essential equivalence" in all "factors which contribute to the effectiveness of strategic weapons and to the perception of non-super-power nations." The second was a "force that, in response to Soviet actions, could implement a variety of limited pre-planned options and react rapidly to retargeting orders so as to deter any range of further attacks that a potential enemy might contemplate." The final requirement was "a range and magnitude of capabilities such that everyone—friend, foe, and domestic audiences alike—will perceive that we are the equal of our strongest competitors."[35]

Schlesinger's objective was to have a wide flexibility in the use of nuclear weapons, ranging from small-yield and highly accurate to large-scale weapons capable of counterforce rather than city-busting strikes. His justification for such capabilities was moral and prudential: the countercivilian aspects of assured destruction, the possibility accidental acts, the escalation of conventional conflicts, the irrational leader, and the less probable contingency of a massive surprise attack upon U.S. forces that were introduced into strategic debates with the renewed interest in limited-war ideas. As Schlesinger put it in his Report to Congress:

> Not only must those in power consider the morality of threatening such terrible retribution on the Soviet people for some ill-defined transgression by their leaders; in the most practical terms, they must also question the prudence and plausibility of such a response

when the enemy is able, even after some sort of first strike, to maintain the capability of destroying our cities. The wisdom and credibility of relying on preplanned strikes of assured destruction are even more in doubt when allies rather than the United States itself face the threat of nuclear war.[36]

Schlesinger's so-called "new doctrine" had obvious parallels with McNamara's. The parallels are evident from some of the criticisms brought against it: the doubt that nuclear war once initiated could be controlled; the concern that if it were believed that nuclear war could be controlled the risk of premature resort to nuclear weapons would increase; and renewed fears that counterforce options meant first-strike capability. But there were some important differences that made it difficult to argue against a counterforce doctrine. By this time the former Soviet Union had acquired counterforce and secure second-strike capabilities. Hence possible contingencies arising from these new capabilities had to be anticipated in operational policy. In his Report to Congress for FY 1975, Schlesinger noted that the "Soviet Union now has the capability in its missile forces to undertake selective targets attack against targets other than cities." "This," he added, "poses for us an obligation to be certain that we have a comparable capability."[37]

Perhaps the most significant difference between McNamara and Schlesinger was the latter's mental attitude towards counterforce. Since the beginning of his tenure, Schlesinger emphasized that he wanted to avoid what he considered mistakes which had led McNamara to retreat from the counterforce/no-cities doctrine and adopt assured destruction. Schlesinger thought McNamara failed to understand the role that perception of military strengths and weaknesses play in international politics. In the early 1970s, analysts had become interested in the causes and consequences of misperception in the decision-making process and were impressed by the difficulties in ensuring clarity of communications brought about by cultural, bureaucratic, and psychological factors. Psychological studies which focused on the pressures of group think, on defense mechanisms, loyalty to organizations, and the way in which world-views limit understanding provided an empirical basis for stressing the role played by perceptions in the military balance. Edward Luttwak, for example, noted:

"The political utility and military effectiveness of a given structure of armed forces exist in different worlds: one, the world of appearances, impressions, and the culturally determined value judgements of international politics; the other, the world of physical reality in actual warfare."[38]

This line of thought is evident in Schlesinger's insistence on an "essential equivalence between the strategic forces of the United States and the USSR—an equivalence perceived not only by ourselves, but by the Soviet Union and third audiences as well."[39] The essence of Schlesinger's doctrine of deterrence was not only possession of the physical capability for a "series of measured responses to aggression which bear some relation to the provocation, have prospects of terminating hostilities, and leave some possibility for restoring deterrence."[40] It also depended on the effort to impress upon ourselves and others that the U.S. had both the will and requisite forces to counter any level of aggression. "The Soviets," he said, "must be under no illusions about our determination to proceed with whatever responses their actions require."[41] They should have no misunderstanding of American resolve and capability to respond across the entire spectrum of possible hostile action.

Despite initial dissatisfaction in the Carter administration with counter-force ideas and the expectation that it would return to a doctrine of assured destruction, the concepts and doctrines adopted under Secretary of Defense Harold Brown were those inherited from Schlesinger. Emphasis upon flexibility and "essential equivalence" were retained as a guard "against any danger that the Soviets may be seen as superior—even if the perception is not technically justified."[42] In July 1980, President Carter signed Presidential Directive 59 which gave more refined limited options, withheld a larger reserve force, expanded the target list, and planned for the possibility of fighting a nuclear war over an extended period of time. Fundamentally there was nothing novel about PD-59. It was an elaboration of strategic postures adopted during Schlesinger's tenure, that developed from McNamara's early counterforce/no-cities doctrine based on the analyses carried out at RAND in the 1950s.

In sum, since the beginning of the nuclear age, the general concepts and the types of targets included in U.S. deterrence policies have remained remarkably constant and marked by a persistent strategic and moral paradox. Deterrence policies and war-fighting plans have included enemy's nuclear and conventional forces, its urban-industrial base, and centers of political leadership. Existing or anticipated technologies, the need to accommodate nuclear weapons to different operational tasks, and moral sensibilities have by and large determined whether a given presidential administration emphasized war-fighting or deterrence-only policies. Any one of these factors engenders insoluble strategic and moral dilemmas that have become a fact of modern life. Among the requirements for a credible deterrence, withholding attack from civilian population centers has been of singular importance, making undesirable the doctrines of massive retaliation and assured destruction. During McNamara's early years and then throughout Schlesinger's tenure, sparing civilian populations was rationalized strategically and morally in terms of flexible response. This posture had an initial strategic and moral respectability. Yet it was fraught with dangerous destabilizing first-strike connotations and retained the threat of subsequent widespread civilian slaughter imposed by the possession of a large nuclear reserve force. In the next section I examine one type of moral argument that attempts to render the limited use of nuclear weapons and the hostage-holding feature of deterrence if not morally acceptable, at least tolerable within the confines of the tradition of civilized war.

4.2 MORAL ARGUMENT FOR THE NECESSITY OF DETERRENCE AND LIMITED USE OF NUCLEAR WEAPONS: JOHN COURTNEY MURRAY AND PAUL RAMSEY

The structure of the debate on strategic doctrine reviewed in 4.1 is reflected in the arguments advanced among a group of moralists whose main effort has been to render the new technologies and strategies of war compatible with the moral principles of the just-war tradition. There is a striking symmetry between the moral arguments for the necessity of deterrence and limited use of nuclear weapons and the strategist's thesis that military force must be subordinated to political goals, and that those goals are to be of a limited scope.

This section sketches in broad strokes the main elements of the moral argument for the necessity of deterrence and limited use of nuclear weapons—what I have designated as the war-fighting party. The central tasks of this party are (i) to show the relevance of the moral principles of the just-war tradition to a nuclear-armed world, (ii) to point to a just conduct in nuclear warfare, and (iii) to subordinate nuclear weapons to politically purposive force. The claims that the ethical and political imperative of the nuclear age is to make just war possible, and that the just-war tradition is the only moral doctrine that can give direction to national policy and limit the use of force within the political purposes of a nation distinguish this from every other moral response to the nuclear dilemma. As John Courtney Murray put it, "since limited nuclear war may be a necessity, it must be made a possibility. Its possibility must be created."[43] While more recent moralists have also advanced this position, and done so with considerable rigor of analysis,[44] my remarks will consider only the relevant writings of Murray and Ramsey. Murray is significant because he was among the first to address the above tasks and anticipated the general direction of the moral argument for limited use; Ramsey's importance lies in his theoretical comprehensiveness, his influence on the moral debate on arms policy, and his personal commitment to interpret for a nuclear-armed world the tradition of civilized warfare. As Richard B. Miller notes, Ramsey's "work constitutes the *Ursprung* from which subsequent efforts in Christian ethics [to assess the morality of nuclear weapons] have explicitly or implicitly taken their cues."[45]

In the essay entitled "Remarks on the Moral Problem of War," Murray sought to establish what he referred to as the "right terms for argument on public policy"[46] in light of the facts of modern international life and technological development. It is important to note that what Murray has to say here about the moral problem of war is part of a larger and more fundamental effort to trace the moral roots of American democracy and to show the compatibility of American national identity and purpose with the ethical principles of what he called the "tradition of reason," namely, natural-law morality.[47] If American democracy is, as Murray asserts, at least compatible with if not an embodiment of this morality, then the crucial question in any discussion on U.S. involvement in modern war is how to defend and promote those values that are essential for the protection and continuation of a democratic political community. Part of Murray's point is that a state whose legitimacy is derived from the consent of the governed and protects a wide range of individual liberties is under a moral obligation to employ as a last resort the available instruments of force for the sake of the common good.   In this regard, Murray continues the tradition of just war begun by St. Augustine and developed by medieval and early-modern Catholic writers.   Elsewhere he says that the "essential significance" of the just-war tradition "is that it insists, first, that military decisions are a species of political decisions, and second, that political decisions must be viewed, not simply in the perspective of politics as an exercise of power, but of morality and theology in some valid sense."[48]

In "Remarks on the Moral Problem of War" Murray does not provide a sustained discussion of the morality of deterrence or limited nuclear war. He agrees with Pope Pius XII that the morality of deterrence or, what amounts to the same, the "legitimacy of defense preparations" is derived from two facts of modern international life: the absence of a world authority "possessing a monopoly on the use of armed force in international affairs" and "the threat of brutal violence and lack of conscience." Murray notes that Pius's acceptance of deterrence says "nothing about the morality of this or that configuration of the defense establishment of any nation [and] does not validate everything that goes on at Cape Canaveral or at Los Alamos."[49]   But it is safe to assume from Murray's remarks on limited nuclear war and his reference to limited-war theorists—Kissinger, for example—his approval of a deterrence policy with counterforce features similar to McNamara's and Schlesinger's.

Murray begins his essay by noting three possible starting-points for a discussion on morality and modern war.   One can begin, he says, by considering either the technological means of war available today, the historical and political situation "dominated by the fact of Communism," or the desire for an international organization committed "to the preservation of peace by pacific settlement of international disputes."[50]   He argues that none of these singly can yield an adequate understanding of the moral problem of war because each neglects in different ways the complexity of the issues that need to be addressed in order to arrive at an "integral and morally defensible position on the problem of war."[51]   For example, an exclusive concern with weaponry leads to the position that "war has now become a moral absurdity, not to be justified in any circumstances."   One might then argue for a nuclear pacifism of the kind presented in chapter 3. On the other hand, a single-mindedly anticommunist stance could make some version of the concept of "holy war" or crusade and the advocacy of preventive or preemptive war the only possible choice. Or one could come to rely upon an international organization which lacking adequate legal authority and powers of enforcement might "sanction injustice as well as justice."[52]

For Murray, the right terms for a discussion on the morality of war are defined first by an inquiry into the values democratic nations wish to preserve and the means available for insuring the preservation of those values. It then raises the question of "the arbitrament of arms as the last resort."[53] If moral reasoning on the question of war is to function properly and responsibly, it must first inquire into the values "that today are at stake in the international conflict."[54] The values Murray has in mind are those of a just and well-ordered democratic society. Much as St. Augustine did, Murray believes that from the viewpoint of the hierarchy of values "immense sacrifices may have to be borne" by the individual for the sake of the political community. There are, he says, "greater evils than the physical death and destruction wrought by war."[55] The values and ideals that constitute a just political society and informs a people's conception of good order justify for intrinsic reasons the recourse to rationally purposive force. Hence a morally satisfactory approach to the problem of war begins with the imperative to preserve fundamental values of social life. War is, first and foremost, a problem of political morality.[56]

Once the question of values has been addressed, the matter of the plurality of means available for their defense can be considered. Such means include a wide range of state-sponsored activities short of war: summit meetings, technological and agricultural assistance to underdeveloped nations, cultural exchanges, and non-violent methods of conflict resolution that help develop cooperation and trust among nations. Murray repeatedly warned against a premature or exclusive focus on military means that could only make the recourse to war more likely. "[T]he value of the use of force, even as *ultima ratio*, will be either overestimated or underestimated, in proportion as too much or too little value is attached to other means of sustaining and pressing the international conflict."[57] Only after the questions of values and means have been fully explored can one reasonably take up the question of the *ultima ratio* itself, "the arbitrament of arms."

Yet when one considers the possible widespread destruction consequent on the use of weapons available today, what circumstances could ever morally justify the recourse to these weapons even as a last resort? What is the just use of nuclear weapons? Isn't there a moral presumption against the use of instruments of indiscriminate killing? What are the prospects that such weapons be made to fit traditional Catholic just-war thinking?

Nuclear weapons, for Murray, are not a species apart from conventional weapons, and so nuclear war must satisfy the tradition of morally justified war. One cannot, says Murray, "uphold the simple statement that atomic war as such, without further qualifications, is morally unjustifiable, or that all use of atomic weapons in war is, somehow in principle, evil."[58] It is, for Murray, senseless to think that in themselves weapons are either moral or immoral. No matter how destructive a weapon can be, it is not, nor can it ever become, a proper subject of moral appraisal to which we can attribute a mental state, a set of dispositions, the capacity for deliberation and choice by which we can judge it culpable or praiseworthy for its acts. Rather it is the use to which a weapon, nuclear or otherwise, is put that can be judged to be either good or evil, justified or not. That judgment is contingent on the satisfaction of certain conditions.

First, the use of force, whether nuclear or conventional, is justified only if it is indispensable for self-defense. Such justification requires the presence of an "obvious and extremely grave injustice [such as] that the nation should in all truth have been unjustly attacked and menaced in its vital rights."[59] Second, recourse to force must be the last resort, justified only when there are no other means available to protect the values of the political community. The third condition is that of proportionality and involves two considerations: proportionality *ad bellum* and *in bello*. *Ad bellum* proportionality regulates war-making decisions and, along with other principles, grants states the right to go to war. As a moral principle it involves a weighing of the "damage suffered in consequence of the perpetration of a grave injustice, and the damages that would be let loose by a war to repress the injustice."[60] It consists of a comparative evaluation of values "from the viewpoint of the hierarchy of strictly moral values," rather than of physical damages suffered and inflicted upon the adversary. Its goal is to ensure that the damage brought by war to human values is in a balanced proportion to those values that are preserved and protected by the recourse to force. On the other hand, *in bello* proportionality regulates the actual conduct of hostilities once the use of force has begun. Its main function is to define the limits of permissible use of force. Since force is likely to beget more force, careful attention needs to be given to the relation between the levels of force employed and the sought-after end. Finally, the use of force is to be limited by the principle of discrimination between morally legitimate and illegitimate targets of attack. The distinction between targets is especially important when modern means of war are capable of widespread destruction.

Murray admits that this structure of moral reasoning does not yield ready-made prescriptions for when or what level of deadly force is justified. It is, he says, nothing more than a *"Grenzmoral,* an effort to establish on a minimal basis of reason a form of human action, the making of war, that remains always fundamentally irrational."[61] Nonetheless it is a moral framework that performs three important functions. It eliminates, Murray says, the false and dangerous antinomy between moralism or "sentimental pacifism and a cynical hard realism,"[62] rejects the fallacy between the alternatives summed up in the phrase "Better red than dead" by pointing to a path beyond them, and sets the right terms for public debate about specific policy choices. The "right terms" for such debate are reached by a consideration of the moral principles of the just-war tradition and the technological and political facts of international conflict. If there is to be no false division between the orders of morality and politics, that is, if there is to be the possibility of justice in war, then the moral task of the nuclear age is to create military and strategic possibilities in which wars can be prosecuted in a just manner. This means that "the use of nuclear force must be limited, the principle of limitation being the exigencies of legitimate defense against injustice."[63]

Murray concluded his essay by calling for the elaboration of a political and moral doctrine able "to give moral sense and political direction to a master strategic concept," a doctrine capable of bringing together the realms of power and morality. "Power," he said, "can be invested with a sense of direction only by moral principles."

It is the function of morality to command the use of power, to forbid it, to limit it, or, more generally, to define the ends for which power may or must be used and to judge the circumstances of its use. But moral principles cannot effectively impart this sense of direction to power until they have first, as it were, passed through the order of politics; that is, until they have first become incarnate in the public policy. It is public policy in all its varied concretions that must be "moralized" (to use an abused word in its good sense). This is the primary need of the moment.[64]

One individual whose main effort has been to provide the needed political and moral doctrine for the nuclear age is Paul Ramsey. I now turn to his analysis of the problem of modern war.

In 1961, Paul Ramsey published his first of several sustained treatments on the moral problem of modern war, *War and the Christian Conscience: How Shall Modern War Be Conducted Justly?* This was, of course, the year when the Kennedy administration took office and widespread dissatisfaction with the Eisenhower-Dulles doctrine of massive retaliation was voiced. Much of what Ramsey has to say in this book about deterrence and the use of nuclear weapons is compatible with the arguments advanced by McNamara and his circle. But what Ramsey has to say is not a mere repetition of the strategic debate. After all, the moralist, he says, "cannot decide the whole question that must rest with the leaders of government,"[65] but rather tells them how they ought to think about the problem of war.[66] Accordingly, what Ramsey offers is a moral argument against the Eisenhower-Dulles doctrine; an argument the general structure of which, I might add, remained consistent throughout Ramsey's many writings on the problem of modern warfare and is particularly evident in his 1963 pamphlet, *The Limits of Nuclear War: Thinking About the Do-Able and the Un-Do-Able*, and the articles and pamphlets on the same subject collected in his *The Just War: Force and Political Responsibility*.

The claim that Ramsey's view of the problem of modern war remained consistent throughout his writing career might be seen as controversial. The inattentive reader or one who only seeks proof-texts for an argument against nuclear deterrence and the limited use of nuclear force or wishes to fulfill some prejudice might be led to conclude that Ramsey's position in his 1961 book belongs to the disarmament party. There is some truth to this, but it is an incomplete truth. Couple the Eisenhower-Dulles doctrine of massive retaliation with Ramsey's conviction that force must be politically purposive hence limited, and one is forced to a position for disarmament. Many of Ramsey's statements unquestionably lead to this conclusion. He says, for example, that megaton nuclear weapons "are not weapons of war at all but of murder and devastation without limit and that have none of the purposes of war remaining in them."[67] "Responsibility for directing defense to justifiable ends and choosing justifiable means, held together in the traditional [just-war] theory, break apart in the face of warfare today and in the future."[68] "Warfare is not feasible, deterrence is not feasible, and what is more, politics is no longer feasible, unless this central war, with intrinsically unjust means, is abolished."[69] "Therefore, I say simply that any weapon whose every use must be for the purpose of directly killing noncombatants as a means of attaining some supposed good and incidentally hitting some military target is a weapon whose every use would be wholly immoral."[70] What we need now is "some substitute for the kind of warfare that can in no sense be an extension of national policy; and this can only mean the creation of the possibility of limited applications of power."[71]

It should be evident from the last passage quoted above that Ramsey's objection is not against deterrence and nuclear weapons as such. Rather, his objection goes to the use of large-scale and indiscriminate nuclear weapons which had been institutionalized in the policy of massive retaliation or might be institutionalized in any similar policy, whether that policy calls for immediate all-out retaliation to any level of enemy aggression or, as President Bush put it, as a last resort. Again, what needs to be created is "the possibility of limited applications of power." Throughout his many writings on the problem of war, what Ramsey sought above all else was to define the limits within which force can be rendered morally acceptable and politically purposive. This is possible only within what he called the "twin-born" function of justification and limitation on war provided by the just-war tradition, especially by the *ius in bello* principle of discrimination.

Ramsey's effort, then, is to lay before us the "upper limits" of what is morally "doable" as defined by the tradition of civilized warfare. This effort rests fundamentally on a particular understanding of the Christian supernatural virtue of charity. A "love-informed reason," he says, discovers a duty in charity to protect the innocent from harm and aggression and also limits intrinsically the permissible means of force by excluding from direct and deliberate attack that class of persons whose protection justifies the recourse to force. "The western theory of the just war originated, not primarily from considerations of abstract or natural justice, but from the interior of the ethics of Christian love, of what John XXIII termed social charity."[72] It is, Ramsey goes on to say, a work of love to "deliver as many as possible of God's children from tyranny, and to protect from oppression, if one can, as many of those for whom Christ died as it may be possible to save."[73] Thus justification for the use of force lies not, in the first instance, on a political theory or abstract system of rights from which one can deduce a notion of justifiable war. The early Christians had already accomplished the indispensable task of developing a practical social ethic by transforming Stoic conceptions of abstract justice based on a universal human nature through the concrete example of Jesus's self-giving and sacrificial love. For Ramsey, the inner logic of Christian love, compelled to affirm itself in every sphere of effective Christian action, leads inexorably to the duty (of charity) of the strong to defend the weak from aggression and to stand between "the perpetrators of injustice and the many victims of it."[74]

At the same time, the "love-informed reason" that leads the Christian conscience to effective action on behalf of the weak and the victims of oppression severely limits what is permissible in the use of force. As Ramsey puts it, "What justified also limited."[75]

> When out of Christian love or from definitions inspired by love it was concluded that the death of an enemy might be directly intended and directly done for the sake of all God's other children within a just or a just endurable political order by which God governs and preserves human life in a fallen world, this also meant that such love could never find sufficient reason for directly

intending doing the death of the enemy's children in order to dissuade him from his evil deeds.[76]

Shaped by this "love-informed reason" the Christian conscience cannot justify directly taking the life of noncombatants ("the enemy's children") for the sake of those who are oppressed by tyranny or aggression. Alongside love's justification for the recourse to force there is also a morality of means and, more generally, of right conduct intrinsically limiting what is permissible in repelling and overturning injustice. "Thus was," Ramsey says, "twin-born the justification of war and its limitation."[77]

In addition to the moral justification for the use of force and its limitation, Ramsey presents a political theory derived from the same theology of charity. The problem of the use of force can be approached from the perspective of individuals. What I have said so far about Ramsey's just-war doctrine strongly suggests this perspective. Persons who are weak and victims of oppression and violence are to be protected by those who can do so. This is a requirement of charity. For "Jesus did not enjoin that his disciples should lift up the face of another oppressed man for him to be struck again on his other cheek."[78] Just as "by his wound Christ died to save,"[79] so too the Christian informed by this example offers his life for the sake of others. However, Ramsey's concept of just war does not rest entirely on a collection of persons whose defense from aggression justifies individual recourse to force. "Love-informed reason" has also a corporate, public order version that justifies participation in war by referring to the requirement "to maintain a just endurable peace in which [individuals] may live."[80]

In the chapter entitled "The Just War According to St. Augustine" in *War and the Christian Conscience* Ramsey explicitly connects the public order version of a "love-informed reason" with St. Augustine's doctrine of the state and the requirements for its defense. For St. Augustine one central function of the state is to insure order and maintain, sometimes by the recourse to force, the external conditions requisite for the "acquisition of the necessaries of life."[81] When Ramsey speaks of charity as either social or corporate and says that the use of force "is inseparable from the *bene esse* of politics," that force is "inseparable from the human pursuit of the national or the international common good by political means," and that "[y]ou never have good politics without the use of power, possibly armed force,"[82] it is St. Augustine's doctrine of a political community and the requirements for its defense which he has in mind.

War is a collective, political act carried out by persons occupying public roles. Ramsey's doctrine of the just war obligates the Christian and the person of good conscience to take up arms for the defense of the common good. His understanding of charity as forming the Christian conscience and the recognition that a "love-informed reason" will take effective action on behalf of the political community lead to the same conclusion. War has its justification in charity and charity requires that the reasons for and the means by which force is employed be limited, and this in two ways: by the *ad bellum* concern with just cause—e.g., protection of the weak and the victims of oppression—and the *ius in bello* principles of proportionality and especially, given the enormous potential of modern weapons for widespread killing, of discrimination.

It is, however, important to emphasize that Ramsey provides little guidance in and elaboration of the traditional *ius ad bellum* categories. Two significant problems may be noted here. First, Ramsey claims to discover the origins for justifiable Christian participation in war in St. Augustine's treatise, *De Liberio Arbitrio*. Yet the passages Ramsey cites from Augustine's dialogue with Evodius in Book I of this work on behalf of Christian participation in war lead to a different conclusion. Augustine's argument is that killing whether in defense of self or other, or as a public official, represents a desire for things which can be taken away against one's will, and things which can be taken away against one's will ought not to be loved. Augustine's view here can lead to a pacifism with a very broad range that includes not only the condemnation of private recourse to force (a point Ramsey is most insistent on), but also killing in defense of another and as a public official. On the basis of this dialogue, to say otherwise is to assume a radical un-Augustinian position. If this is correct, then Ramsey's contention that charity requires the individual to resist injustice on behalf of its victims rests on a mistake. For Ramsey's claim to hold, he needs to develop his position not on the basis of the dialogue with Evodius, but on some other source, for example, Augustine's work *City of God*, especially Book XIX.

Yet even if Ramsey were correct in his interpretation of Augustine's *De Liberio Arbitrio*, his *ad bellum* considerations have a second, more serious problem. In the case of an individual serving in the armed forces of a nation, decisions on whether the use of force satisfies just-war criteria must normally be taken from the authority of the state. Ramsey's studied reluctance to meddle in the affairs of statecraft, to say to political leaders what exactly is and is not morally permissible in the category of ends of the state in the international arena concedes a great deal to political authorities and yields a highly unsatisfactory relation between the justification and limitation of war, that is, between *ad bellum* and *in bello* considerations. For example, the *ad bellum* principle of proportionality requires that the probable good resulting from a war exceed the probable evil. But in Ramsey the "good" required in this principle lacks a clear referent by which one can judge the justice of going to war and the related *in bello* principle of proportionality in means. In some of the passages I have quoted, Ramsey refers to "tyranny," "resisting injustice," "oppression," or "some evil power." But these are couched essentially in individualistic terms. Since the declaration and waging of war is a public function some reason other than, say, "resisting injustice," is required for the classic just-war preoccupation with the questions "Who decides?" and "For what values and ends?" At least in the modern world something other than an elaboration of Augustine's contractarianism (agreement as to a people's love) is required to settle in a morally responsible way the ends for which war may be fought—for example, some more or less objective conception of justice in war. Otherwise, the collective authority which orders the strong to take arms decides on its own terms the issue of justice in the recourse to force.

It is a puzzling feature of Ramsey's thought that while he found the origins of just-war doctrine in St. Augustine, who gave sole considerations to *ad bellum* criteria and had little if anything to say about the *in bello*, Ramsey's thought is unsatisfactory on the former but very strong on the latter. James Turner Johnson has observed that the development of the just war in the modern period shows a gradual erosion of the *ius ad bellum* and an increased concern with the limitation on the means of war.[83] Ramsey's almost exclusive attention to the *ius in bello* is illustrative of this trend. His insistence on the duty of charity to defend victims of aggression and injustice by the use of force helps guide the conscience of public functionaries by defining what constitutes just conduct in war, the core of which lies in the *ius in bello* principle of discrimination. Ramsey spells out that principle as follows:

> The principle of discrimination is shorthand for "the moral immunity of non-combatants from direct attack." This does not require that civilians never be knowingly killed. It means rather that military action should, in its primary (objective) thrust as well as in its subjective purpose discriminate between directly attacking combatants or military objectives and directly attacking non-combatants or destroying the structures of civil society as a means of victory. The latter is the meaning of murder, which is never just even in war; while the former is the meaning of the killing in war which can be justified, including the collateral and foreseeable but unavoidable destruction of non-combatants in the course of attacking military objectives.[84]

Ramsey makes similar remarks on the principle of discrimination in the chapter "The Genesis of Noncombatant Immunity" of *War and the Christian Conscience*. His emphasis on a charity-based approach to the problem of war and the limitation on violence intrinsic to the principle of discrimination leads him in this chapter to a discussion on Aquinas's principle of double effect. That discussion helps him further define within the limits of the principle of discrimination what is permissible in the use of force.

For Ramsey, the principle of double effect is essentially deontological. It defines abstractly those features that render an action intrinsically morally wrong, no matter what consequences follow, imposes strict restrictions on what is morally doable by establishing the kind of subjective intention on the part of government officials required for the bad effects of an action to be permissible, and protects certain categories of targets from direct attack—e.g., non-combatants and the "structures of civil society." The effect of these restrictions upon military, especially nuclear policy is that they bar recourse to certain means of defense and deterrence. In all his writings on the problem of war Ramsey is insistent that when the means of war are contrary to the absolute principle of discrimination—e.g., thermonuclear weapons—so too is the conditional intention or threat to use them. In *War and the Christian Conscience* he says that "If the war itself is incredible because infeasible as a minimally purposive act of a nation, so also is the deterrent threat."[85] In *The Limits of Nuclear War*, agreeing with Stein and the disarmament party, and asserting that the moral equivalence going from action to intention is "surely a correct finding as to the moral law," Ramsey says "it can never do any good to do wrong that good may come of it. Neither is it right to intend to do wrong that good may come of it."[86] What cannot morally nor politically be done, or is, in Ramsey's words, "infeasible," cannot be directly intended.

But there is a difference between Ramsey's treatment of what is permissible in the use of force and other proponents of WIP (see 3.2), namely, while the principle of discrimination serves as a regulative device in decision-making by specifying exceptionless features of morally permissible conduct, for Ramsey the *in bello* principle of proportionality "admits the possibility of significant reference to consequences."[87] It allows, and perhaps requires, the political actor to aim at a net benefit of gains by military action over costs, and thereby introduces, albeit constrained by the principle of discrimination, a consequentialist style of moral reasoning to Ramsey's doctrine of the just war which nuclear disarmers are wont to reject. This commingling of what David Little has called deontological *prohibitiva* and consequentialist discretions sets Ramsey's style of moral reasoning about what can be done in war apart from the disarmament party and creates a more flexible and inclusive approach to the moral problem of war.[88] Public functionaries can, within the absolute restrictions of discrimination, determine policy with respect to a comparative evaluation of outcomes. Decision makers, Ramsey says, "will count the cost of one effect upon the other, will ask how much disorder is worth a calculable preservation or extension of justice or will ask how much of the injustice of the world it is his responsibility to expunge politically, at the cost of disordering the political system in which alone political justice obtains embodiment."[89]

Here lies the reason for Ramsey's studied reluctance to determine policy, to answer the *ad bellum* query "For what ends?" Given the "reference to consequences" Ramsey allows in the *in bello*, there is no standard independent of politics to determine the application of just-war principles now to many future ends or consequences a state might pursue. The deontological principle of discrimination regulates the range of choices in which policy makers may morally operate. It states how to think about the problem of war by "clarifying and keeping wide open the legitimate options for choice."[90] But because the consequences of political action are largely uncontrollable and indeterminate, the principle of proportionality leaves to the discretion and creativity of the "political rulership"[91] the ends to be pursued.

These remarks anticipate what, according to Ramsey, is required for a morally acceptable doctrine of the possession and use of nuclear weapons. A nation can justifiably possess and use such weapons if and only if they are aimed at targets unprotected by the moral principle of discrimination. This led him as early as 1961 to favor what he referred to a "rational, politically beneficial armament," that is, the production and possession of weapons that can be used within the limits of politically purposive and morally acceptable force.[92] It is true, as I have noted, that in *War and the Christian Conscience* Ramsey felt that given the doctrine of massive retaliation a policy of nuclear disarmament coupled with a build-up of usable conventional arms was the only morally acceptable alternative. But it is also true that Ramsey felt inclined to admit the moral permissibility of rational nuclear armament confined to the lower registers of destructive power aimed at acceptable targets. By 1963, when Ramsey published his pamphlet *The Limits of Nuclear War*, this inclination had become an acceptable doctrine for him.

The single event which seems to have convinced Ramsey of the possibility of justice in the possession and use of nuclear weapons was McNamara's commencement address. Ramsey approvingly quoted portions of this address and expressed his grave dissatisfaction with Christians and non-Christians alike that not one rose up to say, "That is certainly the upper limit of what we ever want done on our behalf, if for no other reason than that it is clearly the upper limit of what can be done in defense of anything."[93] How does Ramsey justify the use of nuclear weapons and their political use as a deterrent? How does he reconcile the foreseeable and possibly widespread destruction consequent on the use, however limited, of nuclear weapons with his insistence on a "love-informed reason"? Are the hostage-holding features of deterrence compatible with the principles of civilized war? Can nuclear weapons pass the test of love?

The key to Ramsey's response to these questions lies in the expression "counterforce not countercivilian warfare." When Ramsey heard Mc-Namara's declaration that "principal military objectives, in the event of a nuclear war stemming from an attack on the Alliance, should be the destruction of the enemy's forces, not of his civilian population" he understood this proscription as "the oldest and most well-established rule of civilized warfare."[94] His 1963 pamphlet, *The Limits of Nuclear War*, endorsed McNamara's no-cities doctrine as an acceptable political and military possibility and then proceeded to provide it a moral justification. The thesis Ramsey defends in this pamphlet is "that counterforce nuclear war is the upper limit of rational, politically purposive military action."[95]

This thesis is compatible with Ramsey's 1961 statement that what must be created is the "possibility of limited applications of power." What had changed in this brief span of time was not so much Ramsey's opinion on the possession and use of nuclear weapons. Rather it was that the United States had now declared as official operational policy a doctrine compatible with the tradition of civilized war. Hence it was now possible to think about the preparations for and the use of new instruments of war within the rational limits of morally acceptable and politically purposive force; that is, within the restrictions of the *in bello* principles of discrimination and proportionality. These, Ramsey says, "are regulative of [policy] decisions, so long as war remains in any measure a definite purposive political act."[96]

Accordingly, Ramsey offers in this pamphlet some "suggested policy decisions" which he thinks are "imperative at this hour for the free world's security."[97] Recommending policy decisions is somewhat contrary to what I have called Ramsey's studied reluctance to venture into the ends of statecraft. Ramsey reiterates his opinion that not "every important decision is an ethical decision many exceedingly important choices are the business of statesmen and of experts other than the moralist."[98] But he submits his recommendations hoping that U.S. and Allied policy-makers by unilateral initiative will act upon them at this perilous time. These are four. I will restrict myself to a brief summary and commentary on them.

Ramsey's first suggestion is that "[t]his nation, and other nations of the West need increasingly to procure forces for subconventional and conventional warfare, and at the same time to repair in public consciousness, a doctrine of the possible and just use of such forces."[99] I have already said enough to explain why Ramsey or any other just-war moralist, whether of the war-fighting party or not, finds a morally acceptable role for the use of conventional and other discriminating forms of force. What is distinctive about Ramsey's proposal is that his recommendation for a build-up in conventional arms is a feature of a broader "morally do-able" and politically purposive doctrine of the possession and use of nuclear weapons. It is, one might say, part of a grand moral and political strategy in which the different kinds of available weapons are given their distinctive roles. Ramsey further suggests that conventional forces should not be armed with tactical nuclear weapons so that a clear and firm firebreak be placed between conventional and any nuclear force.[100]

Second, Ramsey recommends that "[t]his nation should announce that as a matter of policy we will never be the first to use nuclear weapons—except tactical ones that may and will be used, against forces and only and not strategically against an enemy's heartland, to stop an invasion across a clearly defined boundary, our own or one we are pledged by treaty to defend."[101] Two features of this proposal need clarification. The strategic rationale for this proposal rests on Ramsey's reading of limited-war theorists—e.g., Paul Nitze, Leo Szilard, and Thornton Read. These theorists agree on the value of the distinction between conventional and nuclear weapons and on the defensive first use of the latter against invading forces and only over one's own territory, thereby preserving the limit set by national boundaries and strengthening the credibility of deterrence. This use, Ramsey says, "is certainly a clear case of just conduct in a first use of nuclear weapons. It is counter-forces warfare, surrounded by the additional limitation of the aggressor-defender distinction."[102]

Moreover, since the use of nuclear weapons advocated in this proposal is restricted to one's own invaded territory, it provides us a powerful incentive to limit such use and to depend as quickly as possible on conventional forces "either to hold the border or to slow an invasion so that civilians could be evacuated from between the lines."[103] It should be added that Ramsey thinks this limited use of nuclear weapons, by assuring U.S. and Allied resolve to the defensive use tactical nuclear weapons, also provides a powerful incentive to any nuclear adversary "to renounce the first [offensive] use of tactical nuclears in the European theater."[104]

The third suggestion is that a "[n]uclear capability be maintained for use in counter-forces strikes over an enemy's territory."[105] Ramsey claims that such strikes have a dual purpose: first by destroying enemy forces they deny him the capability to prosecute the war. Ramsey has in mind here an enemy's conventional and counterforce weapons, including "munitions dumps, supply lines, bridges, etc.," either in one's own or enemy territory. The second purpose is to punish any violation of the restriction on first offensive use of nuclear weapons, which, Ramsey says, will not be tolerated even in answer to first defensive use.[106] Ramsey's justification for this kind of use is that an enemy's first use of nuclear weapons grants a nation the right to nuclear self-defense, so long as this right is executed by limited means and is "declared again and again and communicated to both the enemy and neutral nations."[107]

Ramsey's final proposal addresses the most difficult problem of nuclear war-fighting and deterrence plans. He says, "There should be a firebreak between conventional and tactical nuclear warfare and another between strikes against tactical targets and strikes against strategic forces."[108] By the latter Ramsey means enemy missile bases, homeland tactical forces, other military installation, and the like, not enemy cities. The purpose of this proposal is not, as Schelling would have it, "to raise the risk of general war" by embarking upon a policy that deters or limits war by preparing to retaliate massively against enemy cities, but to deter and limit by raising "the risk of counterforce strategic war." "One must have the ability to carry limited counterforce warfare to the enemy's own territory in order to bargain effectively about the limits and rules by which war is to be fought."[109] The risk of waging a counterforce war on an enemy's territory has "the additional purpose of reducing his will to fight by indicating our possible willingness to go higher still," the capstone of which is the "deterrence of city destruction by the threat of city destruction."[110]

McNamara's Ann Arbor speech clearly set him apart from the Eisenhower doctrine of massive retaliation, even if, as I indicated in 4.1, the latter contained counterforce features and a graduated plan of attack. But the counterforce/no-cities doctrine announced at the University of Michigan had ultimately to depend on the threat of countercivilian war. Nothing short of that can guarantee deterrence. "The very strength and nature of the Alliance forces," McNamara said, "make it possible for us to retain, even in the face of a massive surprise attack, sufficient reserve striking power to destroy an enemy society if driven to it." Similarly, Ramsey's "counterforces strategic war" deters by risking extensive civilian damage. Can Ramsey square "the threat of city destruction" with his deontological principle of discrimination?

The key to understanding Ramsey's justification of deterrence lies in what he has already said about what is permissible in fighting a war: weapons and war-fighting plans should be restricted to what is morally feasible to employ. Consequently, deterrence must be based on what is doable in war. Only insofar as a particular kind of war is morally possible can deterrence based on such a war be morally justified. In 4.1 I examined how for civilian strategists at RAND and then among those in the Pentagon calling for flexible response the credibility of deterrence was thought to rest on the feasibility of the threats—e.g., it was argued that a deterrence based on immediate massive retaliation in response to any level of aggression lacks credibility. For Ramsey the same rationale links a deter-the-war with a fight-the-war policy: namely, only what can morally be done can be morally intended.

What has then to be shown for a morally acceptable deterrence is that the kind of war envisioned be, as Ramsey puts it, "morally do-able," and such a war is one limited by the absolute moral principle of discrimination. Because this principle never permits the direct killing of civilians, no morally justified deterrence policy can include the choice to target them, to hold civilians hostage, either for the sake of a stable deterrence or, should that fail, for intrawar deterrence and bargaining. The rules that apply to war as a contest of strength apply also to deterrence as a "game of wills." No countercivilian warfare is ever justified. Ramsey insists that "neither deterrence nor warfare with these immoral means [weapons whose targets are civilian centers] is or can be made feasible."[111] The nuclear age,

Ramsey says, has written a footnote to the general axiom that ends do not justify the means: "it can never do any good to do wrong that good may come" neither can it do any good "to intend to do wrong that good may come of it."[112]

I have already suggested one way in which Ramsey's adoption of WIP does not lead him to the same conclusion as that of the disarmament party. There is another way in which this is so. In his remarks on Stein's book, Ramsey disagrees with its authors on what he refers to a "a certain finding of fact," and in so doing points to the essential feature of his justification of deterrence, a justification which can include widespread civilian deaths as a secondary, perhaps tragic, but nonetheless morally acceptable "side-effect" of a legitimate "fight-the-war" policy.

In his discussion of Stein's book, Ramsey agrees with the disarmament party that if our having nuclear weapons involves intending what is immoral to do, then deterrence is clearly unjust. However, Ramsey thinks that Stein and his collaborators have failed to recognize that there are several ways of having nuclear weapons. One of these ways is the so-called "argument from bluff," in which the having of these weapons is, as Ramsey puts it, *"praeter intentionem"*; that is, without the actual intention to use or aim them on civilian or military targets. Absent any intention to use these weapons, no immorality is entailed by their possession. Ramsey goes on to propose that the argument from bluff has some additional merit. Apart from any subjective intention to use or refrain from using these weapons the mere fact of having them produces on an adversary a certain unintended deterrent effect, namely, fear of widespread collateral civilian damage. Ramsey is more explicit about the deterrent effect of unintended collateral damage when he presents a second and more convincing way to have nuclear weapons by coupling their possession with the conditional intention to use them within the confines of civilized war. He thinks that the collateral civilian damage that would result from a counterforces attack is in itself sufficient for deterrence and, should that fail, to deter escalation from going beyond the limits of counterforces nuclear war. In that case, he says, "deterrence during the war and collateral civilian damage are both indirect effects of a plan of action in war which would be licit or permitted by the traditional rules."[113] Ramsey's point is that whether the deterrence configuration is mere possession without intention, i.e., bluff, or both possession and conditional intention to use within the range of acceptable employments of force, what deters in any case is the "indirect effect of the foreseeable indirect effects of legitimate military conduct."[114] In this rather tortuous phrasing lies the core of Ramsey's justification of deterrence.

In a footnote added to the 1968 edition of *The Limits of Nuclear War*, Ramsey admits that his choice of words in the above quotation for expressing the idea of "collateral deterrence" resulting from legitimate military operations is "inadequate." Instead, he says, "this deterrent effect should have been described as a direct and a wanted effect of the unwanted, indirect, collateral consequences of even a just use of nuclear weapons."[115] Now, how is this possible? How can one want the direct effect (of deterring both the enemy and ourselves) without at the same time wanting the indirect collateral damage (of widespread civilian deaths)? Here Ramsey makes a distinction between wanting the direct effect of foreseeable but unwanted consequences of legitimate military practice (i.e., wanting deterrence), and wanting the indirect, foreseeable consequences themselves (i.e., wanting the collateral damage). What does Ramsey mean by this?

The principle of double effect draws a distinction between the direct and indirect foreseeable effects of action. Direct effects comprise the ends one intends to bring about, while in the class of indirect effects belong the unintended but foreseeable consequences of action. When applied to situations of war, this principle helps to make a distinction between killing and murdering civilians—i.e., the foreseen but unintended death resulting from legitimate military operations, and the direct death of noncombatants either as an end or a means. This distinction between killing and murder drawn on the basis of the principle of double effect serves as the cornerstone of Ramsey's distinction between the direct and wanted from the indirect and unwanted effects of the just use of nuclear weapons. Let us look at each of these separately.

In the first belong what is intended: the wanted and indispensable primary goals of legitimate strategic counterforces nuclear war. Those goals involve the destruction, whether in one's own or enemy territory, of all targets unprotected by the principle of discrimination and necessary for the enemy's capacity to fight. In the class of the physically unavoidable and morally unwanted—i.e., the indirect and non-essential or, elsewhere, secondary—effects of fighting a just nuclear war fall the destruction of human life and structures of society, including cultural, economic and industrial resources, as well as short- and long-term damage to the natural environment not directly intended nor chosen as means to ends but consequent on legitimate counterforces nuclear war. It is, Ramsey says, this second class of effects and the fear of extensive collateral damage which it evokes that mutually deters and that, moreover, we should want as the "deterrent effects of the prospective of collateral damage, which itself remains unavoidable yet is and remains radically unwanted in fighting a modern war."[116] "Deterrence," Ramsey says, "is at work as an immediate effect of the prospect of extensive damage collateral (and thus a 'side-effect') even in justly targeted nuclear war."[117] And this effect of collateral damage is what we want and seek in a deterrent.

But there is a problem with this reasoning. Is it possible to preserve in the order of intention the distinction between the unwanted and the indispensable? Can we really want the deterrent effect consequent on extensive collateral damage without wanting the collateral damage itself? Ramsey, of course, thinks we can because if the link between a legitimate, morally "doable" "fight-the-war" and a "deter-the-war" policy is intact no immorality has accrued. This view has some initial plausibility. If what is intended in a deterrence policy is within the limits of what is feasible in war, then no immorality accrues. This follows from the moral equivalence of action and intentions. However, I am going to suggest that it is impossible to form an intention to want the effects of some course of action and withhold the intention for that which brings about in a causal way the desired result. That is, if I want the deterrent effect consequent on the fear of extensive collateral damage I am in some real way committed to wanting, and hence morally complicit in the (collateral) damage itself. What needs to be understood here is that there is a necessary connection in the order of intention between wanting the effects of a course of action and wanting their causes, unless the latter is entirely accidental to and unessential for the desired end. If I am correct, then Ramsey's justification for deterrence fails because it depends on an intention contrary to his absolute principle of discrimination.

Consider that there are two ways in which it can be said that one intends something.[118] One can in the order of subjective intention directly want the purpose or end to which one's action is aimed, or one can intend or want what in the objective order is a consequence of a course of action lacking subjective intention. This second kind of wanting or intending an object consequent on a prior course of action or events not subjectively intended can be referred to as intention *in causa*. In the first the agent intends the end as such, while in the other what is sought is the consequence or indirect object of an unwanted chain of events. It is this second sense of intending that is especially relevant for my discussion. For convenience I will refer to these ways of wanting or intending as intention in the strong and the weak sense, respectively.

What is important about this distinction is that the intention (in the strong sense) to some purpose or object to which action and thought are directed, and the less settled determination on a course of action but intention (in the weak sense) for its effect are both products of one's volition and as such both are subject to moral appraisal, but in different ways. The primary moral index of an action is the agent's intention in the subjective order—i.e., intention in the strong sense. In this regard Ramsey is quite correct to say that the principle of discrimination defines the range of permissible moral conduct in war. Any plan of action that directly and willfully intends the death of protected targets is murder. But Ramsey's deterrence, like other deterrence theories with counterforce features, ultimately relies on the intention (in the weak sense) to kill very large numbers of civilians. Ramsey himself presses home this point when he says in a passage already quoted that "apart from intention, [the] capacity [of strategic forces] to deter cannot be removed from them. No matter how often we declare, and quite sincerely declare, that our targets are an enemy's forces, he can never be quite certain that in the fury or the fog of war his cities may not be destroyed."[119] It should be stressed that by "apart from intention" Ramsey means apart from intention in the strong sense. But the fact that one having nuclear weapons knows and wants the deterrent effects consequent upon the extensive collateral damage their use would bring about constitutes an intention in the weak sense. The counter-force-plus-avoidance deterrence configuration Ramsey advocates deters because the nuclear weapons necessary for that deterrence are designed to bring widespread destruction, even if the death of civilians is by indirection.

It is frequently suggested, for instance, that a physician who is opposed to euthanasia and whose patient is dying in great pain may administer a pain-killing regimen of morphine even though the morphine will certainly as a side-effect hasten the patient's death. So long as the death is not directly intended (in the strong sense), the principle of double effect relieves the physician of any moral responsibility in that death. Here she is acting to reduce suffering rather than to achieve death. Indeed she would not be disappointed were the patient to survive. But if she administers the pain-killing regimen of morphine *because* in addition to its palliative value it will also hasten death, then she is intentionally (in its weak sense) ending the patient's life. And this, by her own reckoning, cannot be done. It cannot be done because she is acting not only to reduce pain, but also to hasten death, even when death is the indirect effect of a course of action that is otherwise—i.e., without the indirect voluntary, or, as Aquinas puts it, "*voluntarium in causa*"—morally permissible.

Similarly, if the threat to civilian life is a necessary feature of deterrence and deterrence is the desired end-result of a causal chain that begins with the collateral damage consequent on strategic counterforces war, by my definition of intention in the weak sense Ramsey's justification for deterrence is committed to wanting not only the deterrent effect of collateral damage, but the (collateral) damage itself—unless the threat or fear of the collateral damage is unessential for the deterrence. Ramsey, of course, will not agree to this. But notice that when he addresses the point whether the mere possession of nuclear weapons will be sufficient to deter an aggressor, he suggests that we should "cultivate" the "appearance of being partially or totally committed to go to city exchanges."[120] What Ramsey means by "cultivating the appearance" is not clear. Perhaps he is already aware of the important role of perceptions in international politics and nuclear deterrence, and means by this expression something similar to the dynamics of what Defense Secretary James Schlesinger later called "essential equivalence." Whatever it is that Ramsey tries to get at with these remarks, one possibility he makes available is a doctrine of deterrence that relies on massive retaliation without planning nor intending (in the strong sense) to carry it out. We are offered the possibility of a counterforce-plus-avoidance policy whose ultimate guarantee depends on the cultivated appearance of a willingness to go all-out. To rule this possibility out of the scope of moral appraisal only tends to obscure the fact that the desired deterrent effects are intrinsically related to the unintended (in the strong sense) consequences (i.e., collateral damage) of legitimate military operations both in a physical and moral sense. The one is established by a causal chain of events and the other by the "foreseeability" and voluntariness (i.e., non-accidental nature) of the collateral damage which, to the extent that its deterrent effects are intended (in the weak sense), is morally imputable. In short, Ramsey's deterrence, like McNamara's or any other deterrence doctrine that invokes even without the actual subjective intention and only as a last resort the threat of massive retaliation, partakes of the wickedness of countercivilian war.

4.3 THE NULLIFICATION OF A REQUIRED CONDITION

Ramsey has performed an invaluable service to those who are convinced that the realms of power or force and of morality can in a very real way be compatible with each other. Nevertheless, I am inclined to believe that the risks of massive and indiscriminate destruction consequent on a protracted exchange of any, however limited, nuclear weapons even on counterforce targets lying outside urban centers is disproportionate to any politically purposive or morally acceptable goals that may be won. Once the nuclear "firebreak" has been crossed, the risks of escalating the spiral of nuclear destruction render these weapons militarily "unusable." When we consider the possible extensive collateral damage of a counterforces nuclear war double-effect expressions such as "incidental," "secondary," "unintended," "unwanted," as well as the difference between ends and means, all crucial to Ramsey's justification of deterrence, run so much into each other that the distinctions they are meant to preserved are nullified. As John C. Ford observed: "There comes a point where the immediate evil effect of a given action is so overwhelmingly large in its physical extent, in its mere bulk, by comparison with the immediate good effect, that it no longer makes sense to say that it is merely incidental, not directly intended, but reluctantly permitted. It is not a question of the physical inevitability of the evil effect. It is a question of its incidentality."[121]

In this concluding section I briefly argue two things. First, that Ramsey's justification of deterrence nullifies the distinction between counterforce and countercivilian warfare; and second, even if the distinction were preserved the alleged fact that counterforce warfare is morally acceptable by the principle of discrimination does not yield the conclusion that a counterforces-plus-avoidance deterrence is morally permissible. That is, one cannot infer the moral character of a deter-the-war policy from that of a fight-the-war policy. What makes for a morally good war-fighting policy does not necessarily make a morally good deter-the-war policy. I maintain that there is a morally significant difference between fighting (or doing) and preparing (or intending) to fight a war. The only way to salvage Ramsey's defense for the practice of deterrence is to retreat from WIP and endorse the principle that establishes the permissibility of action (war-fighting) on the morality of intentions (deterrence). In 5.4 I develop this point.

The distinction between counterforce and countercivilian war may be drawn on one of two bases, either physical or moral. The first involves force structures and targeting policies. Strategic debates on flexible response and city-avoidance are illustrative of official government attempts to prepare for nuclear war in accordance with the tradition of civilized warfare. The moral basis of this distinction is the principle of discrimination coupled with the moral difference between direct and indirect attack. In 4.2 I expressed one possible line of criticism against Ramsey's interpretation of justifiable deterrence. I wish now to press a second and deeper dissatisfaction with it. I will demonstrate that Ramsey's use of the double-effect categories of ends, means, and side-effects to draw a distinction between legitimate (counterforce) and illegitimate (counter-civilian) targets of attack is incoherent.

The principle of double effect (PDE) wishes to distinguish between intended and unintended effects of action, and distinguishing one from the other is the work of certain categories. For example, I perform an act A which intends good G and foresees some evil E consequences. Assume that I want to bring G about and have no wish for E nor is E part of my deliberations. E just happens. PDE is ready to say that I am in no manner morally responsible for E, which is merely a side-effect even if foreseen. But the matter is very different if E is a means for G. If E is a means by which G is produced, I intend E. And using evil means even for a good cause makes the act morally wicked.

Charles Fried has suggested that the counterfactual test may help to identify when the evil effects of a good action are merely accidental side-effects or means to the sought-after end.[122] We can ask the agent whether she would perform A if the result is either (i) only G and not E or (ii) both E and G. If the answer to the first is "Yes" and to the second "No," then E is a genuine side-effect and not a means to G. In the matter of deterrence if it is known that a particular configuration would be chosen even if its activation would not produce the fear of extensive collateral damage, then whatever civilian damage follows the activation of the deterrent or whatever fear of civilian damage is evoked is truly collateral or incidental—i.e., is not a means—and hence is sanctioned by PDE. On the other hand, if deterrence depends on the threat of civilian deaths—if G in some real way requires E—then the latter is not a mere side-effect but a means. And this makes deterrence immoral.

Now Ramsey maintains that countercivilian war either as an end or means is evil, while counterforce war is doable within the limits of civilized war, even when civilians are indirectly killed. But when he moves from fighting to deterring war (that is, from doing to intending), he shifts the function of civilian damage from that of unintended and foreseen consequences to what is enabling and empowering of the deterrent threat. Again, what deters is the "prospective collateral damage [of] fighting a modern war."[123] But while the death of civilians and damage to the structures of society are collateral in fighting a counterforces war, they are required as means for a credible deterrence. Without the "prospective of collateral damage" Ramsey's counterforce-plus-avoidance deterrence would be pointless.

The above anticipates my second argument. Let us assume that Ramsey's judgment of civilian deaths as a side-effect and not a means of justifiable strategic nuclear counterforce war is sound. Can a strategic nuclear counterforce war define what is morally acceptable in a deterrence policy? Can we move from what is acceptable in fighting to what is permissible in deterring a war?

In 3.2 I argued that the moral equivalence going from actions to intentions is, contrary to our initial intuitions, deficient and unable to provide the relation of implication requisite for the judgment that it is wrong to intend what is immoral to do (i.e., WIP), at least when it comes to nuclear arms policy. The crucial step in that argument was that intending and doing are separate acts and each can therefore be morally appraised independently of the other. I want now briefly to explore this argument along a slightly different line. I will suggest that we are not required to infer the moral character of deterrence (or intentions) from that of a war-fighting plan (or action). Because a counterforce war may be permissible according to the principle of discrimination, it is not the case that a counterforce deterrence is similarly permissible. If this is correct, then the link Ramsey makes between a fight-the-war and a deter-the-war policy is unacceptable.

Assume Ramsey's deontological principle of discrimination and his assertion that counterforce is morally superior to countercivilian war. It is however evident to Ramsey that the destruction of counterforce targets will produce extensive civilian damage. This damage, he says, is permissible by double-effect, and then he goes on to assume that if counterforce war is permissible, counterforce deterrence threats are equally so. However, this assumption is false. I argued above that for Ramsey's counterforce-plus-avoidance deterrence civilian damage is either intended (in the weak sense) as an end or required as means to the goal of deterrence. That is, the risks to an adversary's civilian population counterforce threats present are either included in a substantive way in the definition of a credible deterrence or instrumental in reducing the probability of an adversary's first strike. If we then introduce the double-effect categories of side-effects, means and ends, the threat to civilian populations is not incidental, a side-effect of a legitimate course of action, but a means for deterrence. Even if one agrees with Ramsey that the civilian deaths which follow a retaliatory counterforce attack are morally permissible, the risks to an adversary's civilian population presented in counterforce deterrence threats are an essential feature of his deter-the-war policy. Insofar as those threats are essential to deterrence they either run together just those things the principle of double effect is suppose to hold apart—namely, action and its side-effects—or use civilians as means. Those deaths, therefore, are not morally permissible. Here Ramsey is forced to his conclusion in *War and the Christian Conscience* that nuclear deterrence is immoral and, unless he retreats from WIP, to the absurd position that some nuclear weapons may morally be used, but their use may never be intended.

NOTES

1. House Committee on Appropriations, *Department of Defense Appropriations for 1983* (Washington, D.C., 1982), pt. 4, 522.

2. *International Herald Tribune*, 9 May 1978.

3. Desmond Ball, *Deja Vu: The Return to Counterforce in the Nixon Administration* (California Seminar on Arms Control and Foreign Policy, Santa Monica, CA, 1974), 10-11.

4. To my knowledge, Ralph B. Potter was the first to observe the parallel structure of moral and strategic arguments in the nuclear debate. By developing an analytic scheme adapted from Talcott Parson's general theory of action and Robert A. Levine's typology of arms policy in *The Arms Debate* (Cambridge: Harvard University Press, 1963), Potter was able to break down the spectrum of Christian responses to the nuclear dilemma. These show a remarkable congruence with Levine's "schools of thought." See Potter's "The Structure of Certain American Christian Responses to the Nuclear Dilemma, 1958-1963," unpublished doctoral dissertation, Harvard University, 1965. The parallel structure of strategic and moral debates is also noted in J. Bryan Hehir's contribution to *The New Nuclear Debate* (New York: Council on Religion and International Affairs, 1976) and, more recently, in Robert E. Osgood's *The Nuclear Dilemma in American Strategic Thought* (Boulder and London: Westview Press, 1988), especially chapter 2, "The Spectrum of Approaches to the Nuclear Dilemma."

5. For the relation between facts and moral reasoning see Ralph B. Potter, *War and Moral Discourse* (Richmond, VA: John Knox Press, 1969), chapter 2, and "The Logic of Moral Argument," in P. Deats, ed., *Toward a Discipline of Social Ethics* (Boston: Boston University Press, 1972).

6. The respected columnist James Reston expressed the then common understanding that what the United States was telling the Communists was that "in the event of another proxy or brushfire war in Korea, Indochina, Iran or anywhere else, the United States might retaliate instantly with atomic weapons against the USSR or Red China." *New York Times*, January 16, 1954. On March 14 of that year, the same paper reported Vice President Nixon as saying: "Rather than let the Communist nibble us to death all over the world in little wars we would rely in the future primarily on our massive mobile retaliatory power which we could use in our discretion against the major source of aggression at times and places that we choose." Nixon, however, later abandoned this view (if he ever truly believed it) in favor of flexible response.

7. For some of the historical material in this section, I am indebted to Lawrence Freedman's *The Evolution of Nuclear Strategy* (New York: St. Martin's Press, 1981) and Fred Kaplan's *The Wizards of Armageddon* (New York: Simon & Schuster, 1983), esp. chapters 11-13, 17-18, and 22.

8. Paras 6b and c.

9.   David Alan Rosenberg, "The Origins of Overkill: Nuclear Weapons and American Strategy, 1945-1960," in Steve E. Miller, ed., *Strategy and Nuclear Deterrence* (Princeton: Princeton University Press, 1984), 165.

10. Rosenberg, "Origins," 165.

11. John Foster Dulles, "Policy for Security and Peace," *Foreign Affairs* (April 1954), vol. 32, no. 3, 356.

12. Dulles, "Policy," 357.

13. Dulles, "Policy," 358.

14. Robert E. Osgood, *Limited War: The Challenge to American Strategy* (Chicago: University of Chicago Press, 1957), 242.

15. Henry A. Kissinger, *Nuclear Weapons and Foreign Policy* (New York: W.W. Norton & Co., 1969), Abridged Edition, 120.

16. Of the limited-war theorists mentioned above, Lidell Hart was the first to develop his views on this subject as early as the 1940s, and were elaborated during WW II. But it was with the development of atomic weapons that his ideas on limited war were widely accepted. For a bibliographical essay on limited-war theory during the 1950s, see Morton H. Halperin, *Limited War*, (Cambridge: Harvard Center for International Affairs, 1962).

17. Kaufmann, "Introduction," *Military Policy and National Security* (Princeton: Princeton University Press, 1956), 29.

18. Kaufmann, "Introduction," 249.

19. Kaufmann, "Introduction," 118, 113, 234.

20. Quoted in Fred Kaplan, "New Look From the Pentagon," *Inquiry* 22 (September 1980), 10.

21. In Richard Stebbins, ed., *Documents In American Foreign Relations* (New York: Harper & Row, 1963), 233.

22. On this McNamara said: "Relatively weak national nuclear forces with enemy cities as their targets are not likely to be sufficient to perform even the function of deterrence." In Stebbins, *Documents*, 232.

23. Raymond Aron, *The Great Debate*, trans. Ernst Pawel, (New York: Doubleday & Co., 1965), 75. Aron goes on to say that "it took the McNamara doctrine to force Europeans into realizing that their situation was ultimately not identical with that of the United States and that there was less truth than wishful thinking in the old bromide about all of us being in the same boat."

24. Desmond Ball, "Development of the SIOP, 1960-1983," in Ball and Jeffrey Richelson, eds., *Strategic Nuclear Targeting*, (Ithaca, New York: Cornell University Press, 1986), 63.

25. William Kaufmann, *The McNamara Strategy* (New York: Harper & Row, 1964), 52.

26. Robert S. McNamara, "The Military Role of Nuclear Weapons: Perceptions and Misperceptions," *Foreign Affairs* 62 (Fall 1983), 79.

27. Albert Wolhstetter, "Optimal Ways to Confuse Ourselves," *Foreign Policy* XX (Autumn 1975), 198.

28. See, for example, Barry Carter, "Nuclear Strategy and Nuclear Weapons," *Scientific American* (May 1974), 20-31.

29. Quoted in James Schlesinger, *Annual Report to the Congress on the FY 1975 Defense Budget and FY 1975-1979 Defense Program* (4 March 1974), 35.

30. Fred Ikle, "Can Nuclear Deterrence Last Out the Century?" *Foreign Affairs* 51 (January 1973), 272, 281.

31. Ikle, "Century," 282.

32. Ball, *Deja Vu*, 13.

33. James Schlesinger, *European Security and the Nuclear Threat Since 1945* (Santa Monica, CA: RAND, 1967), 12.

34. Schlesinger, "Flexible Strategic Options and Deterrence," *Survival* (March/April 1974), 86-90.

35. Schlesinger, *Annual Defense Report FY 1976* (5 February 1975), II-3, II-4.

36. Schlesinger, *Report*, 35.

37. Schlesinger, *Report*, 4. For William Kaufmann's contribution to the Schlesinger doctrine, see Fred Kaplan, *Wizards*, 372-374.

38. Edward Luttwak, "The Missing Dimension of U.S. Defense Policy: Force, Perceptions and Power," in Donald C. Daniel, ed., *International Perceptions of the Superpower Military Balance* (New York: Praeger, 1978), 21-23. See also the excellent study by Robert Jervis, *Perceptions and Misperceptions in International Politics* (Princeton: Princeton University Press, 1976).

39. Schlesinger, *Report*, 6.

40. Schlesinger, *Report*, 38.

41. Schlesinger, *Report*, 42.

42. Harold Brown, *Department of Defense Annual Report Fiscal Year 1979* (2 February 1978), 5.

43. John Courtney Murray, "Remarks on the Moral Problem of War," *Theological Studies* 20 (March 1959). Also published as "The Uses of a Doctrine on the Uses of Force," in Murray, *We Hold These Truths* (New York: Sheed and Ward, 1960), 271. Citations are taken from the 1960 edition.

44. Representatives of the "war-fighting party" are James Turner Johnson, *Can Modern Wars Be Just* (New Haven: Yale University Press, 1984); William V. O'Brien, *The Conduct of Just and Limited Wars* (New York: Praeger, 1981); Michael Novak, *Moral Clarity in the Nuclear Age* (Nashville, TN: Thomas Nelson Publishers, 1983); David Fisher, *Morality and the Bomb* (London: Croom Helm, 1985); and Joseph S. Nye, *Nuclear Ethics* (New York: The Free Press, 1986).

45. Richard B. Miller, "Paul Ramsey on the Morality of Nuclear Deterrence," *Journal of Religious Ethics*, vol. 16, no. 2 (Fall 1988), 201.

46. Murray, "Remarks," 270.

47. For Murray's thought on these matters see, "Remarks," 1960. Recent discussions on Murray may be found in David Hollenbach, ed., "Theology and Philosophy in Public: A Symposium on John Courtney Murray's Unfinished Agenda," *Theological Studies*, 40:4 (December 1979) and George Weigel, *Tranquillitas Ordinis: The Present Failure and Future Promise of American Catholic Thought on War and Peace* (Oxford: Oxford University Press, 1987), chapter 4.

48. John Courtney Murray, "War and Conscience," in James Finn, ed., *A Conflict of Loyalties* (New York: Pegasus, 1968), 21.

49. Murray, "Remarks," 264.

50. Murray, "Remarks," 249-250.

51. Murray, "Remarks," 251.

52. Murray, "Remarks," 250, 251.

53. Murray, "Remarks," 252-253.

54. Murray, "Remarks," 252.

55. Murray, "Remarks," 261.

56. Murray says: "[T]he morality proper to the life and action of society and the state is not univocally the morality of personal life, or even of familial life. Therefore the effort to bring the organized action of politics and the practical art of statecraft directly under the control of the Christian values that govern personal and familial life is inherently fallacious. It makes wreckage not only of public policy but also of morality itself." "The Doctrine Is Dead," in *We Hold These Truths*, 286.

57. Murray, "Remarks," 253.

58. Murray, "Remarks," 260.

59. Murray, "Remarks," 260.

60. Murray, "Remarks," 261.

61. Murray, "Remarks," 263.

62. Murray, "Remarks," 265.

63. Murray, "Remarks," 270.

64. Murray, "Remarks," 273.

65. Ramsey, *War and the Christian Conscience* (Durham, NC: Duke University Press, 1961), 166.

66. Ramsey, *The Just War: Force and Political Responsibility* (New York: Charles Scribner's Sons, 1968), 11.

67. Ramsey, *Christian Conscience*, 229-230.

68. Ramsey, *Christian Conscience*, 153-154.

69. Ramsey, *Christian Conscience*, 269.

70. Ramsey, *Christian Conscience*, 162.

71. Ramsey, *Christian Conscience*, 166.

72. Ramsey, *Just War*, 142.

73. Ramsey, *Just War*, 143.

74. Ramsey, *Just War*, 143.

75. Ramsey, *Just War*, 143.

76. Ramsey, *Just War*, 151.

77. Ramsey, *Just War*, 152.

78. Ramsey, *Just War*, 143.

79. Ramsey, *Christian Conscience*, xx.

80. Ramsey, *Just War*, 143.

81. St. Augustine, *City of God*, XIX.17.

82. Ramsey, *Just War*, 5.

83. See James Turner Johnson, "Ideology and the *Jus ad Bellum*: Justice in the Initiation of War," *Journal of the American Academy of Religion* 41, no. 2 (June 1973), 212-228 and *Ideology, Reason and the Limitation of War* (Princeton: Princeton University Press, 1975), chapters 3 and 4.

84. Ramsey, *Just War*, 429.

85. Ramsey, *Just War*, 314.

86. Paul Ramsey, *The Limits of Nuclear War: Thinking About the Do-Able and the Un-Do-Able* (New York: Council on Religion and International Affairs, 1963), 46. Also found in Ramsey's *Just War*, 211-258.

87. Ramsey, *Just War*, 102.

88. David Little, "The Structure of Justification in the Political Ethics of Paul Ramsey," in James T. Johnson and David H. Smith, eds., *Love and Society: Essays in the Ethics of Paul Ramsey* (Missoula, Montana: Scholars Press, 1974). In addition to the noted distinction, I have benefitted from other points in Little's discussion of Ramsey's political ethics.

89. Little, "Structure," 29.

90. Little, "Structure," 19.

91. Little, "Structure," 19.

92. It should be noted that biological and chemical weapons that satisfy the restrictions on targeting set by the principle of discrimination are allowed. See Ramsey, *Christian Conscience*, 320.

93. Ramsey, *Limits*, 7.

94. Ramsey, *Limits*, 7.

95. Ramsey, *Limits*, 10.

96. Ramsey, *Limits*, 31.

97. Ramsey, *Limits*, 31.

98. Ramsey, *Limits*, 31.

99. Ramsey, *Limits*, 31.

100. Ramsey, *Limits*, 39.

101. Ramsey, *Limits*, 32.

102. Ramsey, *Limits*, 34.

103. Ramsey, *Limits*, 34.

104. Ramsey, *Limits*, 38.

105. Ramsey, *Limits*, 38.

106. Ramsey, *Limits*, 38.

107. Ramsey, *Limits*, 39.

108. Ramsey, *Limits*, 39.

109. Ramsey, *Limits*, 39, 40.

110. Ramsey, *Limits*, 40.

111. Ramsey, *Christian Conscience*, 234.

112. Ramsey, *Limits*, 46.

113. Ramsey, *Limits*, 48.

114. Ramsey, *Limits*, 48.

115. Ramsey, *Limits*, 252-53n.95.

116. Ramsey, *Limits*, 318.

117. Ramsey, *Limits*, 319-320.

118. This discussion is based on Thomas Aquinas, *Summa Theologiae*, I-II, q. 6, a. 3. See also Aquinas on "circumstances," *Summa*, I-II, q. 7.

119. Ramsey, *Limits*, 49.

120. Ramsey, *Limits*, 50.

121. John C. Ford, "The Hydrogen Bombing of Cities," in William Nagle, ed., *Morality and Modern Warfare* (Baltimore, MD: Helicon Press, 1960), 101.

122. Charles Fried, *Right and Wrong* (Cambridge: Harvard University Press, 1979), 23.

123. Ramsey, *Just War*, 318.

5 The Deterrence-Only Party

"a pact with the powers of hell"?

Raymond Aron[1]

The counterforce deterrence endorsed by the war-fighting party is unacceptable because it necessarily intends (in the weak sense) the death of innocent civilians. The principle of discrimination, endorsed by this party as an absolute constraint on what we can morally do, prohibits the direct killing of civilians and, by way of WIP, any intention to do so. However, in 3.2 I argued that deterrence intentions have some moral justification. I want to inquire further into the justification of deterrence here. The authors considered in this chapter argue that the possession of nuclear weapons for the sake of deterring a similarly armed adversary can be justified but not the activation or use of the deterrent. Can one morally justify forming an intention for what is immoral to do?

The French and German Catholic bishops offer two of the clearest responses to this question.[2] In their letter of 8 November 1983, the French bishops unambiguously condemn the use of nuclear weapons. "No reason," they say, "could ever justify the unleashing of [nuclear war], since the survival of humanity is at stake."[3] Yet they are moved to support the countercivilian threat of France's policy of nuclear deterrence—what they refer to as a "deterrence of the strong by the weak, a poor man's deterrence"—despite the "firm and unequivocal" condemnation of "anti-city" deterrence by the Second Vatican Council. To justify their position, the bishops argue that a nation threatened in "its life, liberty, and identity"[4] has the duty to "defend itself against unjust aggression"[5] by an "effective counter-threat,"[6] even when the counter-threat involves nuclear force. They note that the "threat of force is not the use of force"; moreover, it is "not evident" the "immorality of use render[s] the threat immoral."[7] The bishops agree with Archbishop Beck of Liverpool that the possession of nuclear weapons constitutes what traditional Catholic moral theology calls a "near occasion of sin," but one that is a "necessary occasion" given that at this time a nation "cannot really give up its deterrent without grave risks for its liberty as well as its cultural and spiritual values."[8] The very probable evil consequences attending disarmament require a policy that in no uncertain terms seeks to prevent them. The bishops conclude that "in the midst of the present distress,"[9] we lie in grave moral tension between the threat to civilian life required for a credible deterrence and the good of preserving the political integrity of the state.

The West German Catholic bishops reach a similar conclusion in their letter of 18 April 1983. Given the destruction consequent upon the use of modern instruments of warfare, the call for peace among nations has, the bishops say, "assumed a special degree of urgency"[10] that requires the adoption of an "emergency set of ethics."[11] What creates the need for an emergency ethics is the "great dilemma"[12] at the present time between (i) the right and duty of states to "an ethically permissible defense"[13] of the existence and freedom of the political community "against aggression and extortion from outside"[14] and (ii) the basic dignity and human rights to life and liberty of all individuals that are threatened by the possession of and conditional intention to use modern means of warfare.[15] This "great dilemma" leads the bishops to a cautious if not anguished acceptance of nuclear deterrence and "to the need for an emergency system" enabling us to choose "from among various evils the one which, as far as it is humanly possible to tell, appears the smallest."[16] David Hollenbach suggests that descriptions of the nuclear age as a condition of emergency indicate "not only that the realities of contemporary nuclear strategy may be in conflict with the traditions of Western and Christian ethical thought, but also that we may be faced with policy choices that are simply not analyzable in terms of traditional moral categories. If this is the case [e]thics would itself be in distress."[17] Along similar lines, Michael Walzer in *Just and Unjust Wars* says that nuclear deterrence contemplates "an immorality we can never hope to square with our understanding of justice in war. Nuclear weapons explode the theory of just war. They are the first of mankind's technological innovations that are simply not encompassable within the familiar moral world."[18] Walzer, however, argues that even if deterrence is a "bad way" of coping with our condition, "there may well be no other that is practical in a world of sovereign and suspicious states."[19]

In this chapter I examine a style of thinking that makes frequent use of expressions such as "tragedy," "distress," "crisis," "duress," and "emergency" to describe the moral condition of the nuclear age and to salvage, as Richard B. Miller aptly puts it, despite the many obstacles along the way, "deterrence as a plausible moral institution."[20] The first two sections of this chapter examine different attempts to reconcile under a principle of emergency the special moral requirement on the state and its functionaries to preserve the political community and the general moral requirement not to engage in action that is violative of an individual's right to life. Inherent in this attempt is a dilemma between the moral requirement not to form the evil intention of threatening innocent civilians and the moral requirement on the political leadership to protect the liberty of the state by effective action.

The prodeterrence views examined in those sections take advantage of the two dominant approaches available in recent moral theory. One approach adopts the consequentialism principle that actions are to be judged by the overall benefits of alternative courses of action. If a course of action turns out to produce the better state of affairs, it is, by this account, the rational thing to do. But that a course of action turns out to be the rational thing to do might not entail that it is the morally right thing to do. It might indeed lead to great immoralities. In the context of discussion on war, an unrestrained consequentialism might counsel the direct killing of innocent civilians so as to save lives and bring war to a speedy end. The other approach emphasizes as fundamental to morality individual rights to life and liberty and a categorical constraint prohibiting the direct killing of civilians, no matter what comes. The Pauline principle that evil may not be done that good may come of it and the Kantian principle that persons are to be treated as ends in themselves, and not as mere means, capture the central feature of this approach to the morality of deterrence. Yet to salvage the institution of deterrence, this approach requires an escape clause that permits overriding categorical rules in those conditions where their observance leads to catastrophic consequences. Sometimes in conditions of extremity, this view holds, we must act in ways that violate traditional limitations on the use of deadly force.

How the conflict between these styles of moral reasoning is handled by a particular author dominates much of the analysis in the first two sections of this chapter. Walzer (section 5.1) is insistent that the morality he expounds in *Just and Unjust Wars* is "in its philosophical form a doctrine of human rights." Utility, however, is built "into the structure [of this morality] at many points,"[21] particularly in matters of political morality.

"Political leaders," he says, "can hardly help but choose the utilitarian side of the dilemma. That is what they are there for. They must opt for collective survival and override those rights that have suddenly loomed as obstacles to survival."[22] Walzer accepts the view that some acts are intrinsically and categorically wrong. But he obviously accepts the other view that commits him, as he says, to "a kind of blasphemy against our deepest moral commitments"[23] against killing the innocent.

Kavka (section 5.2) also emphasizes constraints against directly killing the innocent when he says that a moral agent has "conclusive moral reasons not to apply [a harmful sanction to innocent people]" if deterrence were to fail. But in that condition he calls a Special Deterrent Situation a moral agent "must intend a harmful sanction to innocent people, if an extremely harmful and unjust offense is to be prevented." Unlike Walzer, Kavka pays close attention to the paradoxes that arise in the special condition of nuclear deterrence and challenge some of our ordinary beliefs about the relation of intentions and action. The paradoxes engendered by our efforts to think morally about nuclear deterrence lead Kavka to important insights about the applicability of agent-centered and outcome-centered moral theories to extreme conditions.

The prodeterrence view of the American Catholic bishops (section 5.3) relies almost solely on the categorical principle of discrimination. Because it is unlikely that any nuclear exchange will remain limited, the principle of discrimination prohibits any use of nuclear weapons. Moreover, because one may never intend what one may not do, it follows that the threat to use any nuclear weapons is equally prohibited. That is the only conclusion warranted by the categorical principle of discrimination. The bishops prodeterrence view is therefore found incoherent. I suspect that any prodeterrence view that takes the principle of discrimination as categorical will be equally incoherent. Now, had the American bishops distinguished between the threat and use of nuclear weapons, as do the French and German bishops, or allowed for consequentialist considerations in a condition of extremity, as do Walzer and Kavka, then their prodeterrence view may not have suffered from incoherence.

It must be noted, however, that the case for deterrence based on the condition of extremity (e.g., Walzer's and Kavka's) might gradually cultivate in us the vice for necessity. Except for the American Catholic bishops, the arguments examined in this chapter rely on just that condition to reconcile conscience with consequences. To threaten innocent people with annihilation is wrong. But what choice do we have? Disarm unilaterally here and now, and possibly face foreign domination, or threaten what morally cannot be done. Most arguments for deterrence want us to abandon the strict demands of conscience and to decide what ought to be done about nuclear weapons and deterrence on what might happen to us without them. Our liberties might well be at stake, they say, therefore retain those instruments of mass slaughter. But to retain them commits us to grave immorality.

There is a prodeterrence argument very different from those recounted above. It purports to show that if it is morally legitimate to form deterrence intentions, then it is also legitimate to act on them. An obvious merit of this argument is that by rejecting the traditional way of thinking about the relation of intentions and actions, it avoids some of the problems faced by other prodeterrence views. Instead it considers the morality of intentions independently of their corresponding actions, and then justifies actions on the morality of their antecedent intentions. This way of reasoning about the morality of nuclear deterrence may yield some important points for moral theory.

Yet, however rational it might be to form deterrence intentions, we must inquire into what we morally commit ourselves to doing. If those intentions commit us to wholesale slaughter either by direction or indirection, we commit ourselves to murder. And a commitment to murder cannot be reconciled with any moral view. Even when our standard is consequentialist, the good conscience is restrained by what intrinsically and categorically cannot be done. The tension between the demands of conscience and the consequences of our actions may well support Hollenbach's claim that the nuclear age has ushered in a "crisis of moral reason itself."[24]

5.1 THE ARGUMENT FROM SUPREME EMERGENCY: MICHAEL WALZER

Walzer has expressed in its most challenging form the tension inherent in the deterrence-only approach to the moral problem of modern war.

Nuclear deterrence is a response to a permanent condition of "supreme emergency" in which action that is ordinarily evil becomes necessary under conditions that threaten the political community. He says:

> [C]ommunities in emergencies seem to have different and larger prerogatives [than individuals]. I am not sure that I can account for the difference, without ascribing to communal life a kind of transcendence which I do not believe it to have. Perhaps it is only a matter of arithmetic: individuals cannot kill one another to save themselves, but to save a nation we can violate the rights of a determinate but smaller number of people.[25]

In this section I examine Walzer's principle of supreme emergency in the context of the theories of human rights and of international aggression he develops in *Just and Unjust Wars*.[26] Walzer argues that the principle of supreme emergency overrides ordinary morality intuitions about justice in war. However, and this is the point I wish to emphasize, the moral remainder which he clearly shows is present in the historical examples he cites is so large that what a condition of emergency justifies does not eliminate in any significant way ordinary constraints on what we can morally do to others. I explain Walzer's justification for doing in politics what is profoundly morally wrong according to ordinary constraints on action by noting his attempt to resolve a rather deep conflict between two incompatible convictions: the centrality of the individual and the priority of communal life, especially with regard to the responsibility of political leaders. The nature of the conflict in a condition of extremity between what I shall refer to as liberal and communitarian values, and between what we want our national leaders and public functionaries to do on our behalf and the principles by which we hold them accountable for their actions present in a rather stark manner the most profound (and, I think, insoluble) moral problem of the nuclear age.

Walzer's use of the expression "supreme emergency" is borrowed from Churchill's description of Britain's predicament at the beginning of WW II. "We are fighting," Churchill said, to re-establish the reign of law and to protect the liberties of small countries. Our defeat would mean an age of barbaric violence, and would be fatal, not only to ourselves, but to the independent life of every small country in Europe. We have a right, indeed are bound in duty, to abrogate for a space some of the conventions of the very laws we seek to consolidate and reaffirm. The letter of the law must not in supreme emergency obstruct those who are charged with its protection and enforcement. Humanity, rather than legality, must be our guide.[27]

For Walzer, Britain's predicament was a desperate one, and this for two reasons. In the first place, British hope for victory, or even avoiding defeat, was meager at best. And second, the British were facing a unique evil. Only the use of bombers coupled with a policy of mass-terror offered any hope of defeating an enemy who posed, as Walzer says, "an ultimate threat to everything decent in our lives, a threat to human values so radical that its imminence would surely constitute a supreme emergency."[28] Lacking technology and weapons systems adequate for precision attacks against legitimate military targets, the British adopted a policy of obliteration bombing in which cities themselves were directly attacked. Part of Walzer's purpose in *Just and Unjust Wars* is to analyze the concept of emergency and to establish criteria for legitimate claims to it.

Throughout sections of his book, Walzer deliberately opposes the grounds of certain claims made on behalf of military practices that are violative of the tradition of civilized warfare. He rejects, for example, Germany's claims to military necessity during WW I and WW II, first to refuse to act according to the rules of naval warfare and then to invade Belgium in order to protect itself.[29] Walzer rejects Germany's claims because in neither situation was its survival really at stake. However, when Walzer turns to the British mass-bombing of German cities, he defends this practice and elaborates two criteria for legitimate claims to necessity. Before one can justify the killing of innocent civilians, a nation has to be faced with an evil of an ultimate nature. The threat has to be such that defeat of the defending nation will result not merely in the establishment of a new balance of power, but in the triumph of evil, of a power so terribly awful that everything decent would be radically jeopardized. Nothing less than an evil of this kind can justify the claim of necessity. Accordingly, the threat giving rise to the claim must be, first, an imminent danger, and second, the danger must be of a serious nature, not simply the loss of honor, but a danger "of an unusual and horrifying kind."[30]

With the criteria of imminence and seriousness of danger, Walzer distinguishes between the legitimacy of British terror-bombing of German cities between 1940 and 1942, and the continuation of this practice during 1944-45, when the danger of German victory had passed as well as the condition of supreme emergency, making the attacks upon cities at the end of the war immoral. It is an important point in Walzer's defense of British bombing policy between 1940 and 1942 that the wrong against civilian life is not minimized. The decision to bomb German cities was made at a time when Germany posed an imminent and serious danger to the survival of Britain, "a time when victory was not in sight and the specter of defeat ever present."[31] Under such condition the rule of necessity overrides traditional limits on the conduct of war, and "a wager against the rules [of war] might be morally required."[32] But while necessity justifies doing what we all know to be wrong, an important wrong against German civilian life was nonetheless committed, one which Walzer insists is a serious and unforgivable moral wrong, regardless of the consequences.

Here lies the core of the moral problem indicated by expressions such as "crisis," "distress," "emergency," and the like. The problem arises when one is faced with a choice between doing evil (mass-bombing or, in the case of nuclear deterrence, threatening civilian life) in order to defeat or deter a greater evil (Nazism or loss of political liberty), or letting evil triumph by failing to act. If the rights of persons set constraints on what we can morally do to them, how can one justify a policy that violates those rights? How can what is dishonorable and wrong, whether at war or not, also be, under conditions of emergency, tolerable and right in the conduct of war?

Some commentators charge that Walzer's reasoning on this point is morally incoherent. Hollenbach, for example, though sympathetic with certain features of Walzer's moral theory of war, especially its emphasis on human rights, objects by saying that "[m]urder, by definition, is unjustified killing. To declare it morally legitimate is to make a nonsensical statement: this act is both justified and unjustified at the same time."³³   And Stephen E. Lammers criticizes Walzer for, among other things, sanctioning British terror-bombing and (unwittingly) justifying a social practice in which the immunity of noncombatants "is not, any longer, an ultimate value."³⁴ Walzer himself lends support to his critics when he says, near the end of his book, that those who under conditions of emergency violate the prohibition on killing civilians "are murderers, though in a good cause."³⁵

These arguments against Walzer have a strong initial plausibility. The principle of supreme emergency does seem, at first inspection, to be morally incoherent, violently subverting those rights that a moral theory of war seeks to uphold. But I think Hollenbach and Lammers overlook the fact that for Walzer the principle of supreme emergency serves not only to justify the temporary suspension of the constraints rights place upon conduct, but is, at a deeper level, a recognition that in the nuclear age the moral landscape has changed in a permanent and decisive way. Hollenbach is correct when he says that "to declare [murder] morally legitimate is to make a nonsensical statement, [it is to say that murder] is both justified and unjustified." But this is true only if one rejects the inordinacy of, or fails to give proper force to, the principle of supreme emergency. What this principle requires us to do is to think in extraordinary ways about the conduct of war. Walzer's attempt to define conditions of extremity using the criteria of imminence and seriousness of danger to the survival of a nation aims to establish an evaluative basis independent of ordinary intuitions about justice in war. The principle of supreme emergency is not morally incoherent because under conditions of extremity the evaluative basis for murder has decisively shifted from ordinary to extraordinary conditions, even if ordinary moral requirements are still in force and murder carries its usual moral weight. What Hollenbach, Lammers, and other critics of supreme emergency must show is that we don't live in extraordinary, i.e., radically tragic and perilous times. Yet to do so requires an argument either against the risks and dangers of general nuclear war or for a strict correspondence between the norms of the just war and the technologies and strategies of modern war. Curiously enough, the impossibility of the latter is, I take it, what Hollenbach means by the "crisis of moral reason itself."

There is another feature of Walzer's principle of supreme emergency that shows up more clearly the "crisis of moral reason." I have already touched lightly upon it in my remarks on the French and German Catholic bishops' letters. I want now to elaborate on those remarks and show that our present moral condition as defined by Walzer is one in which there is a wide and deep conflict between two basic moral convictions, one giving moral priority to individuals and the other to the survival of the political community. Each of these convictions requires incompatible courses of action and together yield a morally dilemmatic situation. This situation may be illustrated by the competing theoretical views of liberal and communitarian political theories.

One of the central tasks of Walzer's book is to advance a moral theory of international aggression that can help us determine when one state commits aggression against another state and why aggression is wrong. This theory is designed also to help define the foundation of a state's international legitimacy and of the right possessed by states to threaten or to use force against another state. For Walzer, aggression is the act by which one state violates the territorial integrity or political sovereignty of another. It is, he says, "the only crime that states can commit against other states: everything else is, as it were, a misdemeanor."[36] Walzer articulates his theory of aggression by means of what he calls the "legalist paradigm," consisting of six propositions the basic postulate of which is that there is a moral order among free and sovereign states analogous to the domestic order among autonomous individuals within any one state.

The initial power of this domestic analogy is that our judgments and reasoning about the world of states is drawn from the more familiar world of national life. Here individuals have rights to life and liberty which can never be bargained away, utilitarian-style, in pursuit of some principle of maximization or end-state to be achieved, and assign to individuals a certain authority to shape their own lives free from external coercion. Walzer cautions us that he cannot explain how these rights are grounded. It is for him enough to say "that they are somehow entailed by our sense of what it means to be a human being. If they are not natural, then we have invented them, but natural or invented, they are a palpable feature of our moral world."[37]

Just as individuals in domestic society have rights to life and liberty, so too states have analogous rights, to territorial integrity and political sovereignty. These rights, Walzer says, "derive ultimately from the rights of individuals, and from them they take their force."[38] Unlike his reluctance to ground individual rights ("How these rights are themselves founded I cannot try to explain here"[39]), Walzer is clear on the foundation of states' rights:

> The duties and rights of states are nothing more than the duties and rights of the men who compose them. This is the view of the conventional British lawyer, for whom states are neither organic wholes nor mystical unions. And it is the correct view. When states are attacked, it is their members who are challenged, not only in their lives, but also in the sum of the things they value most, including the political association they have made. We recognize and explain this challenge by referring to their rights.[40]

Here is the familiar liberal view that a state derives its legitimacy from the protection it provides to the rights to life and liberty of its citizens. When one state violates another state's rights to territorial integrity and political sovereignty, it brutally violates in a quite concrete way the rights of the latter's individual citizens. It is for this reason that Walzer says the crime of aggression "is to force men and women to risk their lives for the sake of their rights. It is to confront them with the choice: your rights or (some of) your lives!"[41]

Walzer's emphasis on the constraints individuals' rights place upon what we can morally do to them captures basic liberal intuitions about the content of morality and the function of the state. Yet this is not his only view on the foundation of the rights and duties of states. States' rights to territorial integrity and political sovereignty derive also from what Walzer calls "the common life" or "independent community" that a people has shaped over a long period of time. On this view, the rights of a state rest on the consent of its members, a "consent," Walzer says, "of a special sort."[42] It is not a (Rawlsian) hypothetical agreement on a set of principles it would be rational for individuals ignorant of their natural fortune and social circumstances to adopt in a contractual situation, nor a (Hobbesian) social compact by which individuals exit the state of nature under the force of an all-powerful ruler. It is rather a consent through "a process of association and mutuality" in which individuals together make a common life through "shared experience and cooperative activity of many kinds."[43]

This second theoretical perspective tends to give priority to communal values over individual (i.e., liberal) rights. Here a state possesses rights to territorial integrity and political sovereignty independent of its observance of individual rights to life and liberty. On this view, states' rights derive from the "rights of contemporary men and women to live as members of a historic community and to express their inherited culture through political forms worked out among themselves."[44] From this perspective, aggression is wrong not so much because it violates individual rights but because it challenges "the sum of things [we] value most, including the political community [we] have made."[45] As I understand this second formulation, a state's legitimacy depends not on its respect of individual rights, but on "a certain fit between the community and its government."[46] That "fit" is present when "a government actually represents the political life of its people"[47] in accordance with their "widely shared world view or way of life."[48]

It is important to emphasize what is entailed in this second theoretical perspective on the rights and duties of states. On the first (liberal) view individual rights to life and liberty are morally prior to any other consideration and establish constraints on what we can morally do to others. Now when states' rights are founded independent of a given state's "internal political arrangements, whether or not the citizens choose their government and openly debate policies carried out in their name,"[49] the liberal view of individual rights to life and liberty recedes in importance and a second standpoint becomes preeminent, namely, that of the state's self-determination. It is for this reason that on Walzer's "legalist paradigm" a state, regardless of its respect of human rights and no matter how tyrannical it may be, possesses the twin rights to territorial integrity and political sovereignty.

Walzer's defense of British terror-bombing between 1940 and 1942 lies just on that basis. When a state's vital rights to territorial integrity and political sovereignty are threatened in a condition of extremity, they suspend the ordinary constraints of individual rights to life and liberty.

However, the nature of individual rights makes it impossible to erode or undercut them: "nothing," Walzer says, "diminishes them; they are still standing at the very moment they are overridden."[50] "They still stand and have this much effect at least: that we know we have done something wrong even if what we have done was also the best thing to do on the whole in the circumstances."[51] Confronted with a situation of extremity, the prohibition against breaking the rules of war is temporarily suspended. But what is justified under extremity is at the same time also morally wrong.

So, the doctrine of supreme emergency depends on a combination of different and incompatible convictions about the nature and function of the state. One accounts for the "pull" of liberal principles by which a state is said to be legitimate only if it protects the basic individual rights to life and liberty of its citizens. It takes persons as the primary unit of moral concern. Aggression is therefore wrong because it violates individual rights. The other accounts for, and is likely to have a better reception among proponents of, communitarian ideas which invest the political community and the state with a value beyond that of individual rights.

This second formulation of the legitimacy of states is made explicit in Walzer's essay, "The Moral Standing of States." There Walzer accuses some of his critics of having misunderstood the dual reference in the doctrine of legitimacy by which "states can be presumptively legitimate in international society and actually illegitimate at home."[52] International legitimacy, he says, depends upon the "fit" of government and community. Here Walzer appeals to what I have referred to as communitarian ideas and makes no reference to liberal principles. That Walzer thinks the latter set of values provides a states' international legitimacy is clear from the following passage.

[T]he opinions of the people, and also their habits, feeling, religious convictions, political culture, and so on, do matter, for all of these are likely to be bound up with, and partly explanatory of, the form and character of their state. That is why states objectively illegitimate are able, again and again, to rally subjects and citizens against invaders. In all such cases, though the "fit" between government and community is not of a democratic sort, there is still a "fit" of some sort, which foreigners are bound to respect.[53]

On the basis of this passage it is difficult to say what exactly is doing the work of establishing a state's international legitimacy, since several candidates present themselves: for example, the ability of states to "rally subjects and citizens against invaders," or the "opinions of the people, religious convictions, and so on," or the "fit between government and community." Gerald Doppelt argues that a state's ability "to rally subjects and citizens against invaders" may not be the result of a "fit" between community and government. It may instead "reveal a people's longstanding distaste for the intervening nation, mistrust of its motives or simply a justifiable fear of personal consequences of the intervention."[54] It can further be argued that if the foundation of a state's international legitimacy is the ability "to rally" whether or not "fit" is present, then the prospects for a moral justification for the recourse to force are not very encouraging. Emphasizing communal values over individual rights or relying on any of the above candidates for international legitimacy, not only contradicts Walzer's stated purpose of his moral theory of war ("The morality I shall expound is in its philosophical form a doctrine of human rights."[55]), but also could fail to lead to a doctrine of limited war. Liberal morality requires the adoption of binding side constraints that prohibit actions violative of individual rights. When these constraints are superseded by the (higher) value of communal life, the kind of restraint required in a moral theory of war grounded in a doctrine of human rights is potentially weakened, since now the justification and limitation of war rests with the "opinions of the people, religious convictions" etc., "for which individuals are sometimes sacrificed."[56] This tends to make the rational and moral criticism of war dangerously improbable.

Nonetheless it is the "fit" between community and government that provides the foundation for a state's international legitimacy and seems, therefore, decisive for the moral theory of war. Walzer provides an illuminating example of the force of this "fit" independent of a theory of individual rights. In a hypothetical case, Walzer asks us to imagine a country named Algeria in which a revolutionary movement pledged to establish democratic institutions with equal rights to all citizens comes to power. Through factional in-fighting the government actually created is an illiberal military and religious regime repressive of civil and political rights—e.g., women are returned to traditional religious roles under patriarchal rule. Now this regime (unlike a liberal democracy) "fits" the "historic community" and "inherited culture" of the Algerian people, and draws upon the "religious convictions" and "opinion of the [Algerian] people." To the extent that the "fit" is present, even if the status *ante rebellionem* is reestablished, and assuming there were strong moral reasons for overturning the earlier repressive order, the new illiberal regime has all the necessary grounds for legitimacy. What is peculiar about this example is that the liberal democratic government which, lacking the requisite "fit" with the "historic community," would be judged illegitimate.

Walzer asks us further to imagine that a second state, Sweden, has available a wondrous chemical that could wipe out of Algerian minds their "historic community" and replace it with liberal democratic institutions protecting the basic civil liberties of all Algerians. Should the Swedes use it on the Algerians? Walzer responds that no one should use it "because the historical religion and politics of the Algerian people are values for the Algerian people which our valuation cannot override."[57] Walzer rightly notes that this formulation is problematical because it "hold[s] that the Algerian people have a right to a state within which their rights are violated [b]ut that is the only kind of state they are likely to call their own."[58]

Underlying Walzer's "legalist paradigm" is a doctrine of state self-determination with a two-fold function. First, it establishes states' rights to territorial integrity and political sovereignty as the foundation of international morality; second, self-determination provides the decisive basis for the duty of states to preserve themselves, whether or not their domestic structure respects individual rights. On first inspection, Walzer's theory of war appears to have its basis on individual rights to life and liberty. Something like a principle of the moral autonomy of persons seems to support this theory. But upon closer inspection, the rights of states are independent of individual rights and a state's self-determination emerges as the highest good in international affairs. It seems, then, that aggression is a crime not because it violates the rights of individual citizens, but rather because it challenges the right of an established government (liberal or not) to determine itself free from external encroachment.

I want now to consider the dilemma that arises out of the conflict between Walzer's doctrine of human rights and of the rights of states when applied to judgments on war. The question of the morality of the threat and use of force is bound up with the question of state legitimacy. War is, after all, a condition between (legitimate) states. Individuals may have many reasons for fighting wars independent of the kind of regime that rules them—e.g., that they dislike the aggressor or seek vengeance on him. But if states have the right to self-determination, then they have the corresponding duty to protect themselves from external threat and coercion. What are the implications of this duty for the responsibilities of political leaders? In discussing this question I do not assume normal political conditions, but a condition of extremity as defined by Walzer, and attempt to understand within his doctrine of war the moral problem faced by the national leadership of a nation in supreme emergency. That is, I want to understand the special responsibilities of national leaders in the context of a dilemma between the moral claims the community makes upon them and the principles by which we judge their actions.

The type of problem faced by national leaders in a condition of emergency is that of doing some evil act to defeat evil. It must be stressed that this is not a problem confronted by the individual as private citizen, responsible only for her action. It is rather a problem faced by a public functionary entrusted with the protection and preservation of the state, insofar as "fit" is present between the community and the state. To illustrate the problem, Walzer asks us to engage in "a morally important fantasy."

Imagine the choices Churchill saw before him in 1940, and suppose you had to choose for him. Unless Bomber Command could be used systematically against German cities, it is very likely that Britain would suffer defeat and an immense evil power would be let loose upon the world. Not to do what is required for the protection and survival of the state would go contrary to the moral claims politics makes upon public officials. Yet to satisfy those claims one must violate the rights of individuals to live free and undisturbed by force. What should one do? "Should I," Walzer asks, "wager this determinate crime (the killing of innocent people) against that immeasurable evil (Nazi triumph)?"[59] Walzer's question is designed to have us consider whether the intentional killing of German civilians as a means to the defeat of Nazism can be morally justified. He responds that "there is no option [to the bombing of German cities]; the risk otherwise is too great. I dare to say that our history will be nullified and our future condemned unless I accept the burdens of criminality here and now."[60]

In an unpublished lecture given several years ago at the Air Force Academy in Colorado Springs, Colorado, Walzer tries to respond to the skepticism his doctrine of supreme emergency met in philosophical circles. He acknowledges the deep conflict between the prohibition against killing civilians and the requirement upon the state to avoid disaster, whatever it takes. To help explain how we might require criminal action by the state, he introduces a communitarian political theory as the foundation of the doctrine of emergency.

Communitarian theories typically hold a view of politics and morality grounded in the shared values and way of life of particular societies. They emphasize the bonds of community, common purposes and ends, along with the religious and cultural ideals which provide individuals "with some portion of their character, practices, and beliefs."[61] These theories make an important point: our settled identities are derived from an identifiable way of life handed down to us; and for many, the continuation through future generations of that way of life has great value. Indeed, it has such a high value that its possible loss might require extreme sacrifice, including as Walzer says, that its leaders "take on the guilt of killing the innocent."[62] Do whatever is necessary when the heavens are about to fall, but know also that the high moral price of killing the innocent will be paid by all.

But this view is difficult to reconcile with Walzer's insistence in *Just and Unjust Wars* that the crime of war is to force individuals "to risk their lives for the sake of their rights."[63] That account of the crime of war depends on a universalistic understanding of rights, rather than on the incompatible communitarian claim that justification is local and refers always to the shared values of particular communities. In spite of his earlier commitment to individual rights, his more recent insistence on a communitarian political theory strongly suggests that it is the latter which explains how murder may become part of a just war. A political leader cannot stand idly by and watch the destruction of a way of life and its shared ideals. When collective survival is at stake, we must set ourselves against the enemy and take recourse in whatever means are available, including the deliberate killing of innocents. Walzer says:

> A morally strong leader is someone who understands why it is wrong to kill the innocent and refuses to do so, refuses again and again, until the heavens are about to fall. And then he becomes a *moral criminal* who knows that he can't do what he has to do and finally does.[64]

Consider the case of Sir Arthur Harris, chief of Bomber Command from 1942 to the end of the war, that Walzer recounts in his last set of remarks about military necessity in *Just and Unjust Wars*. Although after the summer of 1942 Germany was no longer an imminent and serious threat to the survival of Britain and so the condition of emergency had, according to Walzer, ceased to exist, Churchill, Harris, and others in the British chain of command were convinced that Britain was still in imminent danger of defeat. So British strategic bombing of German cities continued. At war's end the pilots of Bomber Command, unlike those of Fighter Command, received no honors. No plaque recording the casualties of Bomber Command was offered. Their sacrifice went without official recognition. Harris and his pilots were "slighted and snubbed."[65] Yet, Walzer says, the pilots of Bomber Command did "what was necessary and right." They risked their lives to protect the common life of the nation and to prevent a great evil from spreading in the world. Without their contribution Britain may well have been defeated and Nazism triumph over Europe. Shouldn't those who are prepared to sacrifice themselves be honored? Shouldn't monuments be built and their names engraved on the common memory?

The contribution of Bomber Command cannot be recognized because even though its pilots and crew sacrificed their lives while performing duties that in a condition of extremity were necessary and justified by the moral claims of the political community, what they did was also not simply wrong, but murderous. For this they, the political leaders, and the nation must find ways to reestablish a commitment to what was overthrown. How can one restore the rules of civilized warfare if those who have violently overturned them are honored? The refusal to honor the pilots of Bomber Command, to grant them what otherwise would have been their rightful place in the common memory of the British people is, Walzer says, "some small distance toward re-establishing a commitment to the rules of war and the rights they protect."[66]

For Walzer, this example illustrates the moral dilemma typical of a wide range of cases catalogued under the problem of "dirty hands." This is an old, for some an inherent, feature of political life. There are times when a political leader must choose between courses of action both of which are morally wrong. Times such as these leave those responsible for action guilty—and this in a rather odd way: a political leader (say, Churchill in the period 1940-1942) cannot refrain from ordering the evil of killing German civilians, lest the evil of Nazism gain victory. But while Churchill cannot refrain from this evil—cannot refrain because he is required to act by claims of the community—he is nonetheless guilty of grave wrongdoing. It is not simply that because of their role and function political leaders may not morally refrain from wrongdoing—bomb German cities and end the evil of Nazism—it is that they must "accept the burdens of criminality here and now." How can a course of action that is inherently wrong also be morally required? Or, how is it possible to commit an evil by doing what one morally ought to do?

In response to these questions it is not enough to say that in situations of conflict the right thing to do is something which ordinarily is morally wrong. This description is typical of cases of *prima facie* duties treated by W. D. Ross and others, in which one obligation may be overridden by a more pressing one. There the conflict arises between more or less routine obligations. For example, I have promised to meet you at six o'clock for dinner and in my way to our meeting an emergency arises that requires immediate attention. We often and rightly break routine promises to aid someone in need. Some political actions are undoubtedly of that kind. But they are not political acts as such, let alone choices and actions in conditions of extremity. Nor is it enough to say that for the sake of some worthy political objective a politician must act in ways that are morally disagreeable, ways in which an honorable person would be disinclined to act. For example, a politician might find herself involved in concealment, coercion, lying, or the more common practice of making misleading statements, or any of the number of morally disagreeable actions typically catalogued under the problem of dirty hands.

But the kinds of situation that arise in conditions of extremity are simply not accessible with normal moral categories. If supreme emergency defines any class of acts at all, it must be a class of tragic situations where one might say there is *no better thing to be done*; whatever is done is, in a real sense, wrong. Let Nazism triumph even if the heavens fall, or commit murder. Either way, ruin! Yet if one is to take morality seriously, then it must be so taken in the most serious of circumstances—when what is at stake is morality itself. At those times we ought to set ourselves against evil rather than, as Walzer suggests, commit evil and become "murderers, [even if it might be for] a good cause."[67] Have we any right to murder and maim innocent civilians? Ought we become criminals and murder the righteous along with the wicked?

Walzer's doctrine of supreme emergency is not coextensive (indeed, it seems incompatible) with the cosmopolitanism of his theory of individual rights. By his account, the rules of war are derived from individual rights. These, he wants to say, are more basic than considerations of social utility. Yet when the stakes are very high, utility has a certain priority over individual rights. This is true for cases in which "we are face-to-face not merely with defeat but with defeat likely to bring disaster to a political community."[68] But why stop utilitarian calculation there? If utility is going to override rights in these circumstances, why not follow utilitarian calculations all the way and consider the interests not only of one but of all communities? Does Walzer have a way to stop the utilitarianism of extreme circumstances from going to the broadest general interest?

Perhaps a communitarian political theory can stop utilitarian calculations from going all the way. The shared values and traditions of a particular community might not include such global concerns. But Walzer should then have to explain why it is morally preferable that one community survive than another, and that requires him to adopt a universal view from which he can weigh the relative values of different states—precisely what communitarianism rejects.

In my view, Walzer's frameworks for justifying the killing of (or the threat to kill) innocent civilians are unconvincing. If utility overrides individual rights, then it is necessary to consult consequences in a truly utilitarian manner; if it is communitarianism that justifies extreme measures, then he must show why one community deserves to survive over another. Because Walzer fails to satisfy these requirements, he has not proven why the life of innocent persons may be directly threatened. I suspect that any moral theory that tries to accommodate categorical prohibitions of a deontological system and consequentialists discretions will turn out to be equally problematical.

Yet, perhaps that is the message Walzer wants ultimately to convey. Under certain conditions, upholding ordinary morality might have disastrous outcomes. We must, therefore, choose between the demands of conscience or avoiding terrible consequences. But the choice cannot be settled within any one of the two systems. Each will point only to itself and together they recommend incompatible courses of action. Do justice even if the heavens fall or commit yourself to immorality, lest the heavens really fall.

5.2 A UTILITARIAN ARGUMENT FOR DETERRENCE-ONLY: GREGORY KAVKA

In the preceding section I explored the general contours of two interrelated moral dilemmas. One has to do with a conflict between the moral requirement to protect the political community and the individual's right to life and liberty; the other involves a conflict between the moral claims of the political community on the national leadership and the principles by which we judge official actions. In each of these, morality seems to require incompatible courses of action, first with respect to the rights of individuals and those of states, and then with regard to the moral claims of politics and the moral principles that apply to persons as persons. I now turn to some writings by Gregory Kavka, who gives close attention to the incompatibility of the moral principles, both utilitarian and deontological, we use in the evaluation of agents and actions when applied to nuclear deterrence.

In this section I consider two questions. What is the moral basis of a utilitarian defense of deterrence? And what are the "unresolved puzzles and paradoxes" Kavka says are generated by the practice of nuclear deterrence? I want to show the general lines of a utilitarian argument for deterrence-only and how the moral conflicts indicated in the preceding section call into question some common moral ideas. To do this I need not remark on all of Kavka's extensive moral analyses of the nuclear predicament. For my purposes it is sufficient to sketch the argument of several sections of Part I of Kavka's *Moral Paradoxes of Nuclear Deterrence.*

Kavka's examination of nuclear deterrence is carried out within a utilitarian moral theory. He agrees that there are nonutilitarian dimensions to nuclear deterrence that call for careful attention. But he holds that absolutist principles—e.g., the Wrongful Intentions Principle (WIP) or the principle of noncombatant immunity—are unable to provide an adequate starting-point for the moral analysis of nuclear deterrence because they neglect some morally significant facts of this practice for human well-being. There is much that can be said about Kavka's contention here. But I restrict my remarks to how Kavka approaches the choice between two alternative nuclear policies—the deter-or-disarm choice. Each of these policy alternatives potentially brings different negative outcomes. Practicing deterrence might lead to its activation, hence to widespread death, and disarming might lead to foreign domination or blackmail, among other things.

The fundamental principle of utilitarian moral theory is that persons ought to act so as to bring about the greatest utility, where utility is conceived to be some objective quality. In this regard, utilitarian moral theory is an instance of the formalized theory of choice that attempts to resolve conflicts among competing values by weighing the relative importance of these values and computing the probabilities of fulfilling the values by different policy recommendations. If it is possible to assign relative value weights to various policy outcomes (possible loss of liberty under disarmament or loss of life under deterrence), and if the probabilities of those outcomes can be computed, in the sense that one can compute the probability of a die turning up "six" two times in a row, then which of the various policy positions ought to be adopted is a matter of simple arithmetic. A decision maker needs only to know which policy alternative provides the highest expected fulfillment for a particular value.

But the application of this decision procedure to arms policy is not very plausible. Or so Kavka thinks. In the world of arms policy the possibility of assigning relative value weights to deterrence or disarmament policies and computing the probabilities of different outcomes is highly uncertain, and this for at least two reasons. First, the difficulty of determining the relative value of competing arms policy makes their comparative evaluation highly problematical. Values in arms policy are not, as Robert A. Levine has noted, "readily measurable and homogeneous."[69] And second, lacking knowledge about the likelihood of different outcomes, we cannot rely on any set of probabilities. However, a utilitarian theorist might say that when the outcomes of one's act or particular policy choices are not known with certainty, one should choose that policy having the greatest expected utility or the least worst outcome. Without having to resolve any value conflicts, one can concentrate on a few noncompeting values and look for policies that provide the highest fulfillment of the relevant values. That is, in a situation of uncertainty instead of weighing the relative value of possible outcomes one need only to identify which policy has either the single best or, if all outcomes are bad, which has the single least worse outcome.

Kavka holds that "[n]o generally satisfactory principle of rational choice under uncertainty has yet been found."[70] A rather special situation thereby arises for the deter-or-disarm choice, confronting us with what Kavka describes as "two-dimensional uncertainty." Because we lack factual information on both the expected utilities of deterrence and disarmament and on their probabilities, we are in a rather poor position to know with any accuracy the amount of human well-being or suffering produced by either policy. A utilitarian theorist might suggest that if we gather enough information about an agent's subjective preferences, then we can construct value and probability estimates so that expected utility can be maximized. However, this procedure is unable to solve the deter-or-disarm choice because an agent's expressed preferences are not necessarily meaningful indicators of objective moral values, especially in the face of extreme factual ignorance about the outcomes and probabilities of alternative policies effecting the well-being of a very large population. Nonetheless, Kavka argues that a principle of plausible applicability to choice-situations having similar features to the deter-or-disarm choice is available. Consider the following hypothetical choice-situation between two disasters of "roughly the same order of magnitude."[71]

Kavka asks us to imagine a forty-year-old man diagnosed with a rare and almost certainly not fatal disease that often causes life-long paralysis but leaves its other victims otherwise normal. Experts are only able to offer a rough estimate of the probability of paralysis. They say there is a 20 to 60 percent chance. Now there is an experimental drug that almost certainly cures the disease in some cases, but kills some 20 percent of the population that takes it (the exact number is not accurately known). But the patient can assume that "he is definitely less likely to die if he takes the drug than he is to be paralyzed if he lets the disease run its course."[72] What should he do?

The choice facing this patient is like the deter-or-disarm choice in that absent any reliable quantitative estimates of the relevant probabilities, he must choose between a smaller probability of a greater disaster (chance of death with treatment or annihilation after deterrence) and a larger probability of a smaller disaster (the chance of paralysis without treatment or loss of liberty after disarmament). The principle applicable to choice-situations such as these, Kavka says, is a decision mechanism where the value to be maximized is the avoidance of disaster, or, as he calls it, the Disaster Avoidance Principle (DAP). This principle asserts that

> when choosing between potential disasters under two-dimensional uncertainty [defined as "the chooser has no reliable quantitative estimates of the relevant utilities and probabilities, but has confidence in his judgment of their ordinal rankings"] it is rational to select the alternative that minimizes the probability of disaster occurrence.[73]

The applicability of this principle to the deter-or-disarm choice is highly plausible, Kavka thinks, since the ranking of the probabilities is fairly clear. The probability of foreign domination under disarmament is greater than the probability of nuclear war under deterrence. If foreign domination would not be disastrous, then disarmament is the more reasonable option since it would greatly reduce the probability of nuclear war. But because domination is an unacceptable, though lesser, disaster and the probability of the greater disaster is less, it follows from DAP that deterrence is the preferred choice. Thus Kavka believes that by maintaining a nuclear deterrent there is a good chance of avoiding foreign domination even if there is some likelihood of nuclear war. This choice, he thinks, is a more reasonable and morally acceptable option than disarmament.[74]

Despite Kavka's assurance about the soundness of this conclusion, there is a great moral cost incurred by the practice of deterrence. It leads to serious and insoluble moral conflicts. Consider a typical deterrence situation. An actor A stands ready and willing to commit what is clearly a terrible wrong. Another, B, threatens and intends to use force should A commit the wrong. B has reason to think that should the intention to use force be carried out, a moral wrong will be committed (say, because harm will be brought to many people not directly involved in or responsible for A's action). Is the moral status of B's deterrence intentions wrong in the same sense that it is wrong to bring harm to those not directly involved in A's actions? If activating B's deterrence is wrong because of the harm it will produce, then it seems that intending to bring harm to innocent people is equally wrong. Yet by preventing the wrong of A's action, B's deterrence intentions seem to bring about some good. That is, A's wrong is prevented from occurring. Can the intention to do what one knows to be wrong also be right?

Kavka thinks that an affirmative answer to this question might "appear absurd or incredible on first inspection, but can be supported by quite convincing arguments."[75] Those arguments, however, produce some disturbing moral paradoxes that strongly indicate a basic incompatibility of available moral principles and the practice of deterrence, and that furthermore require us to reject some widely held beliefs or doctrines about the evaluation of agents and actions. What is at stake here are widely accepted moral doctrines—or, as Kavka calls them, "bridge principles"—that connect the moral evaluation of actions and of agents, and also give credibility to the prospects for a consistent moral theory. If the quandaries engendered by deterrence lead us to question the applicability of those "bridge principles," then the prospects for a consistent moral theory seem fairly low. Here, again, the deterrence-only party confronts a "crisis of moral reason."

To demonstrate how the practice of deterrence yields paradoxical moral statements, Kavka sets up a special "paradox-producing" situation. He calls it a Special Deterrent Situation (SDS) (it may also be called "supreme emergency" or "crisis" as defined in 5.1), and introduces a normative assumption about how we ought to reason morally in an SDS. An agent is in an SDS if:

[(i)], it is likely he must intend (conditionally) to apply a harmful sanction to innocent people, if an extremely harmful and unjust offense is to be prevented.

[(ii)], such an intention would be very likely to deter the offense.

[(iii)], the amounts of harm involved in the offense and the threatened action are very large, and the relevant probabilities and amounts of harm are such that a rational utilitarian evaluation would substantially favor having the intention.

[(iv)], he would have conclusive moral reasons not to apply the sanction if the offense were to occur.[76]

These conditions require a brief commentary. (i) through (iii) are factual assumptions about some aspects of moral psychology having to do with intentions and their effects, and about the relevant outcomes and probabilities involved in the threatened action. More precisely: (i) requires that the probability of an "unjust offense" must be significant; (ii) requires that the conditional intention to retaliate be present; and (iii) assumes the amounts of harm in the attack and retaliation are approximately equal. Kavka's Disaster Avoidance Principle seems particularly relevant to conditions (i) and (iii) to the extent that potential disasters "roughly of equal order of magnitude" are present in an SDS. If it can be shown that there is no real threat of disaster, that the amounts of harm in the attack and retaliation are not very large, or that the defender does not hold the conditional intention to retaliate, but is merely bluffing, however successful that practice may generally be, then the agent is not in an SDS. Factually, then, an SDS is a rare if not unique occurrence.

(iv), however, is purely ethical in content. To be in an SDS an agent must have "conclusive moral reasons not to apply the sanction." This is the most interesting of the conditions from the moral point of view because it presupposes that there is, and requires the acceptance of, an "absolute," i.e., deontological, prohibition on harming noncombatants: All direct killing of noncombatants is unjustified. It is murder. Insofar as this principle is required by an SDS, Kavka adopts some deontological constraints on action. There are some things that can never be done, regardless of the consequences. This is a point Kavka shares with the disarmament and war-fighting parties, and is also in accordance with ordinary morality intuitions. However, Kavka introduces a normative assumption that yields a conclusion about the moral status of nuclear deterrence very different from that of the disarmers. That normative assumption states that "any system of ethics must have substantial utilitarian elements"[77] when "a great deal of utility is at stake,"[78] such as is the case in an SDS. The almost certain and very awful consequences of not taking extraordinary countermeasures against a threatened action suspend deontological principles. Why utilitarian elements ought to be brought into consideration when a "great deal of utility is at stake" is because deontological principles fail to take account of some morally important facts. For example, they ignore the disastrous consequences of not forming deterrence intentions when threatened by a nuclear-armed adversary.

The factual assumption that nuclear weapons create a rare or unique state of affairs, and the conclusion drawn from this, that in conditions of extremity certain moral rules are suspended in order to prevent massive harm, is typical of the style of thinking I have designated as deterrence-only. In this regard Kavka agrees with the French and German Catholic bishops, as well as with Walzer and those philosophers who allow exceptions to otherwise "absolutely" binding constraints. What is of great theoretical value in Kavka's analysis of an SDS coupled with his normative assumption are the paradoxes he generates from the application of three widely held moral principles.

The first paradox involves the direct denial of a simple moral doctrine, WIP: "To form the intention to do what one knows to be wrong is itself wrong." WIP says: "we regard the person who fully intends to perform a wrongful act and is prevented from doing so solely by external circumstances (e.g., a person whose murder plan is interrupted by the victim's fatal heart attack) as being just as bad as the person who performs a like wrongful act."⁷⁹   The relation of entailment between actions and intentions is said to hold also for conditional intentions. If I intend to perform an action that is wrong should certain circumstances arise, then I am culpable in the same way and degree as if I had intended the wrong whether or not my intention depends on the condition that certain circumstances arise. WIP seems to capture (i) the strong feeling that if an act is wrong, so too is the intention to perform that act, and (ii) the belief that a single principle can connect the evaluation of agents and of actions.

However, Kavka's normative assumption leads to an entirely different conclusion. When a great deal of disutility is at stake utilitarian elements ought to be brought in. That is, if you can avoid disastrous consequences, then do so. But avoiding disastrous consequences in an SDS requires forming an intention that violates WIP. This leads to the first moral paradox of deterrence. Kavka puts it as follows:

> There are cases in which, although it would be wrong for an agent to perform a certain act in a certain situation, it would nonetheless be right for that agent, knowing this, to form the intention to perform that act in that situation.⁸⁰

Accordingly, in contradiction to WIP, it is right to form the intention to retaliate in order to prevent "an extremely harmful and unjust offense," but wrong to retaliate. In 5.4 I argue that an intention to be efficacious wills not only the end, but also necessarily desires the means and other acts requisite for it. This view establishes a relation of entailment going from intention to actions that I have argued does not hold the other way around, that is, from actions to intentions (3.2).

WIP normally connects the intention of an agent with the morality of the intended act. However, and this is the crucial point in Kavka's argument, forming a deterrence intention has consequences important for human well-being independent of the intended act, and these ought to be incorporated into any morally responsible appraisal of nuclear deterrence. Kavka says, "The first paradox arises because the autonomous effects of the relevant deterrent intention are dominant in the moral analysis of an SDS, but the extremely plausible WIP ignores such effect."⁸¹   The conclusion seems to follow that the "bridge principle" connecting the evaluation of acts with that of agents is not applicable to deterrence intentions in an SDS.

Now assume that the agent who must form the conditional intention to retaliate is a rational and morally virtuous person. Is that agent able to form the required intention? Kavka says that such an agent would want to form the deterrence intention in order to prevent massive harm, but is unable to do so. This leads to a second paradox. Such an agent, he says, "is captive in the prison of his own virtue, able to form the requisite intention only by bending the bars of his cell out of shape."[82] The argument goes as follows. Anyone in an SDS has "conclusive moral reasons not to apply the sanction." Those reasons make any agent in an SDS moral. But suppose that this agent has also good reasons to form the intention to apply the sanction because forming that intention is likely to prevent massive harm. This might seem trivially true, since condition (ii) of an SDS is that a deterrent intention "would very likely deter the offense." The problem, however, is profound. In an SDS an agent has "conclusive moral reasons not to apply the sanction," but has also a second set of reasons that motivate him to form the required intention. How can a rational moral agent form an intention to apply a sanction for which he has "conclusive moral reasons not to apply"? It seems that an agent in an SDS cannot be both rational and moral. Kavka's formulation of this second paradox is:

There are situations (namely SDSs) in which it would be right for agents, if they could, to perform certain actions (namely forming the intention to apply the sanction), and in which it is possible for some agents to perform such actions, but impossible for rational and morally good agents to perform them.[83]

This paradox calls into question what Kavka refers to as the Right-Good Principle which states that "doing something is right if and only if a morally good person would do the same thing in the given situation."[84] This principle seems to be a variant of Aristotle's claim that actions are right when they are such as the good person would do.[85] Kavka says the Right-Good principle reflects widely held ideas about the close connection between right action and the goodness of persons. But in an SDS a morally good person, one who feels the force of condition (iv), might not do the right thing as required by the normative assumption, namely, form the required intention. An agent who feels the force of condition (iv) will very likely not be inclined to form the intention necessary to prevent a great harm, and according to Kavka's normative assumption this is wrong. So a morally good person fails to do the right thing. The close connection between right action and the goodness of persons is dissolved by the demands placed upon an agent in an SDS.

The third paradox is this. Wanting to do the morally right thing, a virtuous person must form an intention to do something for which he has "conclusive moral reasons" not to perform. In the act of intention-formation, he must become the kind of person to which he is strongly disinclined. He must make himself less morally good. Now if he cannot himself become that sort of person, he must create one that will form the required intention. That is, to do the right thing in an SDS the morally good person must, in the first or another future person, corrupt himself. Kavka's formulation is:

In certain situations, it would be morally right for a rational and morally good agent to deliberately (attempt to) corrupt himself.[86]

How can a morally good person do this? Isn't the case, as Aristotle would say, that a just person is just not only toward others but also toward herself? If this is so, is not the good person, by corrupting herself, acting wrongly and unjustly? The problem is that if one is justified in forming an intention that is morally required, then the morally good person would not be sacrificing her moral self-integrity in forming the intention. It seems either that our morally good person was never good, if she corrupts herself, or that she cannot act as is morally required by an SDS, that is, deliberately self-corrupt. And this is morally wrong.

The incoherence produced by the third paradox is one that calls into question what Kavka refers to as the Virtue Preservation Principle: "It is wrong to deliberately lose (or reduce the degree of) one's moral virtue."[87] While this principle seems fundamental to widely held beliefs about morality, its application to an SDS shows how ordinary morality intuitions conflict with the requirements of that situation. The principle makes it a duty to preserve one's moral virtue. But an SDS requires the agent to initiate a process that will enable her to form an intention for which she has "conclusive moral reasons" not to perform. And this intention-formation will result in moral self-corruption.

To demonstrate the incompatibility of this principle with the conditions of an SDS, Kavka asks us to imagine three agents who respond in different ways to an SDS. The first agent refuses to form the intention, and hence to corrupt himself, and allows the disastrous consequences to happen. The second agent forms the required intention and does corrupt herself. And the third agent tries but fails to corrupt himself. To none of them does corruption come easily. This is a sign that they are (or were) morally virtuous persons, but in different ways. From the point of view of the Virtue Preservation Principle, the first is praiseworthy, even if his choice results in great disaster. But we are suspect of him because "of too great a devotion to his own moral purity relative to his concern for the well-being of others."[88]   The second is culpable of acting contrary to duty, but admirable in that her choice to corrupt herself prevents disaster. The last, Kavka says, "may be admired both for his willingness to make such a sacrifice and for having virtue so ingrained in his character that his attempts at self-corruption do not succeed."[89]   Of all three, he felt the tragedy inherent in an SDS, even if he could not prevent massive harm. From Kavka's normative assumption, however, the first agent acts wrongly because he failed to perform the required act; the second acts rightly (but corrupts herself); and the last, pulled by the force of both demands, weakens his moral integrity and fails to prevent massive harm. Only the agent who failed to preserve her own virtue has done the right thing in an SDS, although she has morally corrupted herself.

It may be objected that these paradoxes depend upon some highly improbable factual conditions. Moreover, no morally good agent will put himself in a situation likely to violate the above moral principles. So, however interesting these paradoxes might be, they really do not add up to much. At least they do not come up to the conclusion Kavka wants to draw from them. But I think these objections can be met. Even if an SDS were never to exist, the fact that these paradoxes can be engendered by a hypothetical situation shows at least that the force of our ordinary morality intuitions depends on certain conditions not arising. The world must be such that it precludes the possibility of an SDS or any other similar situation. However, I argued in 5.1 that there is sufficient consensus at least among one group of just-war moralists that nuclear weapons create a condition which clashes with widely accepted moral doctrines, where what we ordinarily think is wrong—e.g., threatening the lives of civilian populations—is morally required in order to prevent a great evil. What is required to overturn the position of the deterrence-only party is either to show that the factual assumption that we live in a state of emergency is false, or that there is a moral system that can at once avoid the paradoxes of deterrence and the disaster likely to follow if one does not form deterrence intentions. I suspect that for such a system to work it would have to exclude the conviction that we ought to prevent massive harm, and hence would have little intuitive force.

That such a moral system, even if possible, is undesirable suggests that a harmony between our evaluation of agents and of acts is "shown to be untenable by the paradoxes of deterrence."[90] If this is the case, then it may well be that neither an essentially agent-centered nor outcome-centered moral system will prove tenable in conditions of emergency. Either one may well require an agent in an SDS to abandon the belief in a coherent and comprehensive moral system. For example, an SDS requires an agent-centered system which depends primarily on the internal state of an agent to incorporate intentions necessary to prevent massive harm, even if doing so is at great cost to one's moral purity. And the same situation demands an outcome-centered system seeking to perform that act with the greatest utility to form an intention the fulfillment of which would be radically unutilitarian. These incompatibilities further suggest that there are wide and deep differences between moral systems that are essentially agent-centered and those that are outcome-centered that cannot be bridged by any one set of moral doctrines or beliefs.

5.3 A DEONTOLOGICAL APPROACH: THE AMERICAN CATHOLIC BISHOPS' LETTER ON WAR AND PEACE

On 3 May 1983, after a long an unprecedented process, the American Catholic bishops issued the final version of their pastoral letter, *The Challenge of Peace: God's Promise and Our Response.* Its stated purpose is "to lift up the moral dimension of the choices [in the nuclear debate] before our world and nation" and to reflect on the global threat of nuclear war through the principles of Catholic teaching on war and peace.[91] The letter is a complex document considering the scriptural, theological, moral, political, and strategic issues that come to bear on the debate about the possession and use of nuclear weapons and the then escalating arms race between the U.S. and the former Soviet Union. The more immediate context surrounding the bishops' deliberations on this letter was the election of a rather hawkish President who held the conviction that the U.S. could achieve superiority in nuclear weapons, and seemed bent on doing so, and a Vice-President who had unequivocally stated that a nuclear war is winnable and the U.S. must prepare to fight and to win one.

The bishops' letter begins with a discussion of the meaning of deterrence in the nuclear age. As they see it, the moral problem of the nuclear age emerges from a specific factual situation. Nuclear weapons and deterrence have brought a new reality to the political and moral understanding of the just use of force, one that is exacerbated by the conditions of world affairs. In its second and third draft, as well as its final version, the overall conclusion of the letter is that the practice of nuclear deterrence has some moral justification, but only on certain limited conditions. The bishops are convinced that nuclear deterrence performs an essential task in "maintaining some sort of peace among nations."[92] But the long-term risks of maintaining deterrence are so great that we can accept this practice if and only if we simultaneously pursue serious efforts towards arms control and eventual nuclear disarmament. To evaluate this position, I raise the following questions: Is the bishops' conditional moral acceptance of nuclear deterrence logically sound? And can the conditions the bishops require of a deterrence configuration be satisfied?

I argue (i) that the bishops' conditional moral acceptance of deterrence does not follow from their premises, and (ii) that the conditions the bishops require for their acceptance of deterrence can be satisfied only by a deterrence policy that is destabilizing and further escalates the arms race. This will prove to be radically at odds with the stated moral imperative to pursue disarmament. On both counts, then, the letter will be found incoherent, unable to support the conclusion the bishops want to draw and making a much better case for why nuclear deterrence should be morally rejected.[93]

The fundamental problem with the letter is that what has been hailed as its great merit—namely, that it incorporates the diverse values present in the nuclear dilemma—is its fatal weakness. The only way I foresee for resolving the problems inherent in the letter is to reject the moral equivalence going from action to intentions. The choice then, it seems to me, is either to reject the letter because its conclusion is unsound, or to reformulate its argument by rejecting the prohibitive WIP. The latter will lead to a conclusion few if any of the bishops will accept.

On reading this letter, one is impressed with the bishops' struggle to find an acceptable moral basis for the justification of deterrence. This struggle is precipitated by three currents of thought among the American bishops that rule each other out. First, with the exception of American involvement in Vietnam, the American Catholic church has traditionally been a strong supporter of U.S. military policy. The Vatican Council, Pope Pius XII, other modern popes, the bishops of the United States, and a long tradition of Catholic social ethics have repeatedly upheld a nation's right to self-defense and its duty to maintain military forces. This right when exercised by proportionate means against an unjust aggressor is an elementary requirement of justice. In 4.2 I sketched the main lines of the argument of one of the most prominent American Catholic moral theologians, John Courtney Murray, whose position is in accordance with the historical tradition, with Augustine, Aquinas, Vitoria, Suarez, and other major Catholic theologians. To renounce the right to self-defense by not taking proportionate means constitutes not only a dereliction of political duty, but might also usher in an occasion for moral evil that allows grave disorder into the concrete circumstances of individual men and women. It would seem, therefore, that the Christian, or at least the Catholic, who espouses a doctrinal pacifism as the basis for national policy goes contrary to this requirement of justice.

Second, recent papal and episcopal statements have "firmly and unequivocally" condemned the use of nuclear weapons but allowed for their possession, yet in different ways. One permits the possession of nuclear weapons coupled with deterrence intentions, the other permits possession but prohibits those intentions. For example, despite his strong opposition to modern instruments of war, Pope John Paul II states that "in current conditions deterrence based on balance, certainly not as an end in itself but as a step on the way toward a progressive disarmament, may still be judged morally acceptable."[94] An important American episcopal statement was John Cardinal Krol's testimony before the Senate Foreign Relations Committee in support of SALT II. In his testimony Krol carried the condemnation on use to entail a negative judgment on the threat to use nuclear weapons, and concluded that possession of nuclear weapons without threat could be tolerated as the "lesser of two evils" provided that meaningful measures were also taken toward their reduction and elimination.[95] It should be noted that Krol's conclusion is rather suspect from a strategic and a moral point of view. He seems to think that one can bluff one's way into security. This view has been discredited by nearly all strategists and many moralists. Moreover, mere possession must at least be perceived by the adversary as an intention to use, the deterrent effects of which might well be wanted. Otherwise possession is pointless. As Cardinal Casaroli, the Vatican Secretary of State, said: "For to argue that the threat can be associated with a desire for their non-use would be to remove its *raison d'etre* and its power of dissuasion."[96] In 4.2 I argued that deterrent effects even if not directly intended are morally imputable.

In the second draft of the letter, the bishops acknowledge that nuclear deterrence involves an intention that is violative of the principles of discrimination and proportionality. This leads them to assert that "not only the use of strategic nuclear weapons, but also the declared intent to use them involved in our deterrence policy, are both wrong."[97] But the bishops assert that under the present state of international politics, deterrence is to be tolerated "as the lesser of two evils," provided that negotiations be pursued toward arms control and disarmament. As Krol put it: "Catholic moral teaching is willing to tolerate the possession of nuclear weapons for deterrence as the lesser of two evils."[98] That a policy considered evil, even if the "lesser of two," be "tolerated" as well as the intention to perform an act whose commission is evil was, however, unacceptable to a number of bishops.

Auxiliary Bishop Lawrence Riley of Boston, for example, charged that the reasoning leading to the toleration of a policy adjudged to be evil justifies on consequentialist grounds doing evil as a means to a good end. This mode of justification and its conclusion, Bishop Riley said, is an approach to moral theology rejected by the church. Germain Grisez, a

Catholic layman and one of the most vocal critics of the letter, gave a more detailed critique of this approach. He argued that traditionally one may tolerate another's evil so long as that evil is not part of one's intention. But no one may tolerate one's own evil. He noted that the second draft called the arms race an "objectively sinful situation," and argued that since American citizens participate in their nation's policies by voting for, or not voting against, elected officials who help maintain our policy of deterrence is to turn an objective evil into a subjective one. He said: "No matter what the bishops say or do not say about nuclear deterrence, they must not both condemn it as morally evil and approve it as tolerable."[99] Grisez, whose critique of consequentialism I rejected in 3.2, also charged that the "theology of toleration" underlying the draft even if defensible, would be very dangerous, allowing for a form of moral reasoning that would excuse "fraudulent practices" on a wide variety of cases.

Grisez's reasoning resonated with a number of bishops who were already convinced of the grave immorality of nuclear deterrence and had adopted at least a nuclear if not a doctrinal pacifism, despite the preponderance of Catholic opinion to the contrary. Bishop Gumbleton, an acknowledged pacifist and member of the *ad hoc* Bishops' Commission named by President Archbishop John Roach of Minneapolis to produce a draft on nuclear war issues, Bishop Leroy Matthiesen, Archbishop Raymond Hunthausen and 57 other bishops were then members of the Catholic peace organization, Pax Christi. These key individuals, who constitute the third and most troublesome current of thought among the bishops, argued successfully for the inclusion and strengthening of pacifist passages in the letter, without which it would have never been passed.

The influence of the pacifist bishops is evident even before the discussions on the second draft. The opening pages of the first draft of the letter convey the very strong impression that the American bishops have adopted a doctrinal pacifism, and this without any reference to the rights of individuals and the values that are at stake in war or in any single conflict between nations. This draft also contains many passages in which what traditionally have been understood as counsels of perfection for individuals are now interpreted as imperatives of nonviolence by which individuals are to evaluate the morality of their nation's policies. "Many heroic persons," the bishops say, "now live by this precept, by renouncing all violence even in personal self-defense."[100] Such interpretation, however, not only gives a wrong emphasis to the meaning of "counsels of perfection," but also is contrary to Catholic doctrine on the use of force when the common good of the political community is at stake.

There is evidence from the bishops' statements during their May, 1983 meeting in Chicago that the difference in opinion between just-war and pacifist bishops went well beyond the first and second drafts of the letter. The majority opinion wished to leave open the possibility of morally acceptable use of nuclear weapons. This possibility is described by J. Bryan Hehir, who played an instrumental role in drafting the bishops' letter, as a "centimeter [or a "sliver"] of ambiguity" about the use of nuclear weapons.[101] Cardinal Bernardin of Cincinnati, who was in charge of running the committee responsible for drafting the letter, said of the third draft that "we never say that any contemplated use of any nuclear weapon would *ipso facto* be immoral. But we are close to that position because of the severe risk factor involved."[102] During discussion on proposed amendments to the third draft, Archbishop Quinn of San Francisco, a leading nuclear pacifist, moved for the inclusion of Amendment 68 which stated that "there must be no misunderstanding of our opposition on moral grounds to any use of nuclear weapons."[103] This amendment would have decisively moved the letter to an unequivocal nuclear pacifism. Bishop Mahony thought that this position was already included in the conclusion of the letter, which called for a decisive "no" to nuclear war. So Amendment 68 passed. But aware that this conclusion was at odds with the position of Rome, Bernardin reopened the question and strongly opposed the amendment saying that "a note of ambiguity must remain" so as not to undermine the delicate argument of the letter.[104] It is an ambiguity designed to satisfy the views of Rome and of the nuclear pacifist bishops who would not have accepted any statement that gave a clear legitimacy to any use of nuclear weapons.

These three currents of thought may well have pushed a frail, or as Bernardin put it, "delicate," argument into incoherence. The effect of this diversity of opinion among the Catholic bishops is the development within the letter of two arguments radically incompatible with each other. In the final version of the letter, deterrence is given a "strictly conditioned moral acceptance" without appeal to a comparative weighing of evils or any notion of toleration. But this position is reached at great expense. Because Catholic ethics draws a moral equivalence going from action to intentions, and deterrence involves the conditional intention to use nuclear weapons, which use is judged to be morally evil, then it is wrong to intend to use them under any circumstance. The bishops say:

> No use of nuclear weapons which would violate the principles of discrimination or proportionality may be intended in a strategy of deterrence. The moral demands of Catholic teaching require resolute willingness not to intend or to do moral evil even to save our own lives or the lives of those we love.[105]

Adherence to this principle of Catholic teaching carries several important implications. First, once it has been determined that the use of nuclear weapons is violative of the principles of discrimination or proportionality, any independent consideration of the conditional intention requisite for the maintenance of a credible deterrent is ruled out. Rejected is the claim made in 5.2 that deterrence intentions though morally problematical have important autonomous effects and so ought to be assessed independent of the intentions' performance. The consequences of the intention, as distinct from the use of nuclear weapons, are for the bishops morally irrelevant to the question of deterrence. However, given the bishops' conditional moral acceptance of nuclear deterrence and their adherence to Catholic teaching on the close connection between the morality of acts and that of intentions, certain types of uses of nuclear weapons must be judged morally permissible. Here the bishops imply a principle of moral reasoning I will present in 5.4. For now suffice it to say that this principle draws a moral equivalence going from the morality of intention and that of actions. If it is permissible (because it is rational and/or moral) to form certain intentions, then to fulfill those intentions is equally permissible. Notwithstanding the bishops' implicit reliance on this principle, once they move from a consideration of "universally and binding moral principles" to prudential judgments on policy choices they fail to draw the logical conclusion of justifying, even if conditionally and despite the "sliver of ambiguity about use," the practice of deterrence, namely, the explicit acceptance of certain uses of nuclear weapons. Finally, the only deterrence intentions which are permissible to form are those which would be acceptable to carry out. This last point suggests that the bishops have adopted a form of reasoning similar to Ramsey's inference of the moral character of a deter-the-war policy from that of a fight-the-war policy. Each of these last two points suggests the real possibility of a morally acceptable use of nuclear weapons.

But there are many passages in the letter that unambiguously prohibit the use of nuclear weapons. "As a people," the bishops say, "we must refuse to legitimate the idea of nuclear war. To say no to nuclear war is both a necessary and complex task. In light of the evidence which witnesses presented and in light of our study, reflection, and consultation, we must reject nuclear war." And, "our no to nuclear war must, in the end, be definitive and decisive."[106] Now, how can one form an intention that would be permissible to carry out and at the same time reject definitively and decisively the fulfillment of the intention? Is it not senseless to say at once that one can intend and carry out an act and that one may not do either?

These questions go to the center of a major incoherence in the letter that results from the inclusion of two incompatible arguments. These are:

ARGUMENT A

1. It is an elementary requirement of justice that nations have the right to self-defense.
2. Given the present condition of world politics, practicing nuclear deterrence enables nations to exercise their right to national self-defense.
3. Practicing nuclear deterrence is necessary for national self-defense.

Therefore,

4. Nuclear deterrence is an instantiation of justice.

But,

5. Activation of the deterrent involves the killing of noncombatants, either directly or indirectly.
6. Directly killing noncombatants is proscribed by the principle of immunity.

7. The very large number of indirect civilian deaths consequent on any use of nuclear weapons is proscribed by the principle of proportionality.
8. Using nuclear weapons is wrong.
9. To form an intention (even a conditional one) for what is immoral to do is morally wrong.

Therefore,

10. We can maintain a deterrence (from 1 through 4), but we cannot threaten its use (from 5 through 9).

ARGUMENT B

1. All direct or disproportionate killing of noncombatants is wrong.
2. All foreseeable uses of nuclear weapons involve the direct or disproportionate killing of noncombatants.

Therefore,

3. All foreseeable uses of nuclear weapons are wrong.

4. To form an intention (even a conditional one) for what is immoral to do is morally wrong.
5. Deterrence involves a conditional intention to use nuclear weapons.
6. Deterrence is morally wrong.

Therefore,

7. We should disarm immediately and unilaterally (from 3 and 6).

Note that Arguments A and B have much in common. A(5) through (9) and B(1) through (5) are essentially the same. A(5) is a factual assumption about (i) the war-fighting capabilities that will be let loose once deterrence has failed and (ii) the effects upon the civilian population, namely, the direct or disproportionate killing of noncombatants. But it is a controversial assumption. It presupposes that the activation of the deterrent, even if it were of a limited nature, would be radically indiscriminate and disproportionate either in its immediate or long-term effects to any morally permissible use of force.[107] B, however, begins with the moral principle of noncombatant immunity, and then moves to the factual assumption that any foreseeable use of nuclear weapons is violative of it. It shares with A the claim that "all direct or disproportionate killing of noncombatants is wrong." B(1) and A(6) and (7), coupled with this factual assumption yield the conclusion embodied in A(8) and B(3): "using nuclear weapons is wrong." So far Arguments A and B concur.

Moreover, A(9) and B(4) adopt the principle which says that it is morally wrong to intend what is wrong to do. In the final version of the letter the bishops repeatedly appeal to the prohibitive WIP. They say: "Specifically, it is not morally acceptable to intend to kill the innocent as part of a strategy of deterring nuclear war." And, "catholic moralists have stressed that deterrence may not morally include the intention of deliberately attacking civilian populations or non-combatants."[108] Given the bishops's factual assumption about the activation of deterrence and their unhesitant adoption of the prohibitive WIP, Argument B draws the conclusion that "deterrence is morally wrong" and we ought, therefore, to disarm immediately and unilaterally. However, A only says that "we cannot threaten [the] use," of nuclear weapons but allows for the maintenance of a deterrent. Here two serious problems may be noted.

The first is obvious. A allows and B prohibits deterrence. A allows for deterrence by incorporating an argument for self-defense and the principle that permits actions the intentions of which are morally acceptable, while B, influenced by the pacifist bishops, does not. The difference seems to be the result of B's factual assumption about the nature of modern weapons, namely, that they are qualitatively different from traditional weapons and pose an unprecedented moral problem. As the letter puts it: "We live today in the midst of a cosmic drama; we possess a power which should never be used. This fact dramatizes the precariousness of our position politically, morally and spiritually."[109] In 3.1 I argued against the assumption that nuclear weapons are of a kind different from traditional weapons and claimed that this assumption leads to a contradiction for which the only foreseeable solution is to leave open the possibility for the moral use of nuclear weapons. Now it may be argued on behalf of B that "[o]ne must distinguish between the intent to use nuclear weapons and the intent to deter their use"[110] such that one should be able to possess nuclear weapons absent any intention to use them. But I have already indicated the defects in this position, the most damaging of which is that deterrent effects are morally imputable (4.2 and 4.3). Even if possession without a properly formed intention to use were possible, the problem stands. Given the weight the bishops give to Argument B and their insistent reliance on WIP—all of which lead to nuclear pacifism—the position that deterrence is conditionally morally acceptable does not follow, unless they retreat from B, which the bishops do not. In the third draft the bishops say:

> We do not perceive any situation in which the deliberate initiation of nuclear warfare, on however restricted a scale, can be morally justified. Non-nuclear attacks by another state must be resisted by other than nuclear means.[111]

That the bishops do not "perceive any situation in which [the use of nuclear weapons] can be morally justified," can only mean that deterrence has no moral justification. And this makes the bishops' acceptance of deterrence, even if conditional, logically unsound and morally unconvincing.

The second problem in the final version of the letter is more complex than the first and is internal to Argument A. It involves two contradictions. First, the evidence of the testimony the bishops cite is inconsistent with the conclusion of their argument. The bishops claim that "some important aspects of contemporary nuclear strategies move beyond the limits of moral justification. Certain aspects of both U.S. and Soviet strategies fail both tests [of discrimination and proportionality]."[112] These passages have an apparent permissiveness since not all but only "some" or "certain" aspects of deterrence strategies are morally unjustifiable. However, when the bishops consider specific examples of deterrence configurations— counterpopulation nuclear war, the initiation of nuclear war, and limited nuclear war—all fail to pass either test. One is therefore left to wonder what sort of deterrence is permitted by the bishops.

The bishops' moral condemnation of counterpopulation war is unambiguous. The principle of discrimination absolutely prohibits intentional attack upon civilians. "[U]nder no circumstances may nuclear weapons or other instruments of mass slaughter be used for the purposes of destroying population centers or other predominantly civilian targets." This condemnation extends to any retaliatory action and deterrence policy that includes direct targeting of civilian populations. "Our concern about protecting the moral value of non-combatant immunity requires that we make a clear reassertion of the principle our first word on this matter."[113]

"Specifically, it is not morally acceptable to intend to kill the innocent as part of a strategy of deterring nuclear war."[114] The initiation of nuclear war is also unequivocally rejected by the bishops. The empirical evidence they cite, based on testimony of former public officials, about the very small probability of limiting nuclear war once begun led the bishops to this conclusion. "The chances of keeping use limited seem remote and the danger of escalation is so great that it would be morally unjustifiable to initiate nuclear war in any form."[115]

One should expect that the bishops' condemnation of counterpopulation and the initiation of nuclear war coupled with their adoption of WIP extends to the rejection of both strategies as a basis of deterrence policy. Since it is immoral to engage in either kind of attack, then the intention to do so should also be immoral. Despite the evidence the bishops cite and their condemnation of nuclear war "in any form," in the section concerning the limited use of nuclear weapons in response to a nuclear attack, they say: "It would be possible to agree with our first two conclusions and still not be sure about retaliatory use of nuclear weapons in what is called a limited exchange."[116]

The bishops then go on to caution that their refusal to give an unequivocal rejection to a limited exchange does not entail a wholesale sanction of a nuclear response of that type to enemy attack. Any military response violative of the principles of discrimination and proportionality goes beyond morally acceptable defense. "Such use of nuclear weapons," they say, "would not be justified."[117] But then what kind of use of nuclear weapons and hence of deterrence intentions are justified?

The bishops do not draw out the logical conclusion of the permissive aspect of the above statement and their implicit adoption of the principle which says that if certain intentions are morally acceptable so is their fulfillment. But it is fairly clear that we can infer from the first that, in some circumstances, the bishops think nuclear weapons would not cause indiscriminate and disproportionate destruction. From the second we can infer that since one can intend a certain act then one can also perform it. These inferences coupled with the argument for a just self-defense (A(1) through (4)) enable the bishops to adhere to WIP, to judge deterrence conditionally morally acceptable, and to leave open a "centimeter of ambiguity" about the moral permissibility of recourse to some forms of nuclear force. However, this conclusion is at odds with their factual assumptions about the extreme danger of escalation once any use of nuclear weapons has begun and the evidence they cite about the uncontrolability of war.

The bishops themselves state that the evidence which has come before them from former public officials and from a study by the Pontifical Academy of Sciences convinces them not only "of the overwhelming probability that major nuclear exchange would have no limits," but also that there is "no persuasive reason to believe that any use of nuclear weapons, even on the smallest scale, could readily be expected to remain limited."[118] It is very puzzling that the bishops are first permissive on the question of "limited use" and then go on to cite studies arguing that it is very doubtful any use of nuclear weapons could remain limited, that is, within the principles of discrimination and proportionality. If the factual evidence the bishops cite is correct, or even if it is only assumed to be so, then given the probable disproportionate and indiscriminate destruction consequent on any use of nuclear weapons should persuade the bishops of the moral unacceptability of nuclear war and, by way of WIP, of deterrence. The only conclusion that follows from the bishops' premises and factual assumptions is that we ought to disarm immediately and unilaterally. Any other conclusion is a *non sequitur*.

I have argued that the bishops cannot conclude that nuclear deterrence has any moral justification. The principles they adopt coupled with their factual assumptions do not logically lead to their conclusion. I think any one who tries to arrive at a coherent position from morally incompatible points of view will encounter the same problem. I want now to turn to a second incoherence in the bishops' letter. I am going to argue that even if the bishops' reasoning were sound, the only type of deterrence that satisfies their criteria is one that will lead, far more likely than any other deterrence configuration, to instability and escalation, and this creates a woefully incoherent position. The incoherence stems from the fact that the bishops cannot accept the only type of deterrence that is compatible with the moral principles of discrimination and of proportionality.

The bishops give the following criteria that must be satisfied for any deterrence policy to be acceptable to them. I have already remarked on two of them—any use of force, nuclear or otherwise, must respect the principles of discrimination and proportionality. The third is that deterrence must be conducive to stability, and this

> depends on the ability of each side to deploy its retaliatory forces in ways that are not vulnerable to an attack (i.e., protected against a "first strike"); preserving stability requires a willingness by both sides to refrain from deploying weapons which appear to have first-strike capability.[119]

The fourth is that

> If deterrence exists only to prevent the use of nuclear weapons by others, then proposals to go beyond this to planning for prolonged periods of repeated nuclear strikes and counter-strikes, or "prevailing" in nuclear war, are not acceptable. They encourage notions that nuclear war can be engaged in with tolerable human and moral consequences. Rather, we must continue to say "no" to the idea of nuclear war.[120]

The final requirement is that "each proposed addition to our strategic system or change in the strategic doctrine must be assessed precisely in light of whether it will render steps toward progressive disarmament more or less likely."[121]

For convenience, I put these criteria into a single proposition: to be morally acceptable a deterrence configuration must (i) be compatible with the principles of discrimination and proportionality, (ii) maximize the value of stability by deploying forces that are not vulnerable to attack, (iii) discourage the idea that one side can prevail in a nuclear conflict, and (iv) vigorously move towards disarmament. Now what sort of deterrence configuration can meet all of these criteria?

A MAD (mutually assured destruction) type deterrence meets conditions (ii) through (iv). For example, if the nuclear superpowers were to deploy only a second-strike submarine-based capability, they would possess an arsenal sufficiently powerful for the purposes of deterrence that is also non-targetable.[122] Since the location of a submarine-based capability cannot be determined given the absence of adequate sonar technology, mutual deterrence of this sort precludes the dangers of possessing a vulnerable land-based system, reduces the pressures that fuel the arms race, is conducive to stability, and facilitates arms agreements. However, this system is immediately ruled out by the principles of discrimination and proportionality, which require the high accuracy of counterforce weapons. Hence it is morally unacceptable.

In 4.1 I recounted some of the debates among strategists who argued that a counterforce deterrence is morally more acceptable than one based on mutually assured destruction or massive retaliation. And in 4.2 I looked at Ramsey's moral argument for counterforce deterrence and the limited use of nuclear weapons. I concluded that this position is unconvincing because it ultimately depends on the threat of massive destruction. The bishops recognize this and other problems with a counterforce deterrence. For example, they say that the "evil and unacceptable consequences" of a counterforce nuclear strike does not by itself constitute a "moral policy for the use of nuclear weapons."[123] They also acknowledge that a counterforce deterrence makes nuclear war more likely, threatens the viability of other nations' retaliatory forces, furthers the arms race, and lessens the probability of a stable international order.[124] The objective of a counterforce deterrence is not only to provide a set of options from which the President can choose at a time of crisis, but also to render an adversary's nuclear and conventional forces ineffective and to limit damage to one's side. One effect of developing a counterforce deterrence is that it gives an adversary every reason to develop similar nuclear forces limited only by what technology is unable to provide. It was for these, as well as for other similar reasons, that McNamara, shortly after his Ann Arbor speech, turned away from his initial counterforce strategy.

If neither a MAD nor a counterforce deterrence strategy is capable of satisfying the bishops' criteria, then it seems that no available deterrence posture can do so. The categorical principle of discrimination does not permit the bishops to accept a MAD-type deterrence, even if one could be deployed which satisfies the other three. We are left then only with a counterforce deterrence. While this type of deterrence is initially morally attractive, insofar as it respects the categorical principle of discrimination, it has the very serious defect that of all possible types of deterrence it is the most unstable and dangerous. It is therefore hard to see how any conclusion other than a complete rejection of nuclear deterrence is possible. The bishops' letter has made a convincing argument, to be sure. But it is an argument for nuclear pacifism, rather than for a "strictly conditional moral acceptance of deterrence." It may well be that any moral theory that endorses a categorical prohibition, no matter what comes, will fail to salvage the institution of nuclear deterrence. This failure might be considered to be special, arising only for the institution of deterrence. I suspect, however, that the inability of a deontological system to justify deterrence illustrates an important point about the scope and limitation of moral principles.[125]

A moral principle, say, the categorical prohibition on directly killing civilians, or the prohibitive WIP, selects from the whole of available facts some types of information and excludes others. It excludes, for example, the type of information about possible consequences that an outcome-centered system considers morally decisive—most notably, the conviction that we ought to prevent great evils from happening. To say that a deontological system excludes this type of information means that certain facts are not permitted to have any influence on our judgments about what ought to be done in a particular circumstance. The American Catholic bishops are insistent that "the lives of innocent persons may never be directly taken [or threatened], regardless of the purpose for doing so. Just response to aggression must be discriminate."[126] If it turns out that a nuclear deterrence cannot satisfy that requirement, it must therefore be rejected, regardless of the consequences that follow. A deontological or agent-centered moral system imposes universally binding constraints on what we can morally do to others. It therefore cannot take into consideration a comparative evaluation of outcomes under different policy alternatives.

But it should be clear form my remarks above that the bishops depart from their own categorical prohibition by allowing, even if only provisionally, a policy of nuclear deterrence. And there lies the source of the letter's incoherence. If, on the other hand, the bishops had adhered strictly to the categorical prohibition, they would have produced a coherent position, but without any justification for deterrence. Or they could have adjusted their categorical prohibition on intentions by incorporating another prohibition, this one on unintended consequences. The possibility they could entertain is of a moral absolutism that ranges widely over both intended and unintended events. When the latter is very large this principle would say that one ought to prevent great evils from happening. To incorporate this principle, however, requires the bishops to adopt at least an outcome-sensitive system.

In chapter 2 I argued that political morality sometimes requires the removal or suspension of deontological constraints on what we do to others, and the adoption of an outcome-centered morality. The bishops could retain the principle of discrimination as a categorical prohibition and still justify some form of nuclear deterrence by rejecting the prohibitive WIP. Deterrence intentions could thereby be justified as the best available means for avoiding adverse consequences and securing those ends that a state is duty bound to protect. What is entailed in justifying deterrence intentions is the subject of the following section.

5.4 INTENTIONS AND ACTIONS RECONSIDERED: THE RIGHTFUL ACTION PRINCIPLE (RAP)

My discussion in this chapter has focused on the way deterrence-only moralists link judgments on use and on deterrence. WIP, which establishes a moral equivalence going from action to intentions, prohibits any intention the fulfillment of which is morally impermissible. I have shown in this and in earlier chapters that deontologists and consequentialists alike adopt this principle. One might say that this principle is neutral with regard to the variety of ethical systems available in the literature. So its acceptance is, one can safely say, fairly wide.

But I have also argued against the soundness of WIP when applied to nuclear deterrence. Two reasons were given. First, in 3.2, I argued that WIP is insufficient to yield a conclusive condemnation of nuclear deterrence. There I took advantage of a distinction between the absolute and *prima facie* wrongness of an act, and went on to say that when an act is only *prima facie* wrong it may still be morally permissible, all things considered. This distinction allowed me to question the relation of entailment between action and intentions presupposed by WIP. And in 5.2, I presented Kavka's very plausible argument that when intentions have important autonomous consequences, they ought to be appraised

THE DETERRENCE-ONLY PARTY

independently of the intended act. This argument led Kavka to doubt some of our moral beliefs about (or bridge principles that link) our evaluation of agents and of acts.

In this section I am going to suggest that if it is morally permissible to form a conditional intention, then it might also be permissible to fulfill that intention, should the relevant conditions arise. The point is small but carries important implications. I will assume that deterrence can be given a plausible moral justification—e.g., of the kind that Kavka advances. If this is unsatisfactory, then one has only to imagine that deterrence might enjoy some moral justification. The question I explore is: what does it mean to say that deterrence intentions are (or might be) morally permissible?

First I restate the paradox of deterrence. The best way of dissuading someone from doing something one wishes to prevent is to threaten retaliation, should that something occur. Bluffs, idle threats, and the like do not count. And this for at least two reasons. First, in 4.2, I argued that possession of a nuclear arsenal without intention to use, or, as Ramsey puts it, "*praeter intentionem*," nonetheless carries an intention to create in an adversary the fear of widespread collateral damage. Otherwise possession would be pointless. This intention (in what I called its "weak" sense) is morally imputable. And second, if we accept the elements in Kavka's description of an SDS, we must assume that "one must intend (conditionally) to apply a harmful sanction to innocent people, if an extremely harmful and unjust offense is to be prevented."[127] There are other, strategic reasons why the argument from bluff does not count. But I do not need to rehearse these to make my point. Assume, then, that for a successful deterrence, one has to form a genuine intention to retaliate because it is the best way of preventing great harm.

Yet it may also be that should the occasion to employ the deterrent arise, one would have compelling reasons not to employ it, either because it would be morally wrong or no good purpose would be achieved. Thus it seems that while forming a genuine intention to retaliate is just, it would be unjust to make good on the intention. That is the paradox of deterrence. To resolve the paradox one might adopt any of the following positions centered on WIP: reject possession altogether, as does the disarmament party; form only those intentions that would be morally permissible to perform and assume a war-fighting position; or, finally, reject the moral equivalence going from action to intentions (i.e., WIP and similar principles) and point to a crisis of moral reason, as do some deterrence-only moralists.

There is, however, another response. One could draw a relation that moves from the permissibility of intention to that of actions. R. B. Brandt has explored that relation. He says: "a deterrence is of great importance; having the deterrence requires willingness to employ it; therefore, employment is morally justified in the total circumstances."[128] How Brandt moves from deterrence to its employment is not clear. But I will take him to mean that if deterrence is morally important and justified, then one thing we are committed to is that we should be willing to employ it, should certain conditions arise.

Brandt's reasoning has recently been challenged by Ian Clark. He rejects Brandt's derivation of the permissibility of an action (employing the deterrence) from the permissibility of the antecedent intention or threat because, Clark says, it involves "a serious chronological confusion." "It seems to deduce the ethical status of the act from the ethical necessity of the threat."[129] Clark's point seems to be that if one is ever in a position to consider executing the threat (i.e., employing the deterrent), deterrence has already presumably failed. So the question about the rightness of use cannot be determined by the permissibility of the antecedent intention.

There is, I think, something right in Clark's point. If all one means to do by retaliating is to show that deterrence was not a bluff, then there is really no sense in employing the deterrent since its conditions no longer obtain. It is simply too late to show here and now that deterrence was not a bluff then and there. It would be a senseless and brutal act of vengeance to employ the deterrent. But I think Clark misses the force in Brandt's formulation of the relation (or moral equivalence) going from intention to actions, namely: if an intention to perform a certain act is justified, then performing that act is also justified.

An intention is different from other mental acts—like wanting and wishing—in that it is a commitment to act in certain ways under specific conditions. A person who forms an intention is, of course, free to change her mind or to form other intentions. It may well be that an intention is never carried out because the conditions for its realization did not arise or the act to which one commits oneself cannot morally be done. Either way, intentions can be the subject of moral evaluation, and we can determine whether a given intention is morally justified. Suppose that forming the intention to retaliate, should certain conditions arise, is justified for the sake of deterrence, then it seems that retaliating, when those conditions arise, is justified.

What is interesting about this relation is that the objections I have noted against the moral equivalence going from actions to intention (i.e., WIP) are not relevant here. The main point against WIP is that when an intention has important autonomous consequences, it ought to be judged independently of the morality of the intended action. But if we think of the moral equivalence of actions and intentions as one that begins with the latter, then WIP and its objections have nothing to contribute to the moral evaluation of the practice of deterrence and retaliation. What counts is this: if in order to deter I have to form a genuine intention to retaliate, and that intention is morally just, then it is morally permissible (although not obligatory) to fulfill the intention. This is, I think, the force of Brandt's derivation of actions from intentions. Call this thesis the Rightful Actions Principle (RAP). RAP says: if an intention is right (because it is moral or rational to form it), then performing the intended act is also (morally or rationally) legitimate.

David Gauthier has advanced a variant of RAP.[130] Very roughly, Gauthier argues that if you "implant an intention in yourself," you must also form in yourself a desire that would motivate and make it instrumentally rational for you to fulfill the intention. Note these two distinct phases of the act. The first is the act of will directed towards a particular end. This act requires deterrence intentions to be committed to retaliation, should certain conditions arise. Any deterrence intention that is not genuinely committed to retaliation would be mere bluff, and hence would be discounted. Though an act of will is necessary, it is insufficient for a genuine deterrence intention. Hence a condition is required to guarantee the genuineness of that intention needed to deter. This is an act by which one forms in oneself a desire that would motivate one to fulfill the intention.

Gauthier's route to RAP, however, is much more complex than this. He wants to defend the rationality of deterrence and of nuclear retaliation.

The structure of his argument is this: "[1] it may be utility maximizing to form the nonsubmissive, retaliatory intention; [2] therefore it may be rational to form such an intention; [3] if it is rational to form the intention it is rational to act on the intention; [4] therefore a rational person can sincerely express the intention; [5] therefore another rational and informed person can be deterred by the expression of the intention."[131]

There is nothing novel about [1] and [2]. They are already conventional wisdom and form the basis of the deterrence-only position. What makes Gauthier's argument unique are steps [3]-[5]. To clear the way for these, Gauthier does two things. First he introduces a terminological distinction: deterrence success is not having to face a nuclear strike by an opposing nation; deterrence failure is being faced with such a strike and being committed to a retaliatory response; and nondeterrence is having to face a nuclear strike without having formed a genuine deterrence intention. And second, Gauthier refutes the claim that deterrence is irrational because carrying out the threat to retaliate is not utility maximizing. The problem with this claim, he maintains, is that it rejects deterrence because of the great costs of deterrence failure. But if one incorporates the costs of deterrence failure into the benefits of deterrence success, and the latter proves to be of greater value than the former, then deterrence can be said to be utility maximizing, i.e., rational. Gauthier says:

> The utility cost of acting on the deterrent intention enters, with appropriate probability weighing, into determining whether it is rational to form the intention. But once this is decided, the costs of acting on the intention does not enter again into determining whether, if deterrence fails, it is rational to act on it.[132]

Gauthier's point is that the rationality of deterrence partly depends on the costs or disutilities of the intended act, namely: retaliating. If despite those costs deterrence is judged to be rational, because it is utility maximizing, then, should it fail, no further considerations are necessary but to retaliate. So, Gauthier's argument hinges on incorporating the costs of deterrence failure into the appraisal of forming deterrence intention.

Let me illustrate the point with an example Gauthier gives.[133] He asks us to imagine a university professor, B, in Boston who is offered a teaching post in Dallas. His spouse, A, wishes to deter him from accepting that position. Dallas is not her kind of city. And she would have to give up her relations along with many projects important to her. In an attempt to dissuade him from accepting the appointment, she tells him that she will leave him if he goes, even though she prefers to go with him to Dallas. Assume that there is a 70 percent chance (or .7 probability) that B will stay in Boston and a 30 percent chance (or .3 probability) that he will go. So there is a pretty good chance that she will not have to leave him, although there is a chance she will have to do so. Assume further that A thinks there is a 50 percent chance (or .5 probability) that B will accept the offer if she goes with him, but only a 10 percent chance (or .1 probability) if she doesn't. This latter set of probabilities is important because deterrence is an interactive situation in which an individual is affected by the beliefs and expectations she has on what the other will do in the relevant situation. The minimum required probability for the success of A's wishes is the 70 percent chance that B will stay. All A has to do then is to adopt a course of action that gains an advantage on this already present likelihood. If A forms a deterrence intention she increases the chances of B staying in town. The probability estimates based on A's calculations are: (.5-.1)/.5 which equals .8. Hence A maximizes her expected utility (.8 > .7) by forming a deterrence intention, and deterrence proves to be the rational thing to do.

Now consider a nuclear deterrence policy. Let us assume the following ranking of preferences for two nations, A and B. A prefers to suffer no strike than to suffer a strike, and prefers no retaliation to suffering a strike and then retaliating. Why no strike is preferable to strike is obvious; the second preference can follow from different sources—e.g., likelihood of escalation, the wish to minimize expected damage, among others. B, however, has the following preferences: to inflict a strike and suffer no retaliation is preferable to no strike, and no strike is preferable to strike and retaliation. B's first preference follows from its desire to get things its way, and the second follows from its wishes to minimize damage to itself, assuming that retaliation by A would be more than the nuclear equivalent of a shot across the bow.

In this treatment of nuclear deterrence, nation B corresponds to the husband whose spouse, A, seeks to dissuade him from an unwanted action. There are at least two important structural similarities in these examples. First, A wants to deter B from doing something undesirable to A—going to Dallas in the first, and inflicting a nuclear strike in the second. And second, by forming a deterrence intention A effects a decrease in the likelihood of having to face an unwanted action by B. Put another way, by forming a deterrence intention A maximizes expected utility. Hence to form the conditional intention to retaliate is the rational thing to do. This satisfies steps [1] and [2] in Gauthier's argument.

But showing that a deterrence intention is utility-maximizing does not yet show how acting on an intention that is nonmaximizing is rational. How can a nonmaximizing response be utility maximizing? Consider step [3] of Gauthier's argument. It says, "if it is rational to form the intention it is rational to act on it." Steps [1] and [2] have already shown why it would be rational to form the intention. Simply put: deterrence intentions are utility-maximizing. So the "if" clause in step [3] has been satisfied. Now it has to be decided whether acting on the intention is also utility-maximizing. To understand how this may be, we need to consider deterrence as an interactive situation. In an interactive deterrence situation, both nations involved, A and B, take into account their beliefs about what the other will do. B's beliefs about how A will act affects B's willingness to face A with having to choose between suffering a strike and not retaliating. If B believes that A is committed to retaliation, should B attack, then B's actions are affected by A's anticipated response. B, if it is rational at all, would under these circumstances choose its second preference, namely, no strike is preferable to strike and retaliation. And so B is successfully deterred.

Note that what deters B is not A's preference ranking. Let us assume that B is ignorant of this. Rather what deters B from taking an advantage over A is B's belief that A will, or may, resort to a nonmaximizing action. Hence forming a genuine intention to retaliate, that is, to act on the intention should the occasion arise, is the rational thing to do. Now, A knowing that B's beliefs have a deterrent effect and wanting to deter B from an unwanted action then forms the intention to retaliate, should B strike. Or, at any rate, A's adoption of an intention that would (otherwise) be nonmaximizing is the only way of increasing B's belief that A will, or may, resort to retaliation. Gauthier says: "[A] can hope to deter only if the other believes that [A] will, or at least may, make the nonmaximizing response. And adopting a genuine policy of deterrence may be the only way of bringing about that belief. Even in this one-shot situation, a deterrent policy, committing one to a nonmaximizing choice should deterrence fail, may be utility maximizing."[134] In this way committing oneself to a nonmaximizing action may be utility maximizing and "a rational person can sincerely express the intentions" (step [4]).

The final step follows. Since B believes that A might resort to a nonmaximizing action, and it is rational for A to commit itself to this action, should certain conditions arise, and A also sincerely expresses a retaliatory intention, B, being rational and informed of these facts, chooses its second preference, namely, no strike is preferable to strike and retaliation. And this satisfies the requirement for deterrence success.

Deterrence-only moralists claim that possession of nuclear weapons for the purpose of deterring a similarly armed adversary is, under present conditions, justified. But there is no moral justification for the use of nuclear weapons. I have argued in this chapter that this view presents a disturbing moral condition. We threaten to do something which cannot morally be done. However, RAP exploits the deterrers' position and exposes two serious defects in it. First, deterrence-only moralists begin their appraisal of nuclear arms policy in the wrong place. Like Ramsey and nuclear disarmers, they assume that if an act is impermissible, so too is the intention to carry out that act. But unlike Ramsey and the disarmers, deterrence-only moralists find morally compelling reasons to intend what cannot be done. Yet if we invert the equivalence of actions and intention and begin our appraisal of nuclear arms policy with the latter, RAP yields a deterrence with retaliatory features that may morally and sincerely be intended. And second, deterrence-only moralists fail to recognize that deterrence is an interactive situation where what deters, in the first instance, is not what a deterrence policy means to do or not to do, but the adversary's beliefs. Hence incorporating those beliefs into one's deterrence policy—i.e., an adversary's belief that one will in fact retaliate—may be utility-maximizing. If RAP is correct, then deterrence-only moralists must either abandon deterrence because it justifies the use of nuclear weapons, or modify their conclusion—the use of nuclear weapons is immoral except as a consequence of a rational intention to deter another's immoral act. An immoral act can therefore be right when it springs from a rational intention.

The world of sovereign nation-states is in at least one limited but important way analogous to domestic life. It is an interactive and cooperative scheme for mutual benefit. Even when I am insufficiently motivated to cooperate—because under certain circumstances self-interest may seem to yield a desired short-term benefit—I may want a long-term benefit that depends on the cooperation of all. If I truly want that benefit and can be assured that others will cooperate, it would be reasonable for me to forego noncooperative action. Nuclear weapons are not likely to disappear. Nor is it realistic to think that nations will disarm, even if a new world order appears. The most we can do is to reduce the likelihood that these weapons will be put to use. The best way of doing so is to assure a potential adversary that the costs of noncooperation are woefully disproportionate to any action whose performance tries to render others worse off than acting otherwise.

This is merely a footnote to ancient Roman wisdom: *si vis pacem, para bellum*. I am puzzled why this paradoxical admonition is not more frequently dismissed. When put alongside other pieces of conventional wisdom it appears as a foolish contradiction. Perhaps this paradox is not more frequently dismissed because in some manner we recognize that a logic quite different from the ordinary one is at work in the justification and practice of war.[135] I think this is true. I also think that some of the moral ideas by which we assess the preparation for and waging of modern war have not been sufficiently adjusted to the confounding logic of nuclear strategy. One piece of ordinary moral reason that cannot stand under the pressures of modern deterrence is the equivalence we typically draw between actions and intentions. RAP seems better suited to our predicament than WIP, if only because it gives us a moral perspective on a practice that increases the probability of deterring a nuclear-armed adversary significantly more than it increases the probability of nuclear war.

A defender of WIP will say that to intend what is immoral to do is itself immoral. If nuclear deterrence intentions are of this kind, then all I have shown is the inherent wickedness of modern war. In general, if a deterrence policy, counterforce or not, requires an intention (in the weak sense) to threaten civilian life, then it involves a commitment to murderous action, even when what is intended (in the strong sense) is permitted by the rules of civilized warfare. Since one cannot intend (in either sense) what is immoral to do, deterrence is to be rejected. We should then immediately and unilaterally disarm.

However, I argued that one cannot draw this conclusion on the basis of WIP: forming an intention is itself an act and may be appraised independently of the intended action. This point is especially important when intentions have important consequences. Having rejected WIP, I introduced a second principle of moral reason, namely, RAP. This principle establishes the moral equivalence between actions and intentions (i.e., WIP) on different grounds. On this second way of understanding the equivalence of actions and intentions, we derive the morality of actions from that of the corresponding intentions. It is an important question whether the applicability of RAP is restricted to nuclear deterrence intentions or has a much broader range. If the former, then we know WIP is limited to nondeterrence situations. But if it is the case that RAP is a wide-ranging moral principle, then we know at least two things. First, our conventional beliefs about the relation of actions and intentions are in some real way mistaken and in need of repair. And second, that no one single principle can connect the different ways in which the morality of actions and intentions may be related to each other.

It needs to be pointed out, however, that once it is determined that a certain act (mental or physical) is the rational thing to do, one still has to determine whether that act is the morally right thing to do. A policy of deterrence requires that we do many things—e.g., that we mine uranium, appropriate money for research, development, manufacture, and stockpiling of nuclear weapons, that we train personnel, as well as form intentions here and now about what we will do in the future, should certain conditions arise. All of these activities which we undertake for the sake of deterrence depend on one's present beliefs and values. One belief about the importance of deterrence is that it dissuades an adversary from attack. In 3.3. I present the fallacy of thinking that deterrence works in just that way. There is also the possibility that one's beliefs and values will change, so that one would not make the commitment to retaliate. In that case, all the activities we undertake for the sake of deterrence might turn out to be neither rational nor moral.

It must also be pointed out that one function of morality is to set constraints on what we may do to others, whether what one does is justified on the basis of preference maximization, national self-defense, or protection of a way of life. If one takes the view that we should be able to justify what we do to those whose interests and lives are adversely affected by our actions, then the crucial question is this: Can we justify to the citizens of an adversarial state the threat to their interests and lives that is essential to deterrence?

There are cases in which the justification for threatening retaliation is obvious. For example, a person is entitled to use or threaten force against an aggressor. But there are limits to the force one may use against an aggressor and to the targets one can choose. I may not threaten your child to protect myself from your aggression. Yet a policy of deterrence requires somewhere along the line that we move from counterforce and other military targets to the urban, industrial, and civilian sectors of society—from the very agents of aggression to those persons (the aggressor's children) who are outside the chain of aggression. The justification of such policy might seem reasonable when addressed to the citizens of the defending nation, that is, the members of one's own moral community. But it will be terribly unreasonable to members of the threatened nation that we aim to bring about their death as a means to secure our own interests. And that, it seems to me, is just what deterrence intentions do.

NOTES

1. Quoted in Maurice Merleau-Ponty, *Humanism and Terror*, trans. John O'Neil, (Boston: Beacon Press, 1969), xli.
2. The Pastoral Letter of the American Catholic Bishops is discussed in 5.3. It should be noted that this letter disagrees with those of the French and German bishops in several important respects, the most important of which is "that it is not morally acceptable to intend to kill the innocent as part of a strategy of deterring nuclear war." National Conference of Catholic Bishops, *The Challenge of Peace: God's Promise and Our Response* (Washington, DC: United States Catholic Conference, 1983), par. 178.
3. Joint Pastoral Letter of the French Bishops, "Winning the Peace," trans. Michael Wren, in James V. Schall, *Bishops' Pastoral Letters* (San Francisco, CA: Ignatius Press, 1984), par. 5.
4. French Bishops, "Winning," par. 20.
5. French Bishops, "Winning," par. 9.
6. French Bishops, "Winning," par. 20.
7. French Bishops, "Winning," par. 26.
8. French Bishops, "Winning," par. 30.n.21.
9. French Bishops, "Winning," par. 66.
10. Joint Pastoral Letter of the West German Bishops, "Out of Justice, Peace," trans. Irish Messenger Publications, in Schall, *Pastoral Letters*, par. 2.
11. W. German Bishops, "Out of Justice," par. 92.
12. W. German Bishops, "Out of Justice," par. 152.
13. W. German Bishops, "Out of Justice," par. 106.
14. W. German Bishops, "Out of Justice," par. 15.
15. See W. German Bishops, "Out of Justice," pars. 113, 115, 124, 131.
16. W. German Bishops, "Out of Justice," par. 153.
17. David Hollenbach, "Ethics in Distress: Can There Be Just Wars in the Nuclear Age?" in William V. O'Brien and John Langan, eds., *The Nuclear Dilemma and the Just War Tradition* (Lexington, MA: Lexington Books, 1986), 13.
18. Michael Walzer, *Just and Unjust Wars* (New York: Basic Books, 1977), 282.
19. Walzer, *Unjust Wars*, 274.
20. Richard B. Miller, *Interpretations of Conflict: Ethics, Pacifism, and the Just-War Tradition* (Chicago: University of Chicago Press, 1991), 189.
21. Walzer, *Unjust Wars*, xvi.
22. Walzer, *Unjust Wars*, 326.
23. Walzer, *Unjust Wars*, 262.
24. Hollenbach, "Ethics in Distress," 13.

25. Walzer, *Unjust Wars*, 254.

26. Much of this section depends on my "Heaven's Fall: Michael Walzer on Killing the Innocent," *International Journal of Applied Philosophy*, 8, no. 1 (Summer 1993), 57-63.

27. Quoted in Michael Walzer, *Unjust Wars*, 245.

28. Walzer, *Unjust Wars*, 253.

29. See Walzer, *Unjust Wars*, 144-151 and 239-242.

30. Walzer, *Unjust Wars*, 253.

31. Walzer, *Unjust Wars*, 258.

32. Walzer, "World War II: Why This War Was Different," in Marshall Cohen, Thomas Nagel, Thomas Scanlon, eds., *War and Moral Responsibility* (Princeton: Princeton University Press, 1974), 103.

33. Hollenbach, "Ethics in Distress," 16.

34. Stephen E. Lammers, "Area Bombing in World War II: The Argument of Michael Walzer," *Journal of Religious Ethics*, 11 (1983), 108.

35. Walzer, *Unjust Wars*, 323.

36. Walzer, *Unjust Wars*, 51.

37. Walzer, *Unjust Wars*, 54.

38. Walzer, *Unjust Wars*, 53.

39. Walzer, *Unjust Wars*, 54.

40. Walzer, *Unjust Wars*, 53.

41. Walzer, *Unjust Wars*, 51.

42. Walzer, *Unjust Wars*, 54.

43. Walzer, *Unjust Wars*, 54.

44. Walzer, "The Moral Standing of States," in Charles R. Beitz, Marshall Cohen, Thomas Scanlon, and A. John Simmons, eds., *International Ethics* (Princeton: Princeton University Press, 1985), 219.

45. Walzer, *Unjust Wars*, 53.

46. Walzer, "Moral Standing," 220.

47. Walzer, "Moral Standing," 222.

48. Walzer, "Moral Standing," 233.

49. Walzer, *Unjust Wars*, 87.

50. Walzer, *Unjust Wars*, 231.

51. Walzer, "Political Action: The Problem of Dirty Hands," in Marshall Cohen, Thomas Nagel, and Thomas Scanlon, *War and Moral Responsibility*, 73.

52. Walzer, "Moral Standing," 222.

53. Walzer, "Moral Standing," 224.

54. Gerald Doppelt, "Statism Without Foundations," *Philosophy and Public Affairs* 9 (1980), 400.

55. Walzer, *Unjust Wars*, xvi.

56. Walzer, *Unjust Wars*, 54.

57. Walzer, "Moral Standing," 234.

58. Walzer, "Moral Standing," 234.

59. Walzer, *Unjust Wars*, 259.

60. Walzer, *Unjust Wars*, 260.

61. Walzer, "Emergency Ethics," ms., n.d., 20.

62. Walzer, "Emergency Ethics," 25.

63. Walzer, *Just and Unjust Wars*, 51.

64. Walzer, "Emergency," 25.

65. Walzer, *Unjust Wars*, 324.

66. Walzer, *Unjust Wars*, 325.

67. Walzer, *Unjust Wars*, 323.

68. Walzer, *Unjust Wars*, 268.

69. Robert A. Levine, *The Arms Debate* (Cambridge: Harvard University Press, 1963), 35.

70. Gregory S. Kavka, *Moral Paradoxes of Nuclear Deterrence* (Cambridge: Cambridge University Press, 1987), 65.

71. Kavka, *Moral Paradoxes*, 68. Kavka's factual assumptions about the deter-or-disarm choice and the applicability of the Disaster Avoidance Principle treated below have been challenged by Douglas Lackey, *Moral Principles and Nuclear Weapons* (Totowa, NJ: Rowman & Allanheld, 1984), and Jefferson McMahan, "Nuclear Deterrence and Future Generations," in Avner Cohen and Steven Lee, eds., *Nuclear Weapons and the Future of Humanity* (Totowa, NJ: Rowman & Allanheld, 1986). Since my purpose in this section is limited to the presentation of a utilitarian argument for deterrence-only, I do not consider these or other criticism of Kavka's position. But the reader is urged to consult the above sources.

72. Kavka, *Moral Paradoxes*, 66.

73. Kavka, *Moral Paradoxes*, 62, 64.

74. For similar conclusions see David Hollenbach, *Nuclear Ethics* (New York: Paulist Press, 1983), 74: "The real question for moral judgment is whether a concrete strategic option will actually make the world more secure from nuclear disaster or less so"; and The Harvard Nuclear Study Group, *Living With Nuclear Weapons* (New York: Bantam Books, 1983), 15: "[I]t would be difficult to argue that taking a small risk of nuclear war would not be justified for the goal of preventing an even larger risk of nuclear war."

75. Kavka, *Moral Paradoxes*, 15.

76. Kavka, *Moral Paradoxes*, 17.

77. Kavka, *Moral Paradoxes*, 17.

78. Kavka, *Moral Paradoxes*, 17.

79. Kavka, *Moral Paradoxes*, 19.

80. Kavka, *Moral Paradoxes*, 19.

81. Kavka, *Moral Paradoxes*, 21.

82. Kavka, *Moral Paradoxes*, 21.

83. Kavka, *Moral Paradoxes*, 24.

84. Kavka, *Moral Paradoxes*, 24.

85. Aristotle, *Nicomachean Ethics*, 1105b5.

86. Kavka, *Moral Paradoxes*, 25.

87. Kavka, *Moral Paradoxes*, 27-8.

88. Kavka, *Moral Paradoxes*, 28.

89. Kavka, *Moral Paradoxes*, 28.

90. Kavka, *Moral Paradoxes*, 31.

91. National Conference of Catholic Bishops, *Challenge of Peace*, vii.

92. Vatican II, *Pastoral Constitution on the Church in the Modern World*, quoted in National Conference of Catholic Bishops, *Challenge of Peace*, par. 167.

93. Much of the argument of this section is derived from the following sources: Joseph M. Boyle, "The Challenge of Peace and the Morality of Nuclear Deterrence," in Charles J. Reid, Jr., ed., *Peace in a Nuclear Age* (Washington, D.C.: Catholic University of America Press, 1986), 323-335; Susan Moller Okin, "Taking the Bishops Seriously," *World Politics* 36 (1984), 527-554; and Norbert Rigali, "Just War and Pacifism," *America* (31 March 1984), 233-236.

94. Pope John Paul II, "Message to U.N. Special Session on Disarmament," #8, June, 1982. Quoted in National Conference of Catholic Bishops, *Challenge of Peace*, iii.

95. John Cardinal Krol, "Testimony Before the Senate Foreign Relations Committee, September 6, 1979," in Robert Heyer, ed., *Nuclear Disarmament: Key Statements of Popes, Bishops, Councils, and Churches* (New York: Paulist Press, 1982), 10.

96. Cardinal Casaroli, in *L'Osservatore Romano* (Eng. ed.) 17 March, 1986, 12.

97. National Conference of Catholic Bishops, *War and Peace*, second draft of a proposed pastoral letter on war, armaments, and peace, special supplement to *The Chicago Catholic*, 1982, 9A.

98. Quoted in "New Draft of Pastoral Letter. The Challenge of Peace: God's Promise and Our Response," *Origins NC Documentary Service* 12, 20 (October 28, 1982), 317.

99. Grisez is quoted in Jim Castelli, *The Bishops and the Bomb: Waging Peace in a Nuclear Age* (Garden City, New York: Doubleday, 1983), 102-104.

100. First Draft, 9.

101. J. Bryan Hehir, "Moral Issues in Deterrence Policy," in Douglas MacLean, ed., *The Security Gamble* (Totowa, NJ: Rowman & Allanheld, 1984), 60, 68.

102. Quoted in Castelli, *Bishops*, 148.

103. Castelli, *Bishops*, 169.

104. Castelli, *Bishops*, 170.

105. National Conference of Catholic Bishops, *Challenge of Peace*, iii-iv.

106. National Conference of Catholic Bishops, *Challenge of Peace*, pars. 131, 132, 138.

107. National Conference of Catholic Bishops, *Challenge of Peace*, pars. 157-161.

108. National Conference of Catholic Bishops, *Challenge of Peace*, par. 178, 169.

109. National Conference of Catholic Bishops, *Challenge of Peace*, par. 124.

110. David Hollenbach, *Nuclear Ethics*, 73.

111. National Conference of Catholic Bishops, *Challenge of Peace*, par. 150.

112. National Conference of Catholic Bishops, *Challenge of Peace*, par. 144.

113. National Conference of Catholic Bishops, *Challenge of Peace*, pars. 147, 149.

114. National Conference of Catholic Bishops, *Challenge of Peace*, par. 178.

115. National Conference of Catholic Bishops, *Challenge of Peace*, par. 152.

116. National Conference of Catholic Bishops, *Challenge of Peace*, par. 157.

117. National Conference of Catholic Bishops, *Challenge of Peace*, par. 160.

118. National Conference of Catholic Bishops, *Challenge of Peace*, par. 165. The bishops here cite M. Bundy, G.F. Kennan, R.S. McNamara and G. Smith, "Nuclear Weapons and the Atlantic Alliance," *Foreign Affairs* 60 (1982), 757.

119. National Conference of Catholic Bishops, *Challenge of Peace*, par. 163.

120. National Conference of Catholic Bishops, *Challenge of Peace*, par. 188 (1).

121. National Conference of Catholic Bishops, *Challenge of Peace*, par. 188 (1).

122. See Herbert Scoville, *MX: Prescription for Disaster* (Cambridge: MIT Press, 1981), especially chapter 17, "A Sea-Based Alternative."

123. National Conference of Catholic Bishops, *Challenge of Peace*, par. 181.

124. National Conference of Catholic Bishops, *Challenge of Peace*, pars. 183, 184.

125. For the informational analysis of moral principles, see Amartya Sen, "Well-Being, Agency and Freedom. The Dewey Lectures, 1984," *Journal of Philosophy* LXXXII, no. 4 (April 1985), and "Rights and Agency," *Philosophy and Public Affairs* 11, no. 1 (Winter 1982).

126. National Conference of Catholic Bishops, *Challenge of Peace*, par. 104.

127. Gregory Kavka, *Moral Paradoxes*, 17.

128. R. B. Brandt, "When is it Morally Permissible to Use Tactical Nuclear Weapons?" *Parameters* (Sept. 1981), 78.

129. Ian Clark, *Waging War: A Philosophical Introduction* (Oxford: Clarendon Press, 1988), 127.

130. David Gauthier, "Deterrence, Maximization, and Rationality," *Ethics* 94 (April 1984), 474-495.

131. Gauthier, "Deterrence," 479.

132. Gauthier, "Deterrence," 486.

133. In the following three paragraphs I am following Gauthier rather closely, but giving only those lines of his argument needed to make my point.

134. Gauthier, "Deterrence," 488.

135. This is, I think, one of Ralph Potter's points in "The Moral Logic of War," *McCormick Quarterly*, 23 (1970), 203-33.

6 Conscience and Consequence

I have dirty hands up to the elbows. I have plunged them in filth and blood. Do you think you can govern innocently?

Jean-Paul Sartre, *Dirty Hands*

Killing in war was differentiated by our fathers from murder. Nevertheless, perhaps it would be well that those whose hands are unclean abstain from communion for three years.

Basil The Great, *Epistle* CL, II, 188.13

There is not presently available a mode of reasoning concerning the justifiable use or nonuse of force that is capable of rendering solutions to our present moral dilemmas. These dilemmas will not disappear even if a new world order appears.

Ralph B. Potter, *War and Moral Discourse*

In chapter 1, I noted an important and fundamental difference between the two dominant styles of moral reasoning available in contemporary ethical theory. One emphasizes constraints on what we can morally *do* to others, while the other is primarily concerned with what *happens* when we pursue a particular course of action. I suggested that the difference between these represents a division of the moral principles by which we judge action, first with regard to private life and then as it concerns public roles. A deontological or agent-centered conception of morality prohibits action that is violative of others' rights, no matter the consequences to the general good. It holds that an agent may never do certain things. By this account, some acts are intrinsically wrong. In contrast, a consequentialist or outcome-centered morality generally rejects the above view and holds that action is to be judged from an impersonal perspective that requires one to produce the best overall state of affairs.

This division in moral reason led me to consider the special nature of action by public functionaries and its corresponding grounds of justification. I argued that the special moral obligations of a political role require the adoption of an outcome-centered form of evaluation. My central claim was that a political role carries with it a unique set of responsibilities for a very large population. I suggested that a public role brings with it the requirement of publicity in reasoning, and of neutrality in the normative grounds of policy decisions. I then concluded that political action is partly liberated from the constraints that in private life prohibit certain kinds of acts, for example, those against the use of force as a means for the preservation of the common good. I was also led to the argument that says the difference between an outcome- and agent-centered moral system yields genuine moral dilemmas where equally compelling, non-overriding moral reasons can be given for incompatible courses of action. Thomas Nagel puts this point as follows:

> If a [political leader] believes that the gains from a certain measure will clearly outweigh its costs, yet still suspects he ought not to adopt it, then he is in a dilemma produced by the conflict between two disparate categories of moral reason. We must face the pessimistic alternative that the two forms of moral intuition are not capable of being brought together into a single, coherent moral system, and that the world can present us with situations in which there is no honorable or moral course for a man to take, no course free from guilt and responsibility for evil.[1]

In this chapter I reflect further on the moral division of labor. In 6.1, I return to the conflict between an outcome- and an agent-centered morality and argue that it represents a profound conflict between incompatible but equally choiceworthy ways of life. This conflict is of significant theoretical importance. It substantiates my argument for the possibility of genuine moral dilemmas, and also strongly suggests that moral theory cannot be made both coherent and complete. In 6.2, I note one possible conclusion to this study: sometimes one must do what one has a moral duty not to do.

6.1 WAYS OF LIFE

Much of contemporary ethical theory is concerned with elucidating principles for action. What is the right principle for someone to adopt under a given set of circumstances? This emphasis on rules, principles, or prescriptions for action tends to distort the more traditional concerns of moral reflection and gives the false impression that there is a universal rule to which the agent can appeal and in turn derive from it a directive for action. In earlier traditions of moral reflection, diverse as these may have been, there was a fairly broad and firm consensus that ethics is primarily an inquiry into questions such as, "How ought one to live?" and "What is a good or virtuous character?" On this view, ethics is fundamentally concerned with the study of types of character as possible exemplars of the well-planned way of life one ought to seek, and of those other ways of life one ought to avoid.

To illustrate the contrast between the traditional and contemporary conceptions of ethics, consider the hypothetical case Bernard Williams uses in a critique of utilitarianism when applied to matters of personal choice.[2] Williams asks us to imagine a botanist, Jim, who, on an expedition somewhere in South America, comes across a group of soldiers about to kill twenty Indians, all randomly chosen, as part of a program to deter further acts of protest against the government. When Jim objects to this, the captain offers him a "guest's privilege" of killing one of the Indians himself. If Jim accepts the offer, the captain will immediately let go the other nineteen. But if Jim rejects, then all will be killed. By Williams' account, utilitarianism is committed to Jim's acceptance of the offer as the "*obviously*" right thing to do: better one than twenty innocents dead. And this, Williams thinks, shows up the central defect in utilitarianism: that it makes a hard, if not impossible, choice seem easy by excluding from consideration non- or contra-utilitarian facts that are morally relevant for Jim's own life-projects and commitment to a certain way of life. Williams' critique of utilitarianism can be generalized to include the contemporary preoccupation with principles for choice in situations of conflict. The problem with this preoccupation is that it rests on the mistaken belief that practical conflicts can be resolved by appeal to a single principle, utilitarian or otherwise.

The point Williams wants to make with this and similar examples is that if we want to know what Jim ought to do in this situation, we should concern ourselves not with principles by which we can evaluate the various courses of action available to Jim. Rather we should be concerned with what Jim wants to be: that is, with the way of life he thinks, given his own projects and commitments, is most choiceworthy. Admittedly, the expression "way of life" is vague. But what is important about it can, I think, be made clear: a way of life is not just a pattern of conduct, as we might expect from a well-mannered person; it consists also of a set of beliefs and values that makes possible a ranking of available alternatives and provides an evaluative basis for choice in situations of personal conflict. If Jim is truly committed to the contemplative life of a scholar, then to engage in action contrary to that way of life would show a lack of integrity and steadfastness on his part. His refusal to join in the political projects of a death squad, even if twenty innocent victims die, is by this account morally justifiable because Jim's own life-projects override whatever (utilitarian) moral requirement he may have to bring about the best overall state of affairs. As Williams puts it: "It is absurd to demand of such a man that he should just step aside from his own project and decision and acknowledge the decision which utilitarian calculation requires."[3]

Throughout this study I have argued that there are important and recognizable differences between matters of personal morality and the basis of moral judgment for state functionaries and public roles. The two central differences are, first, that public action must be concerned primarily with what happens—that is, with consequences—and second, that when one occupies a public role one accepts certain duties which do not necessarily arise, and are in fact often contrary to what we normally expect in purely personal relations. Williams himself has noted these differences. He says: "In politics the justifying consideration will characteristically be of the consequentialist kind." "If the politician is going to take the claims of politics seriously, including the moral claims of politics, then there will be [those] situations in which something morally disagreeable is clearly required."[4] My reason for pointing out these differences again is to underscore the fact that the duties of public office often require action that is incompatible with the ideals of a purely personal way of life. These differences are sufficient for a differential moral analysis that considers it improper or incoherent to justify policy choices by a consideration of the agent's personal history, beliefs, values, or way of life. The occupant of a role may sometimes have to carry out policy requiring a course of action a morally good person is not inclined to perform. He must be prepared for conflicts the solution of which may well exclude a morally decent outcome. So, public morality and the moral requirements of a well-planned way of life collide with each other. How should the occupant of a political role think about engaging in a morally disagreeable course of action?

To address this question, I return to Sartre's example recounted in 2.1. I argue that the moral facts about the dilemma of Sartre's student do not favor one over the other "limb" of his conflict. Though incompatible, each represents equally choiceworthy ways of life animated by different conceptions of the good. What I wish briefly to explore is a radical moral pluralism. My main contention is that there is no principle, hierarchy, nor any common value to which we can reduce the "limbs" of this or any other dilemma and arrive at a satisfactory resolution. Yet a choice between them must be made.

Sartre's response to his student is that since morality cannot provide a solution to his dilemma, he is "free therefore [to] choose—that is to say invent" morality.[5] I think Sartre is correct to say that his student and any agent in a moral dilemma must and is free to choose. But to say that one is free to choose what one will do does not entail that one can invent the judgments by which one's choice is appraised. Judgment on particular courses of action rests on the basis of a set of beliefs and values, of projects, commitments, and loyalties that together form a distinct way of life. Whatever choice this young man makes in his freedom and whatever moral theory he adopts, if he thinks about his conflict at all, he must recognize that it is a conflict between two incompatible ways of life. Animated by different conceptions of the good, each of these yields incompatible judgments on what he ought to do.

Assume that Sartre's student possesses to an equal degree the dispositions towards friendship, benevolence, justice, and the preservation of familial bonds. We can say provisionally that he shows a praiseworthy set of personal and civic virtues: doing things for the sake of a friend, conferring goods on others, fairness in making awards, and recognizing the claims of loyalty to family. But it happens by a turn of events that these several virtues that once provided him with a morally coherent way of life, now make exclusive claims on him. His country has been invaded and a terrible injustice has been done. He must now choose between joining the freedom forces in order to do his part for the vindication of justice, or staying home to care for a loved one. Can the conflict between the requirements of friendship or loyalty to a loved one and of justice be resolved?

Sometimes moral conflicts can be settled. On some occasions sufficient reason is clearly on one side of things, and the agent can be reasonably certain of making a right choice. An overriding moral requirement or superior principle may be invoked for deciding certain types of moral conflicts. But the conflict Sartre's student faces is one that radically calls into question any moral beliefs he may have about a principle for deciding his situation, and especially about a comprehensive and coherent way of life. In his particular circumstance, there is no intelligible trade-off that can be achieved between the virtues of friendship and justice, nor an Aristotelian mean between them, nor yet any utilitarian calculation or categorical imperative that will provide him a resolving moral principle. He either goes or stays. And whatever he decides to do will impair if not preclude the fulfillment of the rejected moral requirement. The conflict he faces is between two choiceworthy ways of life that cannot be reconciled in any reasonable manner because each of them provides equally compelling and non-overriding moral reasons for incompatible courses of action.

The point can be made more precise. This young man must choose between the claims the various virtues make on him to protect family and friends from untoward fortune, or to avenge injustice. This choice represents a more fundamental choice between a life of care and a life of power. The one inspires trust and the other fear. If he chooses to stay home and care for a loved one, the moral claims his political circumstance make on him are not acted upon and the requirement of justice falls out of consideration. In the privacy of his actions, he will nourish a pure, gentle and caring spirit. He will do things for his loved ones, and in doing so possibly risk his own liberty and life. Noble as this is, he would under the given circumstances let injustice and his brother's death go unavenged. On the other hand, to join the freedom forces will lead to a way of life that consists in dispositions and a readiness for frequent and gross injustices, deceit and exploitation, and the courage to shed blood in the streets and battlefields. All this is required of him as a means for a political goal the attainment of which is uncertain. Once Sartre's student chooses to pursue a course of action that moves towards the moral claims his political circumstance make on him, the dispositions towards fairness, friendship, and loyalty to family are inevitably abandoned, even if only temporarily, for a different set of claims and their corresponding actions. In short, the young man must choose between two different kinds of persons.

The conflict can be seen in yet another, and broader, way. A personal morality of sympathy, of benevolence, of sacrificial service to others forms a picture of an ideal way of life that may be aspired to and attained in individual conduct. That morality derives its plausibility from a conception of life as it ought to be, together with a conception of the kind of character we hope to acquire, of the dispositions we ought to cultivate above all others, and of some ordering among them. On the basis of this view, when conflict arises between competing claims, and it inevitably does, one might be able to strike a balance between them guided by the preferred way of life. With time and good fortune in the events of the external world, that ideal conception of life may be realized, and so taken as a whole, a good life will be achieved.

But the realization of an ideal conception of life requires not only excellencies of character, adequate mental and physical capacities, as well as the bonds of friendship and love. It requires also nourishing natural and social circumstances: the necessary and unavoidable external conditions without which a morally choiceworthy way of life, even minimal respect of human worth in ourselves and others, might be impossible. The external social conditions of an ideal conception of life require, at least under present conditions, individuals who are willing to put aside purely private ways of life. Their special role is to secure and to guarantee often by means generally unacceptable and morally unavailable in private life, the external conditions requisite for community. These conditions are inseparably linked to individual ideals; they form the context and the quality of life. But the kinds of action they call for, the means often necessary to secure them, and the morality they contain, differ significantly from what is found in private life. Dirty as these sometimes are, they make a unique contribution to the moral life and have a distinct notion of nobility.

At least since the time of Thucydides, persons of political experience have come to expect that the choices which must be made in public life often conflict with the ideals of a purely private way of life. Given the very large stakes in politics, the unique responsibilities of political office, and the uncertainty of events, where an entire people might suffer if quick and effective measures are not taken, a ruler or political leader must often choose between different evils—say, between action that leaves a sense of moral horror (e.g., threatening civilian populations) and letting disaster come to the innocent and guilty alike. In private life, outside politics, there is an overriding commitment or moral specialization to a given value or achievement—e.g., to science, religion, or philosophy. This commitment has the effect of simplifying and ordering in a ranking of priorities the conduct of life. In Williams' hypothetical case, Jim as botanist is devoted to the pursuit of scientific knowledge. Whatever choices he makes, if he is serious about science, take into account in a singularly important way a moral specialization that cannot be explained by utilitarian calculations nor by a categorical imperative binding on all rational creatures.

The matter is very different for the politician or anyone who assumes a public role, where intrigue, concealment, deceit, aggression, and violence are often indispensable means for the security and survival of the state. The incompatibility between a purely private way of life and the responsibilities of political office, especially of high office, has led writers such as Hans Morgenthau and George Kennan, among others, to warn against what they refer to as "moralistic" attitudes in the affairs of state. Morgenthau, for example, says:

> The very act of acting destroys our moral integrity. Whoever wants to retain his moral innocence must forsake action altogether and, following Hamlet's advice to Ophelia, "go to a nunnery." Why is this so with respect to all actions and particularly so with respect to political actions? First of all, because of its natural limitations, the human intellect is unable to calculate and to control completely the results of human action. [Second], the demands which life in society makes on our good intentions surpass our faculty to satisfy them all. While satisfying one we must neglect others, and the satisfaction of one may even imply the positive violation of another. Whatever choice we make, we must do evil

while we try to do good, for we must abandon one moral end in favor of another.[6]

And George Kennan, in a classic statement of this position, says:

Morality, then, as the channel to individual self-fulfillment—yes. Morality as the foundation of civic virtue, and accordingly as a condition precedent to successful democracy—yes. Morality in governmental method, as a matter of conscience and preference on the part of our people—yes. But morality as a general criterion for the determination of the behavior of states and above all as a general criterion for measuring and comparing the behavior of different states—no. Here other criteria, sadder, more limited, more practical, must be allowed to prevail.[7]

Kennan's and Morgenthau's worry is that those who insist on morality in international affairs might increase tensions between states. Realists concede that state functionaries have commitments and moral duties to the people they represent. As Kennan says, "morality in governmental method—yes." But the foreign policy of a nation must provide for its own security and the integrity of its political life. To attain these ends, there are "no moral standards to which the U.S. [or any other nation] could appeal if it wished to act in the name of moral principles."[8]

The dilemma between a life of political power and a life of sympathy and gentleness is also vividly present in the writings of Machiavelli, who accused Christian morality because of its emphasis on self-denial, purity and gentleness of being impotent with the exercise of power. It was the same charge brought against Christianity in the time of Marcus Aurelius and then revived after the sack of Rome by Alaric, king of the Visigoths. Due to their indifference to political affairs and rejection of the martial virtues, Christians were held responsible for the fall of the city which preserved the security and order requisite for the continuation of Roman values and way of life. It was this charge that St. Augustine sought to overturn in his *City of God* by giving the evangelical precept to love all humanity a political understanding in which the recourse to deadly force is justified for the sake of the common good.[9]

What Machiavelli, Morgenthau, and Kennan have in common with many philosophers and theologians is the stubborn belief that morality consists of an absolute principle for action. This belief shows a deep confusion about the substance of morality and a failure to recognize a pluralism where different moral principles apply to public and to private life. The realist's contention that in the affairs of states moral predicates are either meaningless, naive, or misplaced makes sense only if morality consists of an overriding rule for action. In this respect, Kant's categorical imperative applied to political conduct would substantiate the realist's charge that adherence to morality is corruptive of political decisions. We should then have to agree with Morgenthau that in politics, even when we intend the good, "[w]hatever choice we make, we must do evil." Morgenthau, along with Kennan and other political realists are wont to believe that because a particular course of action is prohibited by the moral absolutism of private action, then political decisions cannot be made on moral grounds. As Arthur J. Schlesinger observed: "If moral principles have only limited application to foreign policy, then we are forced to the conclusion that decisions in foreign affairs must generally be taken on other than moralistic grounds."[10] This view is not only theoretically unsound. It has also the effect of encouraging a cynicism that totally extrudes morality from the affairs of states. A more sophisticated and adequate theory of morality would recognize the "fragmentation of value"[11] or "heterogeneity of morals"[12] which makes any reductive unification of ethics impossible.

On the other hand, if what realists and persons of political experience want to contend is that the special character of public roles and actions partly liberate political conduct from the constraints imposed primarily on private acts, then they have only to show that the specialness of public life renders private and public morality incompatible with each other. Acts which take place in small-scale, face-to-face relations do not have the same moral quality and content as action performed under the auspices of an institutionalized role. Planning a family outing and settling an international conflict are very different sorts of things. But an argument of this kind would not yield the realist's contention of the meaninglessness or inapplicability of morality to politics. It would be an argument for a morality of "innocence" (as Morgenthau puts it) and a morality of experience; it would point to a pluralism in and incompatibility of different ways of life.

Some might object that the incompatibility of these ways of life is symptomatic of the "pathologies of the modern self,"[13] and of the "moral malaise" that is sometimes attributed to modern life.[14] That it is, as MacIntyre puts it, a sign of the "dark times" that are upon us, of "a state so disastrous that there are no large remedies for it."[15] I do not know whether MacIntyre's and similar diagnoses of our moral condition are correct. Nor is it necessary for me to assess them here. The contrast I have drawn between a noble private way of life and a life of politics has occupied the reflections of philosophers at least since the time of Socrates. This is evidence enough that this problem for which "there are no large remedies" is not peculiar to modern times. The dilemma between the moral claims of politics and private morality has remained intact since antiquity, and is very likely to remain so for the foreseeable future. That is why it continues to be of interest to philosophers and theologians.

6.2 CONCLUSION: HAVING TO DO WHAT ONE HAS A MORAL DUTY NOT TO DO

We appear then to have reached an impasse. Efforts to think morally about nuclear arms policy yield two rival ways of thinking: resist aggression by threatening an evil act that might produce wholesale slaughter of human lives or refuse that threat knowing all the while that such refusal might lead to the evil of foreign domination. Either way, we (have to) do something we have a moral duty not to do.

Hegel saw such insoluble moral conflicts as the very essence of trage-dy—in Sophocles' *Antigone*, for example, where Antigone's loyalty to her brother and her duty to give him a proper burial requires her to defy Creon's edict and loyalty to the city, or Aeschylus' *Oresteia*, where Orestes must avenge his father's murder, but to do so must kill his mother. In such cases, as Aeschylus puts it, "right conflicts with right."[16] The debate on nuclear arms policy illustrates the kind of moral tragedy classical Greek literature often depicts as an important and unavoidable feature of human existence: the world is such that it sometimes presents us with situations in which whatever one does, a moral transgression is unavoidable. We are therefore hard-pressed to say what one morally ought to do about the new instruments and plans for war—disarm or deter. If out of duty to the political community and its survival we choose deterrence, we endorse the intention to wholesale slaughter. In acting, we might thereby sacrifice some innocent people for others. Yet there is no morally relevant difference between innocents. On the other hand, if out of respect for the right to life of persons we disarm, our very physical survival might be at stake.

In the preceding chapters, I made much of the inability of contemporary moral theory to resolve this dilemma. From a consequentialism point of view, we weigh the probable suffering or happiness each alternative is likely to produce. Yet the weighing requires a moral indifference that reduces happiness and suffering to the same scale. How much suffering to ourselves or others can we inflict for the sake of our or someone else's happiness? For an agent-centered morality, on the other hand, suffering as a means to some objective can never be directly intended or caused. To do so violates the rule that persons are ends in themselves. The strict conscience required in a deontological system rejects as a matter of principle the use of certain means to achieve morally worthy consequences.

My argument in this book has been that these rival moral claims cannot be brought together in a neat way. No matter which of these claims one endorses, the moral transgression of the rejected alternative is unavoidable. Effective action on behalf of the political community cannot be reconciled with the duties of personal integrity and gentleness in spirit, or with the purity of intention and love for all humanity that are ennobling of our moral character.

It is just that understanding of the moral life Reinhold Niebuhr conveyed when he said: "A realistic analysis of the problem of human society reveals a constant and seemingly irreconcilable conflict between the needs of society and the imperatives of a sensitive conscience. This conflict, which could be most briefly defined as the conflict between ethics and politics, is made inevitable by the double focus of the moral life."[17] For Niebuhr, there is an individual morality which judges all human behavior from an internal perspective. Our actions are right or wrong insofar as they reflect a pure and disinterested motive. Here the ideal to be pursued is a universal and self-sacrificial love that makes no claims to be "socially efficacious."[18] But the way of politics is different. Self-sacrifice and the spirit of disinterestedness that characterize universal love are, Niebuhr says, inappropriate ideals for political morality. Here the dictum that the ends justify the means, and so that no action is in principle prohibited, evaluates human behavior in an entirely different way and "makes a morality of pure disinterestedness impossible."[19] Must then the "true champion of justice," as Socrates says, "necessarily confine himself to private life and leave politics alone"?

That is surely one way to cultivate in ourselves a gentle and pure disposition toward others. Yet one is right in suspecting that this response might point to a self-indulgence that has little of the character of love. For the sake of a worthy political objective, a moral agent might be justified in doing what she has a moral duty not to do. She must weigh and balance the available alternatives. Sometimes the balance will fall on a course of action that must be carried out but nonetheless leaves us with a sense of horror. It leaves us with that sense because we endorse (others) doing (for our sake) what we have a moral duty not to do. That there are some situations in which we have to do what we have a moral duty not to do may tell us something about the scope of moral reason and the limits of human experience. It may tell us, for example, that we should not strive for theoretical completion because the rival moral claims that come to bear on personal and political morality cannot be brought together in a tidy way. It may tell us also that there is precious little opportunity in life for moral perfection.

NOTES

1. Thomas Nagel, "War and Massacre," in *Mortal Questions* (Cambridge: Cambridge University Press, 1979), 54, 73.

2. See Bernard Williams, "A Critique of Utilitarianism," in J.J.C. Smart and Bernard Williams, *Utilitarianism, For and Against* (Cambridge: Cambridge University Press, 1973), 108-118.

3. Williams, "A Critique," 116.

4. Bernard Williams, "Politics and Moral Character," in Stuart Hampshire, ed., *Public and Private Morality* (Cambridge: Cambridge University Press, 1978), 62, 63.

5. Jean-Paul Sartre, "Existentialism is a Humanism," trans. P. Mairet, in *Existentialism from Dostoevsky to Sartre*, ed. William Kaufman, (New York: Meridian, 1957), 198.

6. Hans Morgenthau, *Scientific Man and Power Politics* (Chicago: University of Chicago Press, 1946), 189-190.

7. George Kennan, *Realities of American Foreign Policy* (Princeton: Princeton University Press, 1954), 49.

8. Kennan, *Realities*, 207.

9. See, for example, R. A. Markus, *Saeculum: History and Society in the Theology of St. Augustine* (Cambridge: Cambridge University Press, 1970), especially chapter 4 and Appendix B.

10. Arthur J. Schlesinger, Jr., "The Necessary Amorality of Foreign Affairs," *Harper's Magazine* (August 1971), 74.

11. Thomas Nagel, "The Fragmentation of Value," in *Mortal Questions*, 128-141.

12. Charles E. Larmore, *Patterns of Moral Complexity* (Cambridge: Cambridge University Press, 1987), especially chapter 6.

13. David Levin, ed., *Pathologies of the Modern Self* (New York: New York University Press, 1987), 37.

14. Edmund Pellegrino, "Character, Virtue, and Self-Interest in the Ethics of the Professions," *Journal of Contemporary Health Law and Policy*, vol. 5 (1989), 59.

15. Alasdair MacIntyre, *After Virtue* (Notre Dame: University of Notre Dame Press, 1981), 5.

16. Aeschylus, *Coephroroi*, line 461.

17. Reinhold Niebuhr, *Moral Man and Immoral Society* (New York: Charles Scribner's Sons, 1932), 257.

18. Niebuhr, *Moral Man*, 264.

19. Niebuhr, *Moral Man*, 272.

Index